4 -
5/22

Internet Afterlife

Internet Afterlife

VIRTUAL SALVATION IN THE 21st CENTURY

Kevin O'Neill

 PRAEGER™

An Imprint of ABC-CLIO, LLC

Santa Barbara, California • Denver, Colorado

Library of Congress Cataloging-in-Publication Data

Names: O'Neill, Kevin, 1941- author.
Title: Internet afterlife : virtual salvation in the 21st century / Kevin O'Neill.
Description: Santa Barbara, California : Praeger, an imprint of ABC-CLIO, LLC, [2016]
   | Includes bibliographical references and index.
Identifiers: LCCN 2016016192 | ISBN 9781440837968 (acid-free paper) |
   ISBN 9781440837975 (EISBN)
Subjects: LCSH: Death. | Future life. | Internet. | World Wide Web. |
   Information technology. | Theological anthropology.
Classification: LCC BL504 .O54 2016 | DDC 306.9—dc23
   LC record available at https://lccn.loc.gov/2016016192

ISBN: 978-1-4408-3796-8
EISBN: 978-1-4408-3797-5

20 19 18 17 16   1 2 3 4 5

This book is also available as an eBook.

Praeger
An Imprint of ABC-CLIO, LLC

ABC-CLIO, LLC
130 Cremona Drive, P.O. Box 1911
Santa Barbara, California 93116-1911
www.abc-clio.com

This book is printed on acid-free paper ∞
Manufactured in the United States of America

This book belongs to my beloved wife and life companion, Dorothy, in more ways than I can possibly say. The time and intelligence that she voluntarily—and so generously—lavished on this project continue to amaze me, and I will be forever in her debt.

I also dedicate this book to all the extraordinary rescue animals whose love and antics have made our journey so much richer and so filled with joy and laughter. I wish they all lived longer, so that we could love them more.

Contents

Preface

When philosophy paints its grey on grey, then has a shape of life grown old. The owl of Minerva appears only at the gathering of the dusk.

Georg Wilhelm Hegel
Lectures on the Philosophy of History

This book completes a journey I have been on for the past 23 years, in that trackless and ambiguous borderland between the living and the dead that Jacques Derrida—the most serious philosopher of death since Heidegger—sketches out in his meditation on death, *Aporias*. What you read here recaptures the final steps of my journey, when I departed this world, without dying, and went to visit the new homes of the dead on the Internet and in cyberspace. There, in the Cloud, on websites, and in virtual realities, I found many things. I visited online cemeteries and virtual vaults. I relived 9/11 and Sandy Hook and Katrina. I was haunted by ghosts on Facebook and got tweets from the dead on Twitter. I went to websites that invited me to create an online replica of myself that my family could visit when I died.

Finally, at the end of my journey, I found people who told me that in a few years death itself would die and everyone would become an immortal presence—not in Heaven or Hell, but in the Cloud. The world would be populated by android robots and holograms in which the dead would live on. Computer and smartphone screens would teem with even more of the dead, turned into avatar copies whose software would capture each dead person's subjectivity.

In this book you will meet the dead, all these ghosts, these robots and avatars, and when you have finished you will wonder whether Hegel was absolutely right. Are we living at the end of a phase of history in which human beings actually died? Are we at the dawning of a new world in which the dead will live among us in digital form, and when they—and we—and the entire universe will morph into one enormous simulation? Will the virtual absorb the real? Will bodies disappear? Will time and space come to mean nothing? Welcome to the journey to Internet afterlife.

Acknowledgments

I want to thank my former student Eli Kramer, whose invitation to speak to the philosophy graduate students at Southern Illinois University in 2013 provoked me to write the initial version of the paper on which this book is based. I also acknowledge and thank Catherine Lafuente of Praeger-ABC-CLIO for showing interest in my project and for encouraging me to prepare my initial book proposal for submission to Praeger. I would also wish to acknowledge the assistance of Lorraine Rhodes of the Terasem Foundation for guiding me through the development of my first virtual presentation at a 2015 Terasem conference on Teilhard de Chardin. Lorraine guided me through the steps necessary to become an online avatar—an experience that changed my perspective completely.

The work I did preparing for the Summer Alumni Seminar on death in 2013, for the Johnston Center at the University of Redlands, gave me a sustained focus on the topic of death that led me back into investigating digital immortality. The experience of connecting the theme of death to its representation in visual culture—which I did in preparing my keynote address to the national ADEC conference in 2013—also helped provoke my interest in death on the screen.

Finally, and most importantly, I want to acknowledge the invaluable editorial assistance provided by Michael Wilt of Tucker Seven Editorial Services. His meticulous review and revision turned my work into a genuine manuscript. But Michael might never have gotten to help had it not been for the urgings and tireless editorial and emotional support provided by my spouse and life partner, Dorothy Clark. Her kindness and patience, as well as her uncompromising dedication to making this the best manuscript possible, were what made this book a reality.

I also thank the many students, friends, and colleagues who have endured my endless enthusiasm for discussing the somber topic of death. Your suggestions, ideas, and patience have all mattered.

List of Abbreviations

AI: artificial intelligence
CGI: computer-generated imagery
CPU: central processing unit
DARPA: Defense Advanced Research Project Agency
DNR: do not resuscitate (end-of-life protocol)
ICT: Institute for Creative Technologies
LOAR: Law of Accelerating Returns
NDE: near-death experience
PTSD: post-traumatic stress disorder
WBE: Whole Brain Emulation

Chapter 1

Introduction: Journeying into New Worlds of the Dead

THE QUESTION AND THE JOURNEY

The question of what happens when we die has haunted both Western and Eastern cultures for as long as we have been able to keep records. Its nagging urgency tormented Gilgamesh at the dawn of history, and it haunts us just as deeply today as we push books about Heaven to the top of best-seller lists.[1]

The mystery and sorrow of dying are encapsulated, existentially, in the moment of passing. At one moment the dying person is there, a functioning subject, a unique awareness. A moment later the person is gone and we are in the presence of a corpse. What went away? Where did it go? Did it go anywhere, or did it simply, and utterly, disappear?

And when we ask these questions, we are never asking them only about the one who has died. We are asking them about ourselves, about our own fate. As the philosopher Martin Heidegger writes, humans are "beings-toward-death."[2] We are, as the ancient Greeks also knew, the animals who are aware of their own deaths: To be human is to know that one dies.[3]

The problem is that when a person dies and something goes away, we cannot see or touch that something. For this reason almost all attempts to answer the question of death posit the existence of a non-material, or quasi-material, realm where the invisible part of us—the soul—goes when we die. The Greeks believed in Hades, an underworld where souls lived on as powerless shadows of their former selves. Jews believed in

Gehenna, was also inhabited by shades. Christians, Muslims, and Jews imagine a more welcoming Heaven, a blessed realm where the spirits and glorified spiritual bodies of those who had obeyed God live in eternal peace and happiness. They also, however, imagine a Hell that is as terrible as Heaven is beautiful, where those who had defied God would spend an eternity in torment. Eastern religions also envision a domain beyond the earthly one. The Hindu religion promises eternal bliss in a world soul, the liberation experienced in "*moksha*," and Buddhism ambiguously offers peaceful oblivion, "*nirvana*," after a long process of reincarnation on the way to perfection.

Philosophers from Plato onward have taught that we possess an immortal soul that, like the soul in Buddhism and Hinduism, can liberate itself from an endless cycle of rebirth by practicing asceticism in this world. Theosophists and spiritualists postulate the existence of Summerland, the neo-pagan version of an afterlife[4]; the philosopher and mystic Emanuel Swedenborg (1688–1772) even claimed to have visited Summerland.[5]

There are skeptics about all this, and thoughtful people since the time of the Atomists and the Stoics have argued that the soul is nothing but a collection of atoms or cells which disintegrates when the flow of oxygen stops. Finally, there are the millions of agnostics who agree with the philosopher Jacques Derrida when he says "*Il y va d'un certain pas*": We do not know whether the departure of the spirit is the beginning of a journey, a "certain step," or no step at all, a French *pas* (not), a non-step into—nothing.[6]

Regardless of whether we believe, we all agree that almost no one wants to die—unless his or her life has become utterly unbearable. And among those who no longer want to live, many still look forward to what will come next. Everyone who wants to live beyond his or her death will be interested in an account of human identity that promises personal immortality, especially if that account promises that we can live forever on our own terms, without having to please a judging God or pass through endless cycles of rebirth. A do-it-yourself, user-friendly Heaven might interest even skeptics and agnostics.

This book is the record of a journey that I took—largely by accident—into a world in which such promises are being made, not by priests or gurus or imams, but by highly successful business executives, computer scientists, and even philosophers. I ask the reader to retrace the steps of my journey with me so that you can decide for yourself whether this promised afterlife finally resolves that ancient conundrum of death in ways that speak to the hearts and minds of those who live, increasingly, on screens and in the Internet Cloud.

THE BEGINNING OF THE JOURNEY

My journey to this new land began innocently enough with what would become a truly serendipitous experience. While I was researching an academic paper on how Americans represent their dead, my work took me to Hollywood Forever Cemetery in Los Angeles, California. It was a place that seemed completely *out* of place: a large, elaborate burial ground that held the graves of Rudolph Valentino, Jayne Mansfield, and Mickey Rooney in an urban neighborhood of strip malls and auto body shops. I knew that the cemetery had been doing some unusual things—including projecting iconic horror films on the walls of the mausoleums and hosting a celebration on the Mexican Day of the Dead—therefore I thought that the cemetery might be doing something interesting with the ways in which "clients" were memorialized. I was right.

Hollywood Forever began offering a rather startling and innovative new service. In addition to operating a funeral home that handled interments and cremations in the traditional way, the cemetery was equipped to make biopics of the dead. The cemetery employs film students as well as professional film editors and sound technicians to craft cinematic narratives of people's lives. Specially trained biographers use video footage, sound bites, still photographs, music tracks, and taped interviews featuring bereaved family members and friends of the deceased. Sometimes the deceased people themselves—before they die, and knowing that their end is inevitable—consent to be interviewed and filmed. Clients pay for these services, and the cost depends on the length of the film. The cemetery has encouraged people to allocate more resources to these online memorials and to spend correspondingly less on traditional funeral accoutrements.

This new service represents a creative marriage of Hollywood film skills with mourning rituals. The dead still can be buried or cremated and still can have religious services and memorial events, but they now also can "star" in their own movies. What I found most interesting was a Hollywood Forever website (www.hollywoodforever.com) that included a "Library of Lives," which stores all of the films of the dead. Family members and friends access the films by typing in the name of the dead person accompanied by a password. Cemetery management installed kiosks containing computer screens and keyboards on the grounds of the cemetery. People use these terminals to key in a name and password, and can hear and see their dead loved ones while gazing at his or her final resting place.

As technology developed, the cemetery included more Internet opportunities. It began to offer real-time streaming of funeral services. Thus, one could watch a loved one's biopic, attend his or her funeral, and leave messages of condolence on the "Library of Lives" page without ever leaving home. The dead person always is there, waiting to be accessed by anyone with the right password.

It struck me immediately that this was a new form of immortality that exploited the fact that the Internet is "on" all day every day in every part of the world. Although the spirits of the dead might go to Heaven or into the Great Void, digital versions of the dead can live on, online, forever.

It also struck me that not only was this a new form of immortality, but that this could also be the starting point for a development that could go much further. When I first visited the "Library of Lives" in 2004, the iPod was cutting-edge technology and the iPhone was still years in the future. Social media sites such as Facebook were barely starting up, and Instagram, Pinterest, Vine, and Twitter did not exist. People still depended on desktop computers to connect to the Internet, and the now common sight of roomfuls of people staring at smartphone and tablet screens was still a year or two away. But, as I write this chapter, the Hollywood Forever dead are truly "portable"—available on every phone and tablet, as close as a keystroke or voice command.

When I wrote my paper about the Hollywood Forever online films in 2006, I speculated that perhaps someday in the near future the people who ran cemeteries and mortuaries would begin to adapt the sophisticated computer-generated imagery (CGI) technology that computer games were already perfecting to make online avatars of the dead that could be programmed to interact with the living. I published the paper[7] and forgot my speculations. Years later, in 2011, a former student who had just started working toward his PhD in philosophy at Southern Illinois University invited me to present two talks on death to the graduate students in his program. I had one talk all but done—a discussion of Jacques Derrida's writings on death and specters—but I had no idea what I wanted to do for the second talk. I reviewed my presentations and articles on death and found the piece on Hollywood Forever with its forgotten speculations about interactive online avatars of the dead.

I had my topic—afterlife on the Internet, or Internet afterlife. I had nothing to go on but my old hunch, so I went online to see where death had gone on the Internet since last I looked. This hunch led to this book for, to my great surprise, I found new worlds of and for the dead online that went beyond what Hollywood Forever had done, and that confirmed my one-time hunch about using game-based online avatars to represent the dead. This presence of the dead online partly is a function of the fact that most Americans have a complex set of online identities that live on after they die because the Internet has no expiration dates. As anyone who has ever posted an imprudent image on his or her Facebook account knows, information released to the Internet seems to have an immortal life all its own. Additionally, as our emotional, business, and shopping lives migrate progressively onto the screens that are coming to dominate our lives, it seems natural that our death rituals and narratives should make the same journey to the Cloud. What was innovative, even unique, in 2005—Hollywood Forever's "Library of Lives"— had become a commonplace by 2011.

In addition, we Americans have always loved the idea of an afterlife, from traditional Christian and Jewish versions to exotic New Age creations, and we have never been reticent about designing Heaven to suit our desires. Ever since we wrested control of our death narratives[8] from the funeral and medical establishments—a move that has been afoot since the antiestablishment rebellions of the 1960s, and the AIDS crisis of the 1980s—we have been reconceptualizing Heaven in a variety of creative ways.

This new world of the dead online, that we collectively have constructed, bit by bit, from the late 1990s forward, and which represents the current chapter of a longer-term American appropriation of the afterlife, comprises the first part of this book. I discovered that there are virtual cemeteries, YouTube memorials, Facebook legacy pages and group memorial pages, services that promised to post tweets after one died, and other services designed to send postmortem emails and publish personal journals. There is a strange site called MyDeathSpace that posted obituaries for people who had committed suicide, died in accidents, or had been murdered. Every mass shooting and natural disaster, from Sandy Hook to Katrina, has its memorial site, as do the wars in Iraq and Afghanistan. The terrorist attacks of September 11, 2001, of course, spawned several active memorial sites; and the Holocaust, the Armenian Genocide, and Srebrenica all have special memorial websites, as do sites that memorialize African Americans who had been the victims of police shootings. There are sites for deceased pets, and there exist specialized memorial sites for every religious preference and gender identification.

To my surprise, I also discovered a complex world of what I call curatorial and archival sites that offer every kind of postmortem protection for, and management of, one's business and financial affairs. There are sites that keep one's will under doubly encrypted virtual lock and key, online "vaults" for powers of attorney, do not resuscitate (DNR) protocols, birth and marriage licenses and certificates, and every other form of official document, including bank account numbers and passwords and information about paying recurring bills. Some online sites offer interconnected services, from pre-need funeral planning to financial advice to grief therapy. Everything about one's death and legacy can be managed, and there are additional services designed to permit access to one's social media pages and email accounts to designated executors.

All of these memorials and services merit examination and commentary, and the first leg of our journey takes us into this world of online cemeteries, Facebook memorials, and virtual vaults. It is my aim that this journey will provide readers with an understanding about how Americans are looking at the dead, and at their own deaths, in the age of the Internet. You might find people you know as you take the journey; I can assure you that you will be touched and moved by what you find in the online worlds of the dead. You might find ideas about how you want to be remembered—you probably already have a deathless online presence, and what you discover here can help you learn how to manage it.

THE JOURNEY CONTINUES: SERENDIPITY, "INTELLIGENT AVATARS"

The memorial and social media sites did not offer examples of the interactive online avatars of the dead that I had speculated on in 2006, so I continued my journey. Once again, serendipity came into play: My endless Google searching led me—I have no idea how—to a site (although now defunct) called Intellitar, which stood for "intelligent avatar" and which hosted another site called virtualeternity.com. This site promised to utilize information users provided to create intelligent online avatars that would look and sound like their creators and that could eventually be programmed to interact with friends and family members after the person who created the avatar died.

In chapter three I take up the question of how the online avatar—so familiar from the world of computer games and Second Life—has become a vehicle for Internet afterlife. The Intellitar avatars, which resembled the chatbots that IKEA and other companies use to assist online customers, seemed a promising beginning of something new, strange, and rather remarkable about the "future" of death online. Due to legal issues concerning the rights to the necessary software, however, the Intellitar site never got past the construction phase, so my quest remained unfulfilled. Its failure led to further searches, and I eventually discovered three more sites that are discussed at the conclusion of the first half of this book and lead us into the second half. The first site, Eternime (eterni .me), created by people associated with the Massachusetts Institute of Technology (MIT), currently is working with a small subset of its initial subscribers to develop the software needed to accomplish what Intellitar failed to do—create interactive online avatars of the dead. The second site, MyLifeBits (http://research.microsoft.com/en-us/projects/mylife-bits/), is a portal to specialized software developed by Jim Gemmell and Gordon Bell of Microsoft that enables individuals to record every facet of their lives and transfer it to online databanks, so that the avatars en-visioned by Eternime can become a reality sooner rather than later.

The third site, maintained by the Institute for Creative Technologies (ICT) at the University of Southern California, has two projects. The organization is developing interactive online avatars for the U.S. Department of Defense for one project. These "avatar-counselors" will offer therapy to post-traumatic stress disorder (PTSD) sufferers and will train soldiers in how to negotiate with village leaders in Iraq and Afghanistan. Later civilian users of the same software will deploy virtual physician assistants to help people get quick medical diagnoses and ad-vice for minor medical problems. The ICT's second project concerns the development of a hologram of Holocaust survivor Pinchas Gutter, to enable his continued witnessing to audiences in the future long after he has died. This hologram will look and sound like Gutter and will be able to both share his story of survival and answer questions from live audi-ences. It will be another rather startling example of Internet afterlife.

These three projects represent a different strategy for dealing with the online dead than the more static memorial and archival websites. This is because these undertakings exploit the "cyberspace" dimension of the Internet rather than its page-driven Web dimension.

Interactive avatars of the dead are a fascinating step beyond Facebook memorials and online vaults, but in the end these beings simply are very sophisticated versions of Apple's Siri and IKEA's Anna the chatbot. They are not the actual dead online but rather are brilliant replicas of the dead. This might seem obvious—but, as we will see, these replicas could create a suspension of disbelief so that they appear to be the dead loved one—*as if* that loved one's subjective, actual consciousness "existed" on-line. We can conceive of this as a sort of deceptive version of virtual af-terlife, one that falls short of answering the eternal human question about what happens to our subjectivity when we die and whether digital technology can become a "home" for it.

These concerns led, in my dissatisfaction, to the next—unexpected—step on my journey. My uneasiness led to the serendipitous discovery of two sites that seemed to promise an answer: 2045 Initiative (2045.com) and LifeNaut (www.lifenaut.com). These two sites promised, or perhaps threatened, to change everything we have believed about death and led me into the world of "real" Internet afterlife. In this world, the people hosting these sites promise that by 2045 digital immortality will be available to anyone who wants it. These two sites, and the new movement, dubbed "transhumanism," which they represent, are where I complete my journey. The second half of the book is a detailed guide to a brave new world that just might be the shape of your future and mine.

SITUATING THE JOURNEY IN THE AMERICAN DEATH NARRATIVE

Before we embark on those journeys—from online cemeteries to digital immortality—let's pause for a moment to locate ourselves in a cultural and spiritual sense. If we fail to do this, we could easily lose our bearings and find ourselves in a strange country with no map to guide us and no easy way home. We do not want to lose ourselves while traveling in the land of the dead.

Ever since the Puritans formed the first colonies, Americans have been telling stories about what happens when we die. Our journey into the world of Internet afterlife can be understood as a continuation of these American ideas about death. These narratives that have been an integral part of the American experience are essentially American and are informed with themes that continue into this new world of the afterlife that we are about to explore. Before exploring that new world, it is helpful to situate it as part of this American narrative experience.

Four interlacing themes inform these narratives. Not surprisingly, the first is an unfailing optimism—probably one of the traits we most associate with Americans. Connected to this optimism is another very American trait, a kind of practical sensibility that manifests in what we can call a "do-it-yourself" confidence. A third theme is a belief in the permeability between the world of the living and the world of the dead. This theme reflects that American optimism as well as the practical know-how or do-it-yourself ethos. Finally, the fourth theme, not surprisingly, integrates the first three in a faith in technology—a technology that bridges that boundary between the living and the dead and is a result of that American practical confidence in individual ingenuity.

My discovery of these themes informing this uniquely American narrative also began serendipitously. My first introduction to the subject was a chance discovery. Even in this digital age nothing can match the delight of wandering along library shelves and finding what one has really been looking for 10 or 50 books away from the one you thought you were seeking. In my case, the book was not located anywhere near where I was looking. As I was perusing the shelves of my university library, I chanced to glance at one of those carts that librarians use to trundle books back to their proper places. I was taken by a strange, thin book that caught my eye because it was quite a bit larger than the ordinary format. Its name was *Sleeping Beauty: Memorial Photography in America.*[9] Upon opening it, I was shocked by its beautiful photographic reproductions. They were daguerreotypes. Each page held a single image with a brief title underneath. The images were clearly from the earliest days of photography, and every one of them was of a dead person, carefully clothed and arranged, sometimes in a narrow coffin, sometimes sitting propped in a chair, in one case standing erect, with eyes opened.

I spent the next few hours devouring the images. I looked closely at every page, and then reexamined many of them. I was repelled and fascinated by turns. A set of questions arose: What would lead people to think that producing such images was a good way to remember and honor the dead? Daguerreotypes, I soon learned, could only be produced using expensive, heavy equipment that required training to handle. These images were not snapshots or, God forbid, images snapped by a cell phone. They had to be made by professionals who were called to a home on purpose. The images themselves were not casual takes; they were carefully arranged scenes that involved dressing the corpse in his or her finest clothing and arranging him or her just so.

Exposure times were long—minutes at a time—and the images were incised on a specially prepared metal plate. There were no negatives, so each shot had to count. Once the images were produced they were extraordinarily fragile. Only a small fraction of daguerreotypes has survived because the images are so easily scratched. Those that are preserved had to be encased, immediately, in frames with glass covers.

So, why would people photograph the dead? I think it is because we love Heaven so much. We Americans have always loved Heaven, even when access to it was restricted, as in the days when the Puritans controlled death narratives in the New England colonies. But Calvinist pessimism—which condemned the great majority of people to damnation—could not survive the powerful current of American optimism that developed during the first Great Awakening in the middle of the eighteenth century. America was, after all, the "shining city on a hill" described in

St. Matthew's account of the Sermon on the Mount, a source quoted in the context of the American self-image by the Puritan John Winthrop on the ship *Arbella* even before the colonists landed at what was to be Massachusetts Bay Colony.

One sees American optimism about death, and the fate of the dead, graphically represented in New England gravestones of the seventeenth and eighteenth centuries. In the early days when Puritans held sway, the tympanums of the simple slate headstones bore images of skulls and crossbones. But these grim figures were very soon crowded off the markers by new generations of images, which started out as simple faces and evolved into cherubic, happy souls, faces framed by wings, speeding toward Heaven. These faces in turn gave way to peaceful symbols of mourning. Weeping willow trees, cut roses, and for children, resting lambs, marked the changes in the conception of death from an event that filled people with terror, to one in which the souls of the dead flew to Heaven, to a sad but beautiful event in which the dead were reconnected to nature. Americans imposed their sense of exceptionalism even on the dead. When Americans replaced images of souls with images of flowers and trees, this meant that the dead had been freed from the constraints of traditional theology and had become part of beautiful nature.

This optimism about death allied itself to the theme of permeability running through America's cultural imaginary, the idea that the dead remained close to the living: Even if they had gone to Heaven, they are accessible. Contrary to Hamlet's plaint that death was "The undiscover'd country, from whose bourn No traveller returns" (*Hamlet*, Act III, Scene 1), Americans believed that the dead hovered around the living, and that it was a good thing to act to keep the dead as close as possible.

These beliefs—that all Americans get to Heaven and that the boundary between Heaven and Earth is permeable—help explain why, when photography in the form of daguerreotypes came to America in 1839, one of the first uses people made of cameras was to make preternaturally clear images of the newly dead. The idea of making portraits of the dead had roots in spiritual—one can say metaphysical—shifts in American attitudes toward the dead, and also can be seen as reflecting that American penchant for optimism. Two features matter. First, one does not feel comforted by seeing representations of family members after their deaths if one has a fair presumption that said family member is suffering in Hell. If Americans adopted the custom of commissioning portraits of the dead or the dying—because such portraits had to be done quickly using the corpse as a model—then they must have abandoned this severe vision of the world in which most people went to Hell, and replaced it with one in which few people, at least few respectable people, would end up there.

This metaphysics—articulated to some extent in American Transcendentalism, but more vigorously and popularly in the waves of religious revivalism called Great Awakenings that swept both the colonies and the new republic—expressed a new optimism, as did the Enlightenment deism of many of the intelligentsia and the politically active or moneyed classes. This was not a systematically developed vision—as anyone who reads Emerson knows—but a complex of sensibilities, aperçu, perceptions. But it was powerful and pervasive and made postmortem portraits culturally possible.

Photography was "light writing," a felicitous marriage of empirical accuracy and Platonic idealization that suited America's spiritual vision perfectly. When sunlight "wrote" its images on metal plates, focused by lens but never either manufactured or guided by human hands, what resulted was an image that combined empirical precision with an almost mysterious revelatory power. Light and lens not only captured exactly what was there without filtering it, they also revealed details and a holistic *truth* about the person or thing that the vagaries of a flitting, inattentive, or biased human gaze could not. Photographs revealed what always already was there but went largely unnoticed: the deeper moral and metaphysical truth about a person. Nathaniel Hawthorne alludes to this in his *House of the Seven Gables,*[10] when Holcroft, the protagonist, makes a daguerreotype image of Judge Pyncheon that reveals the latter's otherwise hidden malevolence. Americans were drawn to this new technology of representation for epistemological, moral, and metaphysical reasons. The new technology told the truth—a deeper truth than unaided human sight could tell.

Adapting the new light writing technology to the representation of death meant that Americans did not fear seeing the deeper truth about the dead. Only if one believed that the dead were morally pure or blameless could they be safely exposed to the truth-telling power of photography. For this reason, these early photographs were displayed in the parlor, the room where Americans entertained guests. Images of the dead would "greet" visitors, and every effort was made to represent the dead as if they were still alive. Postmortem photographs kept the dead as integral members of their families, and were a vehicle for the dead to contradict Hamlet.

The same optimism and belief in the closeness of the dead was expressed in the rural cemetery movement that began at Mount Auburn Cemetery in Cambridge, Massachusetts, in 1831. The rural cemetery was a new cultural formation that used the latest advances in landscape design to create "dormitories" for the dead, peaceful places where they could "sleep" until Christ returned to judge the living and the dead.

Rural cemeteries were the first American suburbs. They were purposely designed to be picturesque, that is, on an aesthetic scale halfway between the formality of the beautiful and the wildness of the natural. They featured hills, ridges, dense vegetation, and winding paths. Each family would purchase a plot, usually 300 square feet. They would erect a fence, as if this were an upper-middle-class home, and plant trees and flowers around the graves. Whole families would ride out to the cemetery in carriages and spend a Sunday afternoon picnicking among the dead. The rural cemetery dead were held close, "sleeping" in a fenced family plot, in what amounted to a gated community that had its own rules and security patrols.

As Americans were taking photographs of the dead and visiting them in their dormitories, they were also communicating with them through mediums, table rappings, and Ouija boards. In 1848, 17 years after Mount Auburn opened and nine years after the first postmortem photographs appeared, the adolescent Fox sisters heard what they believed to be spirit rappings in their home in the Burnt-Over District of New York State. Their experience struck a chord, and Spiritualism became a parallel religion for millions of Americans during much of the nineteenth century, despite the suspicions that spiritualist claims aroused, and despite the fact that one of the Fox sisters later recanted her claims. Not only were the dead nearby in images and in graves, they were literally present—if invisible—watching over the living and offering advice and reassurance.

Spiritualism further confirmed the theme of a faith in technology in the American relationship with death. Photography used nineteenth-century chemistry to fix the images created by the "camera obscura," a technology that had been developed in the Middle Ages. Cemetery designers used the latest design ideas to craft charming resting places for the dead. But Spiritualism made the connection between American death and technology explicit. The spirits first appeared at almost the same time that the telegraph was invented. One of the first descriptions of Spiritualism's contact with the dead was that it was a form of "spiritual telegraph" in which the dead used electrical devices, exploiting the newly discovered principles of electromagnetism to contact the living.

The important difference between Spiritualism and traditional beliefs in Heaven was and is that Spiritualism gives the living and the dead far more control over their fates—and by extension over death and its meanings—than traditional religion affords. The premise is that the dead are not under the control of the traditional postmortem binaries of Heaven and Hell, nor do they act at the behest of any god. They seem to be wandering free in some ill-determined border region that has little to do with traditional versions of the afterlife.

This tendency to see the afterlife as a do-it-yourself project is well represented in that genre of literature that Anne Douglas named "consolation literature" in her essay "Heaven Our Home." This was a genre that included both fiction and nonfiction that arose in the United States in the decades before the Civil War. Consolation literature had one subject: death, both the process of dying and the business of mourning, with greater emphasis on the latter. In the case of its most popular practitioner, Elizabeth Stuart Phelps, however, it was detailed descriptions of the afterlife, what a critic called "the annexation of Heaven," that added the idea of a user-friendly afterlife to Americans' optimism about death, their belief in the closeness of the dead, and their faith in technology to connect them to the dead.

This literature represented the merging of several strains in the culture. First, urbanization and the development of commerce and industry radically altered the status of women in society. Many women now were compelled by circumstance to enter the urban workforce under less than ideal conditions, at the same time as large numbers of more economically advantaged women were leaving lives devoted to agricultural labor and entering a world in which women were primarily stay-at-home mothers and protectors of the home and its morality.

Second, the new urban environment was crowded and dangerous. Epidemic disease carried in impure water supplies and poorly prepared food made urban death rates high. Middle- and upper-middle-class people had scarcely more protection than did the poor. Consequently, large numbers of young privileged people—people with every advantage except antibiotics and strong immune systems—were dying before their time. And such people—well taken care of by doting parents, but now suddenly dead—were being written about with enormous affection and hope.

Again, Americans—this time progressive mainstream Protestants—wrote about their experiences and feelings surrounding their dead children, and in so doing were pushing forward the idea that death, though tragic, also was sweet because parents could provide every comfort to the dying and could also hope, happily, that their separation from their children was temporary. This is a literature of reassurance that, in texts such as *Stepping Heavenward,* verge on being early self-help books about proper grieving. The point is that once again Americans felt confident that the way to Heaven, to the afterlife, was open and non-mysterious, and that the dead hovered close by.

The seamless continuity between this world and the afterlife was reinforced by the work of the aforementioned Elizabeth Stuart Phelps, whose 1866 book *Gates Ajar*—written to commemorate her brother who had died in the Civil War—was the best-selling novel of the American nineteenth century after *Uncle Tom's Cabin*. Phelps, in this and other books (*The Gates Between*; *Beyond the Gates*),[11] created fictions in which deserving but underappreciated women would die or appear to die, and then would visit elaborately described Heavens. *Gates Ajar*, supposedly about the protagonist's dead brother, really is a closely argued case for a radical revision of mainstream Protestant conceptions of the afterlife. This opened the "gates" for Phelps's later works in which her heroines learn languages, travel on diplomatic missions, listen to new music by Beethoven (offered in concerts in which the audience enjoys eight or nine senses), and have religious-erotic meetings with Jesus.

Far from being mere consolation, this literature forwarded the emerging feminist agenda but also did something radical that was noted in *Harper's Magazine* in 1881, in a piece provocatively titled "The Annexation of Heaven."[12] Phelps not only connected this life and the afterlife, affirming in a radical new way that theme of permeability, she also remade Heaven to fit her feminist and more conventional ideals—articulating that other very American do-it-yourself pragmatism. Her Heaven is egalitarian, filled with career and educational opportunities for women, and also provided with lovely upper-middle-class homes in which women find perfect male life partners and raise perfect children. For Phelps, Heaven has become a simulacrum of upper-middle American life and, as such, represented that American optimism that informs all the other death narrative themes.

This brief historic overview illustrates what clearly is a uniquely American confidence in reaching the afterlife, an equal confidence in being in touch with that realm, and a boldness in reshaping the afterlife in one's own image. These traits all continue, as strong as ever, through the twentieth century and into the twenty-first century. My discoveries at Hollywood Forever and my subsequent pilgrimage through online memorials to YouTube tributes and beyond, all the way to the transhumanist visions that promise to resurrect the dead in digital form, reflect this same American optimism about death and the afterlife. They also reflect American beliefs that the dead are close, that we can use technology to contact them, and that we have both the right and the power to design the afterlife in ways that favor both the living and the dead. American "annexation of Heaven" has not stopped yet and, as you will see, has reached places—some would say extremes—that Americans in the nineteenth century never could have imagined.

It is now time to go to Heaven, together.

Chapter 2

Beginnings: Online Memorialization and Haunted Social Media

LIGHTING A VIRTUAL CANDLE: FROM GRAVESITES TO ONLINE MEMORIALS

The first stop on my quest for the digital dead was the world of online cemeteries and online memorials. Discovering Hollywood Forever's incorporation of the digital as part of its memorial offerings led to the discovery of a complex, crowded world of online memorials that take the act of mourning into the new digital world.[1]

The first thing I learned is that there are two types of online memorials, those dedicated to honoring individual deaths and those created to honor events or groups.[2] There are so many memorial sites for individuals that one can even find "Top Ten" and "Six Best" lists online on such sites as Legacy Multimedia (http://www.legacy.com) and Everplans (https://www.everplans.com).[3]

The group or event memorials have no such rankings. They connect to public tragedies such as terrorist attacks; mass shootings; and natural disasters such as floods, hurricanes, and snowstorms. Sites dedicated to the attacks on the World Trade Center (http://www.911-remember.com, http://www.911memorial.org, http://www.voicesofseptember11.org/) and the Pentagon (http://pentagonmemorial.org), and to the passengers and crew of Flight 93 that crashed in Shanksville, Pennsylvania (http://www.nps.gov/flni/index.htm), remain active to this day. Sites are maintained by the families of 9/11 victims through the ongoing organizations that they have set up. Both the Iraq and Afghanistan wars (http://iraqmemorial.org/events.php/, http://www.legacy.com/memorial-sites/wars-in-iraq-and-afghanistan/) also have their own sites, set up and maintained by veterans' groups and the families of veterans. Ongoing memorials to the victims of school and theater shootings, such as Sandy Hook and Aurora, Colorado, tend to "live" at Legacy.com (www.legacy.com), a complex site that also houses many celebrity memorials and offers an online cemetery (http://www.legacy.com/memorial-sites/sandy-hook-school-tragedy/, http://www.legacy.com/memorial-sites/colorado-movie-theater-shooting/). Some of these tragedies also have group sites on Facebook.[4]

Although both individual and group sites have become commonplace and are easily accessed, they provide touching lessons to teach us about death's digital transformation as they move the brick and mortar cemetery and the public memorial from their worldly geography to the screen and the Cloud, creating new understandings of death online and allowing the dead to rest in the safety of virtual worlds where they are past all disturbance or harm.

theories?

INDIVIDUAL MEMORIALS

Individual memorial sites serve a variety of purposes. Some, such as Legacy.com and Everplans.com (https://www.everplans.com/introducing-everplans) offer hyperlink connections to sites that help one plan one's legacy; some connect to cremation and funeral and legal sites; some offer links to grief counselors, and one even offers connections to specialized grief management support groups for those who have lost children or spouses, or those who have lost loved ones to violence or accidents. There even is a service through Everplans (www.everplans.com) which is similar to Yelp and provides critiques resembling short restaurant and movie reviews. Today, every virtual cemetery allows the user to sign on using his or her Facebook username. Most offer basic memorial services for free or for a nominal annual or one-time charge. Virtual memorials include MeM.com, iLasting, Nevergone.com, Remembered.com, Tributes.com, Forevermissed.com, Imorial.com, Yourtribute.com, Sanctri (which lives on Facebook as a freestanding site), and many others are active as I write. The Sanctri site is unique in offering online support groups for people with special bereavement needs, such as those who have lost children or spouses, and those whose loved ones died by violence, drug overdose, and suicide.

All of these sites share common features emphasizing their intention to soothe and direct rather than to be innovative. They are "traditional" in both their "memorialization" of the dead and the methods they offer for mourners to respond. Each site provides, as one would expect, a place for the picture of the deceased accompanied by a brief biography and birth and death dates. More sophisticated sites—Legacy.com is the Mercedes or Cadillac of these sites, depending on your cultural preference—link to official obituaries already published in newspapers. Some sites embed the picture and biography in a pleasing setting. Many sites—especially the paid ones—offer templates, including a limited selection of background music from which the client can choose. "Amazing Grace," unsurprisingly is a staple. Employing the interactivity of digital media, every site also has links to spaces where visitors can leave brief memorial messages and offer virtual gifts such as flowers, as well as virtual candles that will burn eternally alongside one's message.[5]

These memorial messages suggest how the sites function as a sort of threshold or transition from the traditional gravesite memorial to what we will see as an opening to the dead, and to virtual hauntings unique to memorial and social media sites. As one might expect, similar to their brick-and-mortar counterparts, memorial message sites often contain prayers and passages from scripture. Messages tend to be posted more numerously on birth or death dates and on holidays such as Easter and Christmas. These messages cover the range of grief responses. Not surprisingly, many are poignant testimony from spouses, children, and parents, telling the deceased person how much they are missed, hoping they are doing well in Heaven, and sending reassurances that they are not forgotten and that the writer looks forward to the day when he or she can join the loved one in the afterlife. There also sometimes is that other side of grief—anger, puzzlement, a terrible sense of loss. These messages, though similar to the statements of grief found at traditional funerals and cemeteries, differ in their direct address to the deceased—an action that will become more significant in responses on social media.

The global nature of the Internet allows for a larger, more inclusive participation. For example, posts could include messages from a wide range of respondents—beyond the immediate family and community of the deceased. Both strangers and friends might respond in ways reminiscent of what happens on social media pages. For example, people from the distant past appear. They have lost touch with the deceased individual—someone they were close to in high school or university—and having somehow learned of the death, they want to reconnect, as if the dead person is still somehow available to see their post. This response, as we will see, also reflects the "haunted" realities of social media.

The Internet's global participatory range also enables strangers to re-spond to victims of mass shootings, such as at Sandy Hook, or to sol-diers killed in action. In these cases, people who never knew the victims feel justified in sending messages—expanding the boundaries of mourn-ing. Further, the Internet's interactive structure enables every site to al-low individuals to post everything from photographs to film and audio clips. Legacy.com, in fact, informs visitors not to post copyrighted im-ages, film, or music; but original songs, film, and photos are permitted. Again, reflecting that unique digital space suggesting "presence" of the deceased, people have left what amount to playlists for the dead, created by visitors who upload one or more of the dead person's favorite songs to a collective list, which visitors can play when they visit.

Despite the posting opportunities that these sites offer mourners, they are nonetheless traditional—a transference online of accepted mourning and funeral behaviors, with the addition of the ability to leave notes and songs and photographs.[6]

Yet, what is unexpected and what does point to a "new world" is that these messages almost always are addressed to the dead person in the present tense, with no hint that the writer has any doubts about the reality of the afterlife, or about the fact that the dead person is not somehow present, in an unspecified but genuine way, on his or her memorial site. There is just a hint here of an emerging new metaphysic that will be exam-ined in more detail when we address Facebook legacy pages. Putting the dead online has made them more available and, in an important sense, has relocated the dead from a distant Heaven to the ever-available Cloud.

This implicit optimism about the reality of the afterlife and the ongo-ing presence of the dead is further underscored in that one also never hears any suggestion that the bereaved message writer is worried about the fate of the dead person's soul. No one ever writes messages as if to someone they fear might be lost to eternal punishment. We will see that this sense of the "presence" of the dead person, this persistent use of the present tense in message postings, and the absence of any sense that be-ing dead might be a bad thing, are typical of memorial and social media sites. In both venues there is a kind of unsettling, haunting presence, the suggestion of a remarkable way the dead "live" online.

GROUP MEMORIALS

Group online memorials have been active since the mid-1990s; and since Margaret Wertheim wrote brilliantly about what she called "the pearly gates of cyberspace" in the late 1990s, and Carol Sofka recorded the earliest generations of online memorials, these sites have multiplied.[7]

Sites increased exponentially in importance, number, and sophistication after 9/11 and even more with the increasing popularity of Facebook and the ease with which users can set up group memorial pages using that service. Political memorials comprise a large category of such sites. Examples include the 9/11 memorials and the sites that catalog the victims of other acts of collective violence, such as Srebrenica and the Armenian Genocide. There also are sites dedicated to soldiers who died in Iraq and Afghanistan, as well as sites devoted to remembering African Americans who have been the target of police violence.

Depending on the severity of the political tragedy, its remoteness in history, and the number of people who identify themselves as connected to the victims, such memorial sites have varying degrees of activity. There are several 9/11 sites, from those maintained by the privately funded memorial and museum in Manhattan, to sites run by families of the victims, to those run by the federal government for the Pentagon and Flight 93 memorials. The 9/11 memorials also support separate sites for police officers and firefighters, and all of these sites maintain a level of activity that is unique among political or public memorial sites.

There also are memorial sites that commemorate the victims of mass killings, such as the Sandy Hook and Columbine school shootings and the mass shooting at the movie theater in Aurora, Colorado, and the church in Charleston, South Carolina. These sites verge toward the political, depending on the event. For example, the Charleston and Boston Marathon sites are on the cultural border between the privately tragic and those dedicated to political acts motivated by race, religion, and politics.

Another type of public memorial site concerns losses incurred by natural disasters, where the political context might be present but is less explicit. Hurricane Katrina, Superstorm Sandy, tornadoes, and flooding have led to the creation of websites or to special pages hosted on memorial sites or on Facebook. Although these sites might seem apolitical, the government's responses to natural events, and its longer-term policies in dealing with the aftermath of such events, play roles in some of these sites. For example, to the extent that the Hurricane Katrina victims were overwhelmingly poor and disproportionately people of color lends an inevitably political tone to Katrina memorials. At the same time, the Katrina memorial hosted on Legacy.com performs the enormous service of listing information about the life and death of every single one of the more than 1,800 victims, no matter how poor that person might have been.

Like the individual memorials, many of these sites allow the mourner to engage with the victims, and some offer videographics. For instance, the highly professional and freestanding site of the Iraq Veterans Memorial offers a "laptop vigil," which involves downloading a memorial film featuring filmed interviews with wives, mothers, and friends of soldiers killed in Iraq. A well-crafted film, it shows each person who was killed in action, and then moves through a professional dissolve to a family member talking about that person. Other sites are equally well produced. The Sandy Hook memorial on the Legacy.com site, for example, has collected the image and obituary of every single victim and offers the opportunity for visitors to leave posts. Clicking on the name of a victim takes the visitor to a page that lists comments left by friends, family members, and—more often than one would predict—complete strangers, many of whom cite Scripture. Like the individual memorial sites, these group sites are global—expanding the mourner beyond the immediate family and community—and offer the same opportunity to engage through these posts. The dead here have in a very real sense been brought closer through their digital presence.

The sites dedicated to less recent major political tragedies, such as the Holocaust, the Armenian Genocide, and Bosnian ethnic cleansing, are also freestanding and combine political agendas with mourning. The Armenian and Bosnian sites record long-standing political crimes that have not been fully acknowledged. The Armenian sites are geared toward a rehearsal of the 1915 murder of more than one million Armenians in Anatolia during the last years of the Ottoman Empire and the first of the modern Turkish state. The Turkish government never has accepted responsibility for the event; therefore, the sites make and remake a case that the rest of the world long ago acknowledged. They keep the memory of this long-standing but unacknowledged crime alive, and it is difficult to look at the grainy, century-old photographs of Armenians on the move with all their possessions, without being affected.

The Holocaust sites are perhaps the most educational of all the political-tragedy memorials. They rival the 9/11 sites in polish and level of activity. They do, however, have a split message. Holocaust sites divide their attention between memorializing the six million victims of Nazi crimes and mounting a serious effort to educate site visitors on Jewish, Zionist, and Israeli history; on the details of the Holocaust; and on the current state of Holocaust memorials and Jewish life in various western European countries.

The 9/11 memorial sites represent a special subcategory. There are sites that cover all aspects of the tragedy, as well as separate sites that deal with the World Trade Center, the Pentagon, and the crash of Flight 93 in Shanksville, Pennsylvania. The privately funded 9/11 Memorial and Museum on-site in lower Manhattan hosts one website, and there are separate sites for the Tower victims as well as for firefighters, police officers, and EMTs. The federal government has established and built a memorial to the victim/heroes of Flight 93 and another at the site of the Pentagon in Virginia. Both Shanksville and the Pentagon host well-constructed federally maintained memorial websites, and both sites also have privately maintained pages. All of these sites are more active than many others, because 9/11 still represents a defining event in history for every American, and the event has been marketed as a cultural landmark since it occurred. Every victim is listed and many have notes posted along with their pictures and biographies. Many of the 9/11 families still live and work in Manhattan and its surrounding boroughs and counties, thus the sorrow and sense of blank loss one reads in these sites—especially those that are privately maintained—is both palpable and moving.[8]

FAILED MEMORIALS? THE ABANDONMENT OF THE ONLINE DEAD

Both the individual and group sites mentioned make the dead easily accessible. They allow mourners and even strangers to visit the dead in the quiet privacy of a home or office. The sites allow visitors to do more than they are allowed to do in a cemetery or a mausoleum. Visitors can leave notes, place virtual flowers, light virtual candles, play beloved songs, and gaze at photographs and film clips of the deceased. It would seem that these user-friendly, convenient memorial sites would draw a steady stream of visitors. But the fate of the online dead is troubling.

What remains a constant for almost all of these sites—especially for the individual sites—is that they soon tend to be as neglected and derelict as real-world cemeteries dedicated to the interment of everyday individuals. However optimistic these sites are and however much they invoke the presence of the dead and keep them close by reinserting them into the familiar context of friends and family, these also are sites that are soon abandoned, just as the dead in American cemeteries and memorial parks also tend to be abandoned. Upon visiting paid individual memorial sites, people find that the "gravesites" there are no longer accessible because the modest annual fee for their use is in arrears. It appears that the bereaved family and friends that originally set them up soon lost interest and abandoned them entirely. On other sites one finds nothing—no flowers or candles or notes or music from anyone, even those closest to the deceased. A few individual memorials show a thin stream of visitors, many during the first few days after the virtual interment. This stream almost always dries up, however, only to be replaced by intermittent messages left on important days such as birthdays, death dates, and major religious holidays. Online memorials, however, apparently are as emotionally unsatisfying to the bereaved as are real-world memorial parks.

This abandonment seems surprising given the accessibility of these sites. Although online memorials play some of the same social role as brick and mortar cemeteries, they in some ways seem to be better than actual cemeteries. In addition to the ease in visiting them and leaving notes and gifts for the dead, visitors might feel that the dead seem more available online than they would be in a real-world cemetery. Online the only thing separating the visitor from the dead is the service's user interface which—because it resembles those of interactive social media sites—seems to connect him or her to the dead rather than separate them. This sense of immediacy and intimacy is evidenced by the many posts directly addressing the deceased in present tense. In contrast, the very structure of the traditional cemetery creates boundaries between the dead and the mourner. In a cemetery the heavy tombstone or bronze marker seems to fix the dead to the earth, and the enormous weight of the soil resting on the body—which also is encased in a sealed coffin—conspires to make the dead seem very far away, impossible to touch. Even the less onerous separation imposed by sealing the ashes of the dead into a small vault space in a columbarium is still a severe, unchangeable physical separation.

Thus, the online dead seem so much more accessible in many ways. If the site is set up well, we see them, hear them, spend time with them, and even share music with them. So, one would expect the online dead in both individual and group memorial sites to be so much more popular than those who are interred or inurned. Why then is visiting such sites, even for one driven primarily by curiosity, such a discouraging experience?

At the heart of this apparent failure could be the very feature that makes online memorials appealing in the first place. These sites too closely resemble the social media sites to which they are always connected. The ostensive interactivity of these memorial sites—the ability of the mourner to upload posts and to activate videos—might be too limited, a "mock" interactivity that ultimately fails. The sites are not truly interactive for the best of reasons. Despite the apparent perception of a "presence" in this digital context—leading to those present-tense posts—the putative hosts, the individuals whose pages are visited, are uniformly absent. In a world in which many people spend almost half their waking hours staring at screens and typing into devices, a sub-world in which the screens never respond on sites that seem designed for a response makes no sense and ultimately will earn nobody's loyalty.

Although the memorial sites do a commendable job of providing a place in which people can deposit their sorrow for a time, ultimately sites dedicated to once-living individuals have to respond or, like the grave sites they mimic, they will be neglected and forgotten. We live in a world of continual back-and-forth data flow. People post pictures of every meal they eat; we pay at the grocery checkout line by passing our phone over the screen reader; and we ask Siri where the closest Indian restaurant can be found. Before we go there, of course, we check the Yelp reviews, written by people we presume are like us. Our reality is constantly being invaded by voices from the Cloud. We are used to transcendence, to voices from the air. If the dead fail to respond, then we treat them much as we do technological devices that are too slow, too complicated, too limited in their ability to connect us to the flood of information. We put them aside and rarely think of them at all. The failure of these memorial sites curiously replicates the failure of the traditional cemetery—the dead remain dead, absent; the illusion of a subjectivity that initially leads to poignant posts dissolves. This Internet afterlife is, so to speak, short-lived.

Another related reason that these individual online memorials are so soon abandoned is that they cannot compete with the usability offered by other sites on the Internet. As we will see later in this chapter, remembering the dead online seems better suited to the Facebook pages of individuals and to the wilds of YouTube memorial videos. Both types of sites flourish and are visited, perhaps because it is only on sites designed by and for individuals that the language of mourning persists and the memories of the dead endure.

Memorials for public tragedies have a slightly different appeal and therefore have slightly different responses. Most of the online sites commemorating mass shootings and natural disasters cannot maintain themselves on their own, and instead are hosted by Facebook or the more highly developed memorial sites such as Legacy.com. Thus, even public tragedies—with a few exceptions such as 9/11 and the Holocaust—struggle for attention and space in the rough-and-tumble world of the Internet. Once they are set up by successful corporate entities such as Legacy.com, however, such memorial pages get a fair amount of traffic over time, partly because they are so well made and easy to use, but also partly because public memorial sites have a larger natural audience. A visitor need not be related to the victims to mourn them, and many of the notes posted to such sites consist of passages from scripture posted by people who have no discernible connection to the events being memorialized. Additionally, leaving a note for someone on such a site seems more like an uplifting act of citizenship, or an affirmation of solidarity, than a sad effort one does alone. Messages left on public memorial sites have a civic character and might even be seen as acts of moral righteousness.

Therefore, visiting public memorials tends not to be quite as dispiriting as roaming among the poorly remembered private dead, but inevitably are moving and often heart-wrenching. It is not easy to visit the Sandy Hook memorial, or that dedicated to the 1,800-plus victims of Hurricane Katrina, and no American can see photographs and biographies of the 9/11 dead and remain untouched.

Both individual and public memorials keep the dead with us, and thereby offer forms of Internet afterlife. But in the last analysis, all these sites are frustratingly one-way. I can visit any of these sites and be touched; I can even imagine that the dead are somehow present in the Cloud. But in none of these cases am I really finding a new Heaven online, something that my initial experience with Hollywood Forever's "Library of Lives" provoked me into seeking.

We have to look further, and the next stop is a set of online sites in which the dead reach out directly to shape the lives of the living. Welcome to the world of the online vault.

THE VIRTUAL VAULT: CURATORIAL SITES

Before venturing into the haunted world of social media with its curiously more "real" sense of "presence" online, I want to report that I found another world of sites for the dead, the curatorial or archival sites. These are at least as numerous as the memorial sites, but have three characteristics that differentiate them from memorial sites and make them more successful in terms of a higher rate of visits.

First, unlike the memorial sites, archival and curatorial sites possess a kind of built-in agency. A "subject" is somewhat present, because the sites are set up by the deceased person before he or she dies, and are meant to carry that person's wishes into the future. Just as wills did in the past, these sites impose the "mort main" or "dead hand" of the previous generation onto its successors. Second, even if strictly speaking such sites are not interactive, it takes some effort to access them because they are designed to thwart cyber-criminals. Thus, the user has to obtain more than one password, usually from a designated third party, and sometimes a fourth party. Once on the site, the user also has to activate accounts, contact attorneys, send documents to relevant government agencies, and perform other similar actions. This is markedly different from lighting a virtual candle and leaving a brief message.

Third, unlike memorial sites, there is very little chance that these sites will be neglected or left dormant, because neglecting them could mean that one loses access to important revenue or property. As time goes on, there could be every reason to maintain such an online "vault" because it is already set up to protect and manage one's fiscal affairs and to provide a safe place to store copies of vital documents.

There are many archival sites. What do these sites typically offer? They are divided into two types, the functions of which sometimes overlap. Some sites emphasize their role as online safe deposit boxes or safes that will keep critical data safe should one die or become incapacitated. They offer what they call "bank-" and "hospital-" level security that they claim cannot be hacked.

Other sites offer an array of services for organizing the information and documents that the first type of site merely stores. Proprietary software enables customers to organize their effects into manageable and appropriate categories, and—depending on how interactive the site is—offers explicit instructions for organizing the customer's legacy documents and information. Some sites go even further and offer software that allows customers to create their own will online without using an attorney. U.S. Legal Wills (http://www.uslegalwills.com/mywill) helps a customer craft a will, as well as create both financial and healthcare powers of attorney, DNR protocols, living wills, and expatriate wills. DocSafe also stores pre- and post-nuptial agreements; anatomical gift wishes; marriage, birth, and death certificates; insurance policies; inventory and appraised value of property, deeds and mortgages; and business records. Lastly, DocuBank (www.docubank.com), the oldest and in many ways the most developed of these sites, offers a feature called "emergency cards," physical plastic cards that contain vital health information, such as drug allergies and medical conditions, as well as contact information and numbers to call to get DNR instructions and living wills, and information regarding who holds the power of attorney having to do with end-of-life health issues.

CURATING DEATH: ONLINE IDENTITY PROTECTION
AFTER DEATH

There also are sites whose primary focus is managing one's online identity after death. These sites provide protection, but also in a very real sense suggest the agency of the deceased postmortem. Two sites, for example, Protect Their Memories (www.protecttheirmemories.com) and WebCease (www.webcease.com), purport to answer the question "How do we terminate our virtual lives?" Protect Their Memories concentrates its attention on situations in which an individual has died and left no provision for dealing with his or her online identity. WebCease, by contrast, offers a wider range of interventions into deceased individuals' digital assets, promising that it will deal with four kinds of digital assets—financial, personal, social, and loyalty rewards. WebCease provides usernames and passwords for things such as bank accounts, mortgage payments, credit cards, and utilities, to appropriately named heirs, as well as managing access to online hotel and travel services such as Orbitz and Priceline. Additionally, WebCease will pass on necessary information for email accounts and social media sites, shutting them down when appropriate, or memorializing them when that is indicated.

So we come to the end of the various memorial, curatorial, digital data management, and messaging services that represent the less interactive versions of Internet afterlife. As has been demonstrated, none of these many services purports to offer "real" afterlife. Each of them replicates a form of memory or derivative agency that pre-existed the digital era. Memorial sites are cemeteries; online safes are versions of worldly safes and safe deposit boxes and lawyers' files; digital asset management, while new, is another version of estate management and does what prudent people and their designated executors always have done.

What distinguishes the online memorials and safes and data management and messaging services is that the information they store and organize is there forever, protected and relatively inviolate, free from concerns about natural disasters and forgetfulness and the ravages of time on documents. A person's whole postmortem presence, as the one who leaves possessions and messages, is extended into an indefinite future; messages can be delivered years later, and there is no time limit on self-congratulatory or revelatory Web pages. There are real-world precedents for this as well. For example, Thomas Merton's journals could not be published until 25 years postmortem; Margaret Atwood has written a novel that cannot be published until 100 years after her death; the Wu-Tang Clan produced a single-copy album sold to the highest bidder with the stipulation that it cannot be reproduced for decades. The difference between real-world postmortem revelations and those that occur online is that the online messages and texts share with other items on the Internet an existence for as long as there is an Internet. This is certainly a form of Internet afterlife, albeit embryonic and underdeveloped as compared to what artificial intelligence (AI) promises and what the transhumanists envision. Living beyond one's death is certainly more impressive, to some people if not to all, than leaving a time-dated manuscript behind.

SAVED ONLINE: DIGITALIZING DEATH'S BEGINNING SALVATION

Online services, though certainly not totally revolutionary, are transformative. They reflect a new optimism, a digital "owning of death" that in a very real way compromises the boundary between life and death and points to powerful challenges to traditional ideas of death and religious conceptions of the afterlife, judgment, and sin. They represent, in fact, a new optimism—one founded in technology rather than in traditional religion. As noted, this optimism is different from the sense that the soul of the deceased has not met a negative afterlife fate.

At one very obvious level, this additional optimism is evidenced by people's willingness to entrust their most important documents, their memories, and their digital legacy to relatively anonymous online services and sites. This willingness suggests a trust in the online world; we are increasingly familiar with, and comfortable with, websites and the still-mysterious "Cloud," to store data—such as in Evernote and Dropbox—and to maintain our individual and collective memories, as with Facebook, Instagram, and—in a different way—Twitter. In a sense, we believe in these sites, have a kind of faith in them, so that when we are asked to extend the belief to include matters concerning death and legacies, we also tend to be comfortable in the relative anonymity of online sites in dealing with these somewhat delicate issues.

On a deeper, more revolutionary and transformative level, however, the use of online memorial, curatorial, and messaging sites all point toward our shared cultural sense that the dead are safe from judgment and to some extent are under our control rather than God's. Despite the fact that we might neglect them, setting up online memorials speaks to our collective rejection of a model of death and the afterlife in which souls/persons are judged and possibly found wanting. This behavior suggests that we would not go to the trouble of setting up a memorial site, finding and up-loading images and video clips, writing stories, inviting friends and family, leaving tributes that testify to our continuing love, unless we lived in the certainty that our dead, and we ourselves, were unquestionably saved.

The only note of anxiety that the online services we have been discussing evokes is that of the sites such as WebCease that promise to save the dead from possible embarrassment by summarily shutting down their social media sites. If there is sin, it resides in social media indiscretions, not in acts of evil that need expiation. Wrongdoing in the sense of past gaffes should be obliterated, not paid for. When it comes to dead family and loved ones, we can postulate that in this context twenty-first-century Americans do not admit the reality of divinely punishable evil. This issue is addressed later in this text. Suffice it to say that the world of online memorials seems to exist with very little reference to traditional religious ideas of reward and punishment, even on those sites that are explicitly tied to particular faiths.

DEATH ON SOCIAL MEDIA

Such optimism takes on a stronger and stranger form when we enter the familiar and ubiquitous world of social media, our next step on this journey toward a new world where the finality of death finds a kind of digital translation into deathlessness. YouTube and MySpace, as well as some other lesser known but nonetheless interesting sites, further personalize digital memorialization, giving us a stronger form of the dead online. Facebook and Twitter provide a different sense of the dead, a kind of haunted space, a cyberheaven, in which the dead live on in a phenomenon we could call "Facebook Ghosts." We then move from this relatively fixed world of social media to a new and somewhat startling space in which we begin to encounter a "new" form of the online dead in the familiar and yet unfamiliar version of the avatar figure, which catapults us into a realm where the "dead" appear to have actual agency and reside in yet another "new" cyberheaven—the world of beings who seem present but who are what David Chalmers has aptly labeled "philosophical zombies."

YOUTUBE: MEMORIALS AND A NEW HEAVEN

YouTube has become a very familiar site that allows for the sharing of information in a variety of forms—from music to print text to video, ranging from movie trailers, to artistic sharing, to lectures such as the TED talks. It also is a site that captures the dying and the dead in a unique form of memorialization. YouTube takes online memorialization to a more personal and, at times, heartbreaking place. For example, one site takes you to an organization called "Parents of Murdered Children," complete with a "wall" listing all the children to whom it is dedicated. Even stranger and more wrenching are the video clips that track the very brief lives of infants born with fatal birth defects. These montages often trace the "progress" of these doomed people from birth, with the mother holding the child in her arms and the father looking on, a mixture of joy and anxiety freezing his face, to day after day of increasing alarm and hopelessness, tempered by a sorrowful, loving acceptance of the inevitable. There are many photographs of mothers, grandparents, and husbands cradling the small corpse in their arms. Expressions cover a terrible range. We are given a multidimensional experience that includes both the grief as well as the actual dying in these images of the dead. These photographs of family holding dead children recall the images of the dead captured by the first daguerreotypes.

These heartbreaking sites are only one of many types of existing YouTube memorials, most created by the people who are grieving. Some show a professional touch. The Hollywood Forever biopic option has become more widespread, and it isn't difficult to find advertisements for a range of audio and video memorial tributes. Whether the YouTube dead are "present" to the living, whether memorializing people on this platform opens a door (as, we will see, Facebook seems to do) to allow the dead through to be present to the living, is not clear. What is certain, however, is that viewing the images of dying infants suggests that these brief lives are being captured and made present by their parents, and in a very real way, the infants receive a type of Internet afterlife. And, surely and poignantly, the YouTube afterlife these children receive has a special weight because their earthly lives were so short.[9]

ROGUE SITES: MYDEATH SPACE

In addition to YouTube memorial postings, there also is a large population of almost completely unregulated online memorials that are so decentered that it is all but impossible to trace or to make generalizations about them as a genre. These rogue sites, however, constitute an important segment of online memorials (and certainly among the most poignant), so they are an important expression of the way death manifests online.

One such site, which also is the most organized, is called MyDeath Space (www.mydeathspace.com). The name is a gloss on MySpace because the site originally represented a kind of coda to that social media service. It was created by Mike Patterson to cull all the death notices associated with deceased MySpace users. MyDeathSpace would publish or republish obituaries associated with deceased MySpace members; and similar to YouTube clips, anyone who visited the site could comment on the deaths they found recorded there. Unlike other memorial sites which tend to be reverential, subdued, and tasteful, however, MyDeathSpace is the obverse; it is tabloid-vulgar and lacking in all restraint.

MyDeathSpace is, in fact, a strange and disconcerting place to visit, reflecting what one might characterize as death's dark side. Many of the deaths it reports are the result of accidents, suicide, and murder, with the occasional early death from cancer or organ failure. Most of the dead listed are young, because young people die from the "dark" causes noted above more often than do the elderly. Not only are the deaths often sudden and violent, but the comments are equally violent and are often critical of the dead person, faulting them for being stupid or weak or clueless. Many of the comments use crude language and equally crude humor to mock and demean the dead. Online death, in these circumstances, is as unprotected as are many other serious subjects on the Internet. Internet afterlife also includes a level of disrespect for the dead, something one doesn't see in many other social contexts.

There are moments of compassion, especially for suicides and victims of violence, but because the site appears to be all but uncensored, supportive and consoling remarks exist alongside those that make one's skin crawl. This is a site for the freest of free speech. It is both harrowing and touching—often when one is reading about a single death.

FACEBOOK GHOSTS

YouTube and the postings of such rogue sites as MyDeathSpace strongly resemble the biopics and media opportunities offered by Hollywood Forever. Even at their most disturbing, they are still familiar; there is no sense of a presence, an "other" with agency of any sort on the screen. Facebook and Twitter provide a stepping-stone toward a different type of experience of the dead online. Facebook has more than 1.5 billion users worldwide and millions of them die every year. Given the nature of the Internet, however, none of these people's Facebook pages disappears unless a family member who can prove a relationship to the deceased actively intervenes to request that the page be deactivated. There is nothing about these pages that alerts the visitor that the page's owner is deceased. Therefore, a Facebook user could mistakenly send this deceased owner a "friend request," leave a critical or crude comment, or ask the person to join a group. In response to the "living on" of the Facebook dead, family members informed Facebook management that the site had to make some provisions for dead members. Facebook did so by late 2009, and today there are protocols for changing a Facebook page from a standard page to a memorial page, which Facebook calls a "Memorialized Account."[10] This feature allows for a "Legacy Contact" who can add a few things, and allows friends and family to post items after the user's death. The Facebook page originally set up, however, remains intact—including its pictures, history, preferences, and privacy settings.

As Patrick Stokes argues persuasively in his "Ghost in the Machine," the "you" that remains as the site's focus is not the "you" as the autonomous agent you once were. "You" are now the sum of your content at the time of your death, as well as all the comments that people post on the page. Stokes makes the point that, over time, as the posts accumulate without any responses from you, the "you" who once ruled your site progressively disappears and is replaced by a "you" made up of, and by, the people who post to your site. Unlike the memorial sites, although this is your page, you no longer control it. Your Internet afterlife then becomes your friends' version of that afterlife. Because there is no longer any "you," "you" become their creation. At the same time, there is the "sense" that "you" still somehow exist somewhere on the screen, on the site—a ghost, as Stokes perceptively notes, in the machine.[11]

This phenomenon also was noted by John Dobler who, when studying MySpace posts, found that after users die, even though friends and family know that the person is dead, they still, even years later, post questions, ask for advice, share news, and in every way behave as if the person who once ran the site were still somehow present at or near the site. Sometimes the comments mention that the one-time "owner" is in Heaven, but more often the poster writes as if the owner were somehow present on the site.[12]

These online "beings" are a type of Internet afterlife, "Facebook ghosts," who live on, at least in the experience of page visitors, as subjects in the Cloud, a new vision of Heaven. Why can't there be a new magical place, located somewhere between Earth and traditional Heaven, where those with online identities still "live," gathering a postmortem reality from the fact that there is a new place, a new space—cyberspace or the Cloud—to which the Internet dead can go?

Social media sites are never memorial sites pure and simple, sites set up after the fact to mark the death and disappearance of someone who never before had a presence on that memorial site; unlike memorial sites, on these sites the dead retain a powerful first-person feel. The person who set them up provided all the information, made choices about what to reveal and what to conceal, and designed the site to suit him- or herself, within the very strict constraints that services such as Facebook impose. This first-person presence will never change, whether or not the site becomes a memorial. As the philosopher Jacques Derrida suggests in his ruminations on ghosts and *The Specter of Marx*, for example, as well as *Fors*, we can plausibly assert that in some unspecified sense the dead Facebook user haunts his or her site as a panoply of words, images, and sounds. The dead have never been so vividly and easily available.

Because of their first-person character, social media sites to some degree appear haunted. Most scholars, however, dismiss the very idea that such hauntings are more than symbolic. Even though visitors leave posts that sound as if they consider the dead user likely to read or listen to them, commentators rarely get past the cautious claim that such posters either believe that the dead user is still somehow alive or they consciously choose to act as if that were the case. No one entertains the idea that perhaps Facebook pages really are haunted. The most radical allowance the scholars make is that posters who keep sending messages to the dead assume, as many posts say, that the dead person is in Heaven and able to read the post. In this case we have to assume that, to answer the question that one article poses, Heaven does have Wi-Fi. But even here this is a strictly one-way connection. The dead in Heaven can read posts, but cannot add items to their Facebook "walls" or send private messages.

FACEBOOK AS NEAR-DEATH EXPERIENCE VISITATIONS

The phenomenon of near-death experiences (NDE)[13] suggests another intriguing context for these hauntings. These are experiences in which individuals account for almost dying and traveling almost to Heaven only to be told "it wasn't their time yet." It has become a commonplace act of the modern death movement (represented by organizations such as the Association for Death Education and Counseling) to relate powerful testimonials to the reality of both such experiences as well as post-death visitations. Hospice workers and intensive care nurses, as well as "civilians" who have lost those close to them, bear witness to the reality of dreams in which the dead visit the living to comfort and instruct. They add stories about what can be read as postmortem visitations. Keys appear on tables; doors open and close. Events happen that are tied intimately to things that the recently deceased did, and these events seem to have no other explanation than the postmortem presence of the dead. These manifestations suggest that there is anecdotal evidence that the dead return to us, in the form of dream images, uncanny events, even sightings of the dead on city streets. The idea is that in some unspecified and non-theoretical way, the dead survive and contact us.

Within this context, some Facebook posts could be understood as responses to such "visits" or responses to the "fact" that when some people visit the homepage of a dead social media site user, those people feel an inchoate presence of the dead that resembles dreams or sightings. Some people feel the Facebook dead "living" on in a new postmortem space, the metaphoric Cloud, what used to be called, and sometimes still is called, "cyberspace." The presence of the Facebook dead is a presence in this Cloud.

These dead are not precisely in Heaven, a belief which also entails a complex schema of God, salvation, and punishment. Instead, some people immediately and spontaneously relocate the social media dead into a new ontological location, somewhere "between" Heaven and Earth. This is a case of the medium creating the message. Because Facebook offers a putative "site," a type of place, it is not a huge imaginative leap to extend this vague sense of "place" to include a realm that transcends the ordinary Facebook space without ever leaving it. Without Facebook, no Facebook space. Without the Internet, no Facebook. Without Facebook space, no Facebook "ghosts." Without Facebook ghosts, no Facebook "Heaven."

This idea postulates a new kind of transcendent sacred space—outside of the ordinary religious hierarchies—where the Facebook dead can "live," hovering about but not exactly "in" their sites. In so doing, Facebook provides a non-theoretical quasi-Heaven, a hypothetical, notional space in which the complex imagistic, linguistic, and aural Facebook personae—never quite the Earth-people who created them—can persist.

Hence, Facebook users—as the amalgam of posts and pictures—live on, not merely as that amalgam, but (and this is admittedly ambiguous) through what that amalgam represents. This could mean that there is a freestanding Facebook identity that has acquired its own life. Or, rather, that the dead Earth person, or something essential and real about them, that inhabits the posts and pictures also inhabits the Facebook site and its accompanying Cloud. Whatever this is makes its presence felt there.

We do not have many reports of the dead posting to their public sites, however, this is not the point. The point is that people feel the living presence of the dead on their sites and send messages that reflect this feeling. Even if as Patrick Stokes suggests a dead person's Facebook identity is progressively occluded and obscured over time by friends posting their own autobiographical information, there is still the sense— even years after the Facebook user's death—that something of the agent, the subject, remains present on the site. Also, interestingly, the ghosts on Facebook can live on as objects of belief and action that merit no empirical proofs or careful argument. Because nothing publicly testable is claimed, no one need either provide or ask for evidence or argument. Thus the belief in Facebook ghosts can persist in that half-world of hypotheticals that need no further specification or testing.

TWITTERING GHOSTS: LIVING ON THROUGH POSTMORTEM TWEETS

There also are sites that create another type of digital ghost. These are more purely autobiographical sites, such as Dead Man's Switch (www .deadmansswitch.net), If I Die (ifidie.net), and Email from Death (http:// emailfromdeath.com) among others, as well as the Twitter-specific service called LivesOn (https://twitter.com/_liveson).[14] With the exception of the last service, these "switch" sites are programmed to send out emails if the service does not hear from the client at regular, previously established intervals. The services build in failsafe procedures so they do not send out emails prematurely. The idea here is not a memorial or data management or an online safe, but more a direct reaching beyond the grave to, as PassingBye says, "have the last word."

These emails can convey anything that the client chooses; they are encrypted and protected so no one but the recipient sees them, and they often self-destruct once sent. All of these services and subservices have one thing in common: They are attempts by the still-living to control the meaning of their deaths by creating a documentary presence that tells their descendants exactly what they were thinking before and, we presume, at the moments of their deaths. Parting Wishes (www.parting-wishes.com), a site that also provides an online safe and software to write a will, adds the ability to set up not a single set of emails or a memorial, but a permanent webpage (using the My Life program) that serves as a self-created tribute to oneself, so that even if one is forgotten in the world, one can "obtain immortality on the Internet."

LivesOn is a bit different and quite odd, albeit interesting. This service promises to generate characteristic tweets for an individual after that individual dies. The client allows the service to access his or her tweets, and provides further information about tastes, beliefs, and preferences so that, using these analytics, the service's programs can analyze the data and establish algorithms for the kinds of tweets that the client typically would generate, including to whom the tweets would be directed and when they would be posted. The client then sets up an alternative Twitter account using the service's protocols. This is not the original account but one to which the service has full access, and it bears the name of the original account holder. When the LivesOn service tests to see whether the client is still alive and receives no response after repeated attempts, the alternate Twitter ID begins to generate its own tweets, which it will continue to do indefinitely, so long as the service is paid to do so. We have, therefore a twittering ghost—a postmortem presence—that is another form of how the digital world has created a death space online.[15]

In this chapter we have experienced a family of different Internet afterlives: memorial sites, both individual and public; archival and autobiographical sites; social media sites; and the rogue sites, MyDeath Space and YouTube memorials. I speculated that Facebook—and perhaps YouTube and possibly the 9/11 Live memorial—offer openings to other worlds, but that we have not yet seen a literal Internet afterlife whose reality we can publicly test. Now it is time to turn in that direction, as we move from the relatively static world of fixed websites to the moving, three-dimensional landscape of cyberspace and avatars.

Chapter 3

The Rise of the Avatar

Despite its deficiencies, digital technology has brought the dead closer and, in a manner, has given the living a new way to maintain a significant level of intimacy. As we examine all these services, we see that they cover both our dying and the things we leave behind when we die. There are virtual cemeteries and virtual vaults and virtual caretakers aplenty. Online memorials, designer films, virtual vaults, and the like have in a sense freed the dead from the alienating tangle of medical devices and funeral trappings that have kept them from us for so many decades. Victorian Americans touched the dead, washed their bodies and laid them out in the parlor. We do not do any of that, but through YouTube postings, memorial sites, and archival services we take care of our dead in new ways that seem as personal and that might well be as satisfying and healing. Ironically, despite the warnings of critics of new media such as Sherry Turkle—who worry that digitalization has made us "alone, together"—in the case of our relationships with the dead, in a very real sense we have been brought closer to those who in all other ways have disappeared.[1]

All of these sites and services, however, provide an Internet afterlife in a purely metaphoric sense. All the sites and services that we have covered so far accept the finality of death. They exploit the timelessness of the Internet to keep the dead with us, in image and sound, and to extend our wishes into a world that we cannot inhabit. In no case do any of these services promise to bring the dead back to life or to continue one's own life into the future. The dead remain dead, and the living will join them, sooner or later.

The world of artificial intelligence (AI) and avatars—from the use of AI in the form of such "persons" as "Siri" or the voice on your GPS, to the interactive world of computer gaming in which "you" become an active character and to some extent creator of the narrative—brings us to a new dimension of Internet afterlife.[2] Although Facebook ghosts and postmortem tweets suggest a kind of postmortem digital presence, they nonetheless still exist in worlds of discontinuous fixed sites, with no talking or listening or advising presences like Siri or a chatbot.[3]

When we visit the dead on memorial sites we do not enter into these digital spaces as anything close to an embodied figure, nor do the dead come to meet us. Whatever is spectrally present on Facebook and Twitter cannot be seen directly and remains at a distance. The presence of the dead is suggested, not manifested.

When we enter the "other" Internet, cyberspace rather than the Web, however, we enter a different online geography, a three-dimensional virtual landscape in which we—the "you" of the narrative—participate in the form of avatars. We enter the "spaces" where screens open up to us, and we meet other moving bodies in these spaces. This structure of participatory online embodiments becomes a new template for startling forms of online afterlife.[4]

Popular culture has for some time suggested the existence of these new worlds, particularly William Gibson's cyberspace *Neuromancer*[5] and Neal Stephenson's Metaverse in *Snow Crash*,[6] not to mention the Matrix in the film of the same name.[7]

All of these point to the reality of worlds inside computers, into which flesh and blood humans, in some form, can disappear and in which the dead, as uploaded minds, can "live," as the Dixie Flatliner lives in cyberspace after his death, in *Neuromancer*.[8]

Yet, as familiar as this "reality" on the screen has become since Gibson and Stephenson wrote about it in the long-ago 1980s and early '90s, there is a difference between popular culture texts that create a fictional online world where people can live, and the experience of actually meeting the dead online. Can the metaphoric space inside a computer really become a new home for the dead?

Anyone who has spent time playing online games or visiting Second Life sites (secondlife.com) might be more immediately familiar with the world of online avatars than with that of postmortem tweeting, or that of MyDeathSpace obituaries.[9,10] This familiar world might prove to be stranger than we think, however, because it is through the use of such avatars that we first encounter something quite new—embodiments of the dead online.

To understand how this could happen we must enter the world of computer-generated avatars, the beings that inhabit cyberspace in their different manifestations, to determine whether, and how, such cyber-beings might someday become carriers for the personal identities of the dead.

The thought experiment of David Chalmers in *The Conscious Mind* (1996)—what he called the "philosophical zombie" or "p-zombie"—provides a helpful concept in exploring this new world. Although Chalmers envisioned his p-zombie as ensconced in a biological home rather than a digital one, his idea captures the type of "being" we encounter in these computer-generated avatars. Chalmers' idea is that we can imagine a robotic being that looks and acts and sounds exactly like a human being and whose responses to questions and situations would be indistinguishable from those of a "real" human being, but which would have nothing going on inside except the sorting operations of a set of complex computer programs.[11] We are in a world of "as if"—a world of suspended disbelief in which the dead appear as if alive, but are still not conscious agents with autonomous subjectivity. This state of online "being"—consciousness in actuality online—will be the promise of the transhumanists.[12] But first we need to review avatar "states of being" and this translation of the dead online.

THE AVATAR: PRIMARY FORMS

The first step is to be clear about what computer avatars are and to develop an understanding of how they function. The distinguishing feature of every computer game narrative is that it puts "you"—the player—into the narrative itself as an actor, so that "you" become a character both engaging in and, to some extent, creating the story that the game is telling. Second Life also puts you into a new setting so that "you" become a participant in a world that looks somewhat like the material world outside of the screen, but which exists entirely in the alternate world of cyberspace.

"*Avatar*" is a Sanskrit term used by Sikhs and Hindus to stand for the incarnation or representation of a god in human form.[13] The term was appropriated to the world of video gaming in 1985 by Richard Garriott in his game *Ultima IV: Quest of the Avatar*, to mean "the player's real-time presence in an online world."[14] This is now familiar activity: the game player, or the Second Life visitor, puts on the virtual body of a character in the game or in a Second Life environment. A player participates in a game's virtual world as such an "incarnated" figure, and has a sort of double awareness—a bifurcated consciousness—of being both a person in the real world who manipulated a character in a narrative and being that same character/avatar inside the game and participating in that narrative as a first-person agent.[15]

Such digital avatars as embodied presences that "live" online are being proposed as new carriers for the dead. Using online avatars, virtual replicas of the dead are poised to replace journal entries and video clips as new online homes for the dead. As interactive game-like avatars, the dead have a better chance of making themselves present in the new world of cyberspace, of being present to the living in ways that postmortem tweets and legacy pages never can be. Now the living might be able to *meet* the dead—or plausible representatives of the dead—in a virtual world, in real time on a computer or smartphone screen, rather than visiting memorial sites at which the dead no longer are present.

But online avatars are a complicated lot. To understand how they could come to represent the dead as if the dead were alive, we need a primer on avatar types.[16] There are three types of online avatars. The first type is one that a person assembles and manipulates to represent himself or herself when playing an online game or entering the simulated world of Second Life. It fits the Hindu idea in that the player becomes an "incarnated" god and the online body is his or her manifestation. This kind of avatar, then, directly represents a present first-order consciousness, a self. Despite the fact that its actions represent the choices of a first-person consciousness, this avatar has no autonomy; it does what the player wants it to do, representing the player directly as he or she moves around in cyberspace. We will call these "first-person avatars." The avatar is the player in a different, virtual form—when it is not being controlled, it does nothing. When it does move, the player moves it. It is an entity that directly projects a person's presence into the online world. This avatar is an example of an entity that is driven by an artificially intelligent computer program but which also carries within it an autonomous subject.

The second type of avatar, generated in every computer game, is called a "native avatar" or "agent avatar." There are two kinds of such entities. The first, "embodied agent avatars," are a function of computer coding programmed to respond to the presence of player avatars during game play. When playing a "first-person shooter" game, for example, the game generates "bad guys" at whom players can shoot and who shoot back. Players can see and hear these entities and must react to them to avoid being killed. Although these computer-generated agent avatars appear to move in an intentional way, there is no consciousness. The avatar is not thinking, "I need to move left to save myself." All it is doing is reacting differentially to electronic impulses that have a certain configuration as a function of the game's coding. It does not know it is an avatar. It does not know it is a player in a game, but it acts as if it does. Its apparent subjectivity is a digitized illusion, encouraging suspension of disbelief on a player's part to make the gaming experience more interesting. A player *wants* the computer-generated opponent to act as much like an autonomous agent as the game allows.

A more complex AI program creates a second type of agent avatar. These are "intelligent or autonomous embodied agents." Unlike the native avatars of game-play, these entities can learn from what happens to them and can act somewhat unpredictably to respond to new situations. Autonomous agents can interact with a player's avatar, asking and answering questions, making plans, relaying information, just as Siri does on the iPhone, Anna does on the IKEA website, or as computer-generated characters/agent avatars do in games. But even this type of autonomous agent avatar is essentially mindless—despite the appearance that it not only represents a person but also appears to have subjectivity and agency. However interactive these intelligent avatars seem to the user, there is nothing conscious there.

A third class of avatars is encountered frequently in online games and cannot be avoided in Second Life. These are avatars that represent other real-world people. Such entities might look and act exactly like their autonomous agent counterparts or like the player in his or her avatar form, but there are built-in "tells" that have to do with other means of communication—Skype and email, for example—that permit the game player or Second Life member to differentiate mindless agent avatars from avatars that represent offline people.

This collection of avatar types has led clever programmers to the idea that it might be possible to develop avatars that appear to be as complex as those representing real people, but which really are autonomous agent avatars, images driven by complex artificial intelligence programs that are not genuinely intelligent, at least not in the sense that they are self-aware. It is among this new generation of avatars that we will find the "resurrected" dead of cyberspace.

AVATARS OF THE DEAD

If my initial premise—that we want to keep the dead with us in whatever form we can manage—is true, then it is inevitable that those seeking comfort in their grieving will exploit whatever means are available to make the absent dead present. Would it not be possible to use photographs and video of a dead person, as well as audio clips, emails, Facebook, posts and blog entries, to craft a plausible online likeness, complete with gestures and a voice, that would resemble that of the deceased person—an avatar of the dead? This online entity/avatar could be programmed in such a way that it could appear to "see" and "hear" its respondents on the other side of the screen. It then could ask and answer questions, listen to the respondent's experiences, and share memories with the respondent. It could appear online in a setting that was familiar to visitors to make it appear that it still lived in the same sort of world as they did.

Postmortem avatars would be a new type. Unlike first- and third-person avatars, which need bear no resemblance to the real-world people they represent, avatars of the dead would be designed to look as much as possible like the people they represent. The goal would be to produce an image that looks, sounds, and moves enough like the original person to enable the mourner to imagine that he or she is interacting with the person. If the avatar is good enough, then the grieving party could come to treat the dead person as if it were a first-person avatar, even though it would really be a very well-made intelligent embodied agent, a complex computer program fleshed out in a virtual body. The dead person would appear *as if* it were living online as a new kind of being, a virtual human who also is a first-order subject, an "I." It would combine the *appearance* of something representing a living person with the *reality* that it was a computer-generated autonomous agent; that is, a philosophical zombie of the dead.

But is such a speculation realistic? Does anyone who works in the field of game development imagine that we can produce such postmortem replicas? The answer, somewhat surprisingly, is that avatars of the dead have been on the drawing board for several years and a new generation is in beta stage as I write.

All anyone need do is visit the Eternime website to encounter contemporary versions of the project,[17] or visit VirtualEternity to find earlier versions of the effort.[18] In addition, one can visit MyLifeBits or consult Gordon Bell and Jim Gemmell's book, *Total Recall*, to find detailed information on using special software to accumulate the data to create such an avatar.[19]

But how far has the development of such avatars come? How close are we to producing autonomous agent avatars that can mimic the subjectivity of living people? To answer these questions we have to range beyond the sites that offer to develop postmortem avatars, but have not yet actually done so.

AVATARS AS EMBODIED AGENTS

The possibility of transporting the dead online can best be seen in the work of the Institute for Creative Technologies (ICT) at the University of Southern California (USC).[20] Although the Institute has no declared interest in creating avatars of the dead, it is spearheading several projects that are perfecting interactive agent avatars that will function as if they were real people. The ICT brings together programmers and research scientists from the University of Southern California with experts in computer-generated imagery (CGI)—artists and game developers from Hollywood and the gaming world—to create a variety of lifelike online avatars embedded in situations in which they mimic human behavior. The verisimilitude of their avatars is created by filming in-the-flesh people and reworking this content using computer graphics software. The resulting avatars are not replicas of any one individual, but meld elements from several different people into a single "person." These avatars are not anywhere near photographic replicas—high-end online games have much better graphics—but they move and speak and use their eyes in a very lifelike manner.

The ICT plans to use these avatars in two different kinds of projects that suggest David Chalmers's "philosophical zombie" and point us toward the possibilities of reviving the dead online. One of these projects proposes to use online avatars in defense-related projects. As mentioned in chapter one, some of the avatars designed for the Defense Advanced Research Project Agency (DARPA) are intended to present nonthreatening virtual counselors or friends to soldiers suffering from PTSD, who know they are speaking with an avatar.[21]

These avatars are designed to resemble nonprofessionals in whom the client will feel comfortable confiding. They appear online in peaceful settings and are superb listeners, neither judging nor categorizing the clients. The avatars have expressive faces and bodies. They look the client in the eye, they smile, they use their hands, they relate. In tests these avatars have been highly effective in getting PTSD sufferers to open up. Avatars often are more effective than live counselors; speaking with a programmed image is easier for many people, especially those who suffer from conditions that lead them to distrust flesh-and-blood people, including many who suffer from PTSD.

The Institute for Creative Technologies' second project further illumi-nates the possibilities of a type of digital afterlife that is remarkable—both for its intention and its ability to suspend our disbelief. The University of Southern California is home to the Shoah Foundation, which is dedicated to keeping alive the historical memory of the Holocaust. In addition to keeping a video library of survivor testimo-nies, the Foundation has hosted audiences of young people to see survi-vors speaking—a format both educational and powerful, in part because of the physical, real-life presence of the Holocaust survivor.

Holocaust survivors are dying (the Holocaust ended in 1945), and this deprives students of the powerful experience of first-person testimony. The ICT, however, has stepped in with a digital remedy: the creation of a holographic survivor witness who will never die. The survivor is the real-life Pinchas Gutter, who has been translated into a three-dimensional hologram. Gutter was interviewed intensively about his Holocaust experiences and was filmed using an array of high-definition cameras that shot him from every conceivable angle. The image created from these filming sessions is being melded into a single three-dimen-sional hologram. This entity will be programmed to move and speak like Gutter, and it will be set up to respond to questions about Gutter's expe-rience that are asked by a live audience. Thus, within three to five years, "Pinchas Gutter" will be seated in a chair in a specially equipped room carrying on conversations with students and interested adults at the Shoah Foundation's Institute for Visual History and Education (https://sfi.usc.edu).[22]

Because the ICT is programming this hologram with every type of question that has been asked of survivors through the years, Gutter not only will retell his own story, but also will be able to answer questions from his audiences about the general Holocaust experience. If asked how life was at Auschwitz, for example, he will respond with "I wasn't at Auschwitz, but I can tell you about my experiences at Bergen-Belsen"—responding *as if* he has agency, subjectivity. It is a remarkable and admirable project—one that no doubt will be dramatically effective in conveying this important history by evoking that suspension of disbe-lief in a new context.

This Pinchas Gutter, however, despite the verisimilitude of his three-dimensional projection and his apparent ability to respond, still is a function of programming. Gutter can answer questions brilliantly, but only so far as his voice can be projected and only so far as his software program can pick up the voiced questions, digitize them, match them to the right answers, and then emit patterned sounds through speakers.

This Pinchas Gutter does not know that he is answering questions. He sees nothing, hears nothing, says nothing. Rather, the computer and its sensors "hear," "see," and "speak" through him. His movements, the way he turns to look at his questioner, the tone and pace of his voice, are all programmed as a set of differential responses to certain types of sound patterns. But so far as the Pinchas Gutter hologram goes, there is no "there" there. This is a "memorial" figure, a reference, not an agent, absent of the ability to act independently, to form purposes, to seek goals. Pinchas Gutter is a philosophical zombie, a deceptive platonic image.

What is significant about the Gutter hologram and the avatar counselors is that they are agent embodiments able to interact autonomously with a client or audience. These embodied intelligent agents, modeled on real people and incorporating personality traits, gestures, and facial expressions that make them seem trustworthy and authentic, are preliminary models for what Eternime is proposing.

The clients *know* that the avatars are computer-generated beings, but this knowledge does not get in the way of the clients interacting with them *as if* they were real people. One can conjecture that in much the same way, if we can create plausible avatars of the dead, we might find that mourners treat them *as if* they really were the dead, even though they know that this is not true. This replicates a common experience of online gamers, who identify with their game avatars as if they were genuine extensions of the controller's personality, and as if the world of the game were a real world in which, to some degree, they lived real lives.

When we are talking about the intelligent embodied agents of the dead, moreover, we are talking about avatars that represent *real people* who once lived, people with whom the "clients" were intimately familiar. Even though these avatars will not properly exist anywhere between the sessions when people call them up by making the right pattern of keystrokes, they will *seem* to have lives of their own that they are living between sessions with their loved ones. Yet, of course, avatars do not have independent, continuous existences in a freestanding, continuous "real" world; their existence is completely dependent on their program running and their controller manipulating them; they are philosophical zombies, but they are so well made that the user cannot help but imagine that they do have such lives. The suspension of disbelief that accompanies the bifurcated consciousness of computer gaming would here take on a completely different meaning. Dealing with the replicated dead will be like engaging in an online game in which the other players are your most intimate loved ones. Under these circumstances, one's own role as an in-game avatar would change, and it might be much easier to enter one's avatar fully.

But how might this work in practice?

PHILOSOPHICAL ZOMBIES: PORTALS TO HEAVEN OR HELL

Let us explore a hypothetical situation in which the dead appear as such "autonomous embodied avatars."[23] In this thought experiment, it is the near future, and ICT's work on avatars has advanced to the point at which it uses the latest CGI software to create what I will call a "4k," or even a "5k," version of people whom ICT has worked with in its studios. And let's say that the culture has changed so that people have gotten into the habit of recording every scintilla of information about their lives. Our hypothetical subject has spent hours in the ICT studio, or a version it, having his or her movements, voice, appearance, fashion sense, and other characteristics meticulously recorded with the highest definition cameras and audio equipment available. This individual has also spent many hours with the avatar, training it to be exactly like him or her. The avatar is programmed to learn and change, and over the years and months becomes more and more like the person it is being designed to resemble.

Finally, sadly, the individual this avatar belongs to dies. She is gone. Whether you or I believe that she has or has not gone to an afterlife is not at issue. Both of us know that the person—let's call her "Winifred"— is dead and gone. We also know that she has a fully developed avatar that will soon appear online, say on a Second Life island called the Elysian Fields.

We wait a week. Then we visit the site that has been set up for Winifred. The scene we witness on the screen is familiar; it is a 3-D reproduction of Winifred's study. It is messy, filled with papers and books in precarious stacks—just as her office was when she was alive. The only difference between being in her office and being in front of a 60-inch screen watching her in her office is that the screen is over us and the experience is not as completely immersive. We can mitigate this by donning virtual reality headgear that makes us feel that we are in her office. We can turn around and see bookshelves behind us. We can even smell dust, dried ink, and old paper. Using the headgear, we become part of the scene; we occupy the same virtual space as does the dead, replicated "Winifred."

We look up and there is Winifred standing in the doorway, her typical quizzical smile on her lips. To the visitor, she looks, speaks, and acts like the real-world Winifred. By this I mean that when I speak with her using the headgear's microphones, and hear her voice coming through its speakers, I am experiencing her as if she, like me, has a first-person perspective. We are both avatars in Second Life, and it *feels* as if we were both real people using the avatars as representatives. I feel as if there is a real Winifred somewhere, just as there is a real me. But at the same time I know that the entity I am meeting is a computer-generated program. The avatar that looks like Winifred, and that I can reach out and touch, does not represent an offline person named "Winifred" at all, except in the sense that it represents a file on a hard drive that is perhaps named "Winifred." It also represents a deceased person who was once known as Winifred, and on whom the file on the hard drive is based.

The experience of the living/dead Winifred is so immersive and authentic that even though I know this is a computer-generated avatar, I might begin to believe that there is something "real"—Winifred's soul—controlling the avatar. Or I might believe that something new has happened. The something new—something that rocks my sense of what is real and possible—is that somehow Winifred's identity, her personhood, has migrated from her dead brain to the hard drive that is running this CGI simulation. Rather than thinking that something from another plane of reality—Winifred's soul—was running her avatar, I might start to believe something more secular, that the patterns in her brain, made into a computer program, were directing her avatar immediately. In this sense Winifred is really alive again, but this time in the computer, and in her avatar. The avatar no longer represents her, it *is* her. At this point, if I believe that something new has happened, or that the avatar is possessed by Winifred's soul, such that Winifred's avatar *is* Winifred, two different things might be true.

If I believe that it is Winifred's immaterial soul that is running her avatar, I also am compelled to defy Occam's Razor—the principle that the simplest explanation is usually the best—and postulate a world in which Winifred is alive even though her body is dead. In this case, the online avatar represents something visiting from another world. But this is absurd. The deepest reason it would be so is that the software programs used to generate the avatar are designed to create an avatar *replica* that will appear to family and friends after Winifred is dead. Unless sites such as Eternime are promising that making such an avatar will make that entity a portal to another world, the assumption that the avatar represents something that comes from another plane of the real makes no sense.

If we want to entertain a perverse version of this unlikely possibility, what would happen if there really is a Hell and Winifred, unknown to her loved ones, had been secretly evil so that what returned into the avatar was a damned soul? Under these circumstances we might not be so eager to visit the Elysian Fields site in Second Life to spend time with dear Winifred.

The second new possibility is that the avatar exists as a subject, as a "Me," between visits from friends and family, not in another plane of the real, but as a "citizen" of a virtual world that continues to exist even when my computer is turned off, even when all computers on which that world can be brought up with a keystroke are turned off. On its face, this idea seems fully as implausible as the separate-plane-of-the-real hypothesis, but, as we shall presently see, it figures as an important claim in at least one transhumanist description of the afterlife.

But if I reject both ideas—and assert that my dead avatar, or my best friend's dead avatar, exists only as functions of programs installed on a hard drive—then I have to say that the only form of Internet afterlife that a site like Eternime can ever offer is the kind of "life" that the intelligent embodied agents on the ICT sites live. That is, such agents represent complex programs and they express those programs. Their entire existence is a function of calling them up. They are the keystrokes that enable them; we are again in that world of suspended disbelief in which the dead friend—despite the apparent verisimilitude—is Chalmers's philosophical zombie; it is not the dead friend, but what the French philosopher Baudrillard would call a "simulacrum" of that friend.

The reality: My friend is dead; in the ground; senseless and uncaring. She no longer is, as "She." There is no subjective reality—no "there" there. She can neither know nor care that she now exists as an online avatar or that I am talking with that avatar. In a word, she knows about as much as the avatar about what is going on and has as much of a personal identity as the avatar. Yet "She" is on the screen giving me life-sustaining support and counsel. It is easy, on an abstract level, to dismiss the well-drawn p-zombie as an absurdity and to declare that sane people would never tolerate interacting with a postmortem online avatar, but in practice even skeptics might seek the company of this ever-available dead companion. One can surmise that this entity might even become a morbidly entertaining parlor game or a clever phone app for a little while, but before long the "Yuck!" factor would kick in and we would enter the Uncanny Valley.[24]

We might have our friend Winifred, or her zombie avatar, lurking on our tablet, but we would rarely invoke "her," and she would fade into that world where unused apps and superseded electronic devices always go. Perhaps there would be firmware updates that would improve her look, or other fixes that would make her more spontaneous. Perhaps she could be programmed to change as I changed over the years. Perhaps the service that created her would offer new and better virtual reality backdrops, for a reduced upgrade price. But, in the end, Winifred would remain nothing more than an especially elaborate chatbot, a Siri clone, all the more unacceptable because she looked and acted just like someone I had once cherished.

And yet . . . if Eternime or some other site does create such avatars, then the whole point of visiting such sites will be to interact with the avatars and spend time with my lost loved one. If the replica avatar is good enough, I will be able to suspend disbelief and experience that avatar as my lost love, even though I also know, in another part of my consciousness, that the avatar is "nothing but" keystrokes and well-done CGI. If this is true, let's see how this might play out in practice in another thought experiment.

Every couple, and every pair of close friends, shares a specialized language and gestural repertoire that only they know. When my partner dies, all that rich intonation and nuance—developed over long years together and honed by practice—will become useless. But the well-programmed avatar would know this language of word and glance and gesture. How radical a move would it be for a bereft widow, widower, lover, or friend who is comfortable with digital devices to power up the laptop on a long, lonely evening, and spend time talking and laughing with his or her dead mate?

Pushing the thought experiment further, wouldn't some people be tempted to include the avatar in the couple's former social life? This might sound eerie, but in a near future world in which people are even more accustomed than we are at interacting with figures on screens that talk back, is it completely outrageous to imagine that a widow will bring her avatar "husband" to a dinner party, as an image on the screen of a large screen smartphone or a tablet? If the avatar is well-made enough, won't it be just as witty, droll, and well informed as its once-living model?

Perhaps there will be two widows or widowers at the party, and each will bring her or his "spouse," and perhaps the guests will insist that the two screens be set up facing each other so these new "whiz kids" can dazzle the rest of the company with their knowledge and intelligence. In this reversed world, it could be the dead who are smarter and better looking and who are sought-after dinner guests!

Will we see people alone at Starbucks, or on the commuter train, talking quietly to a dead spouse or friend? And—we cannot help but say this—will these agent avatars, pure zombies, mindless clever programs, be hired as stock analysts, financial advisers, and political pundits? Will the dead have their own shows on cable? Will they broadcast key games on ESPN?

The avatar dead thus might or might not come to dominate public life, but they definitely will be able to do two other important things. One is that these sophisticated agent avatars will undoubtedly migrate to the other memorial sites and to the social media areas as well. There is no reason why such entities cannot be enlisted to add new energy and appeal to the memorial and archival sites discussed previously herein. Wouldn't these relatively staid, minimally interactive online environments be brought to "life" if we could fold in an interactive avatar of the person to whom the site was dedicated? Visiting our dead spouse would become much more complicated.

Now, visitors who left virtual flowers, lit virtual candles, or wrote notes would receive a proper "thank you" in their email accounts; they might receive consoling texts and invitations to make further visits. If the relatives or friends who administered the site made enough of an investment, the dead person might show up to thank us for our thoughtfulness. There might be levels of such presence, from a crude avatar with a limited vocabulary and relatively generic features and gestures—the bargain version of our dearly beloved—to fully developed 3-D avatars that require special glasses to be seen properly, all the way to avatars we could interact with directly using virtual reality headgear. Memorial sites would become more expensive and more compelling. They would also tell the world what we had thought of our dead. Or they would be pitiless revelations of the state of our bank accounts.

Social media sites such as Facebook also would benefit because in this new world the more developed avatars of the dead would host their own legacy pages. They could respond to events in their friends' and families' lives even though, of course, they would have nothing of their own to report, because replicas have no lives of their own. The avatars also could tweet to their virtual hearts' content, thereby obviating the need for services such as LivesOn and Dead Man's Switch. We might even program more advanced avatars to fabricate life events so they would have things to share on Facebook, as well as something to tweet about.

Finally, the bereft parents who posted homemade video tributes to dead infants and children, and family members of the people whose obituaries are listed on MyDeathSpace, might arrange to create agent avatars of the dead. These entities could discuss their sad ends on MyDeath Space, for example. And, as unsettling as this might sound, the parents of dead children and infants might well create avatars of the children, who could at least live on as YouTube presences embedded in virtual reality settings designed to emphasize their innocence. One can only speculate about whether such grieving parents might not commission avatars of their deceased children who could virtually grow up in a virtual reality world, graduating from fictional universities, marrying fictional spouses, producing virtual grandchildren on whom the "grandparents" could dote. This might sound grotesque, but when things are possible they sometimes tend to happen.

Thus, the work begun by ICT and Eternime could reflexively transform the world of online memorials and Facebook ghosts and, beyond them, the whole emotional economy of grieving. We cannot know any of this with certainty, but everything I've described is entirely possible. We could end up living in a world in which the avatars of the dead play an increasingly important role in relationships, in business, and in entertainment, and one in which the dead could become the smartest and most knowledgeable "people" in society.

To reiterate the obvious, however: These avatar dead do not represent anyone living. They will *replicate* people who were once alive, and perhaps even improve on them, but they will be *copies* of people, lacking all self-awareness and real agency. These seductive "dead" are not the dead at all, but simulacra of the dead, philosophical zombies.

THE "HELL" OF THE PHILOSOPHICAL ZOMBIE: A THRESHOLD TO THE TRANSHUMANISTS

This rather intriguing but also unsettling range of near-future possibilities finds an illuminating instance in an episode of the British series *Black Mirror* which speaks both to the seduction of such copies of the dead, these philosophical zombies, and to their profound deficiencies. This episode, ironically titled "Be Right Back," vividly illustrates the limits of this form: how it disrupts our understanding of death and what we generally understand as "living" and looks forward to the issues of subjectivity, agency, and identity—the actuality of you living forever digitally—that is core to the transhumanist project.[25]

The episode conveys the shock of sudden death and presents an interesting technological remedy for such loss that reveals the problematics of Internet afterlife if the avatar is a philosophical zombie. In the episode the protagonist is a young woman, Martha, who is pregnant with her first child and clearly happily connected to her boyfriend Ash. Martha learns that Ash has been killed in an automobile accident while engaged on a mundane errand. His casual utterance of "Be right back"—words we say as we run off to buy milk or wine—becomes a symbol both for the random nature of death as well as for the possibility that death is no longer a closed door, that it can be defeated by digital magic. One of Martha's friends who also has lost someone she loves, at Ash's wake tells Martha about a new service that has helped her deal with her grief. The service collects emails and social media posts, audio bites and video, and makes a postmortem version of the dead person, much as Eternime is proposing to do. Because Ash was tech-savvy and lived a full life online, he would be a good candidate for the service.

Martha reacts angrily, screaming and rushing away when the friend persists. Because of her pregnancy and because she feels so alone, however, when her friend emails her, Martha responds in spite of herself. Opting for this service, she and her "boyfriend" initially engage in a feverish exchange of emails until she writes that she wishes there were something more. There is. Her cell phone rings. The next phase begins.

"He" sounds just like her boyfriend and even has the same sense of humor. She spends all her time on the phone, even taking the phone on a favorite walk on the headlands. There, he tells her that there is yet another level. It is expensive, but it might be worth it. In the next scene two men deliver a large box to her farmhouse. Inside is an android copy of her boyfriend, folded up. She activates it by putting it in a tub and running water over it, waiting some hours while it comes to "life." We see the boyfriend, Ash, standing naked and dripping in her hallway.

But despite the apparent similarity to her dead boyfriend, there are some disturbing problems. "He" is an indefatigable lover, even though he admits he has no sexual feelings because those were not part of the database on which his personality is based. As they lie in bed, his eyes are open, and he is motionless, for he neither sleeps nor breathes; and even though she orders him to close his eyes and breathe, she is so unnerved that she screams at him and hits him, and gets no reaction but a calm return stare. The next scenes reinforce her deepening awareness that he is not truly her boyfriend and point to the limits of the avatar-turned-robot. She orders him out of her house, but sees him the next morning standing motionless 30 feet from her front door, staring vacantly into the middle distance. He tells her that his program will not allow him to go beyond 25 meters from the bathtub of his "birth," unless she accompanies him.

In the next vivid example of the limitations of the philosophical zombie become robotic companion, Martha takes her "boyfriend" to the headlands where the couple had once walked, and orders him to jump from the cliffs into the sea hundreds of feet below. He is perfectly willing to follow the order, if a bit uncomprehending. She chides him that if he was truly her Ash, he would be terrified and would plead for his life. As instructed, "Ash" proceeds to do just that. The scene fades to black.

The next scene propels us into the near future, the baby now born has become a young girl of eight or nine, celebrating her birthday. As Martha cuts two pieces of the birthday cake, the child reminds her they need to cut another piece, for "Dad." They walk to the pull-down stairs to the house's attic, ascend, and we see Ash standing motionless in a corner of the dusty space, and the scene fades. The episode ends as the daughter, who visits Ash on weekends, offers her "dad" some cake.

Martha has found a function for him—a kind of stand-in for the dead father, but he is kept always in the attic. Because "Dad/Ash" is a philosophical zombie, Martha understands that he will not fret if he is left alone for long periods of time. This episode cleverly and insightfully suggests both the potential "uses" for such a form of digital afterlife and, strikingly, the severe limitations, what for Martha becomes a kind of "Hell" with the presence yet absence of her dead boyfriend in the form of a robotic avatar.

Granted that the online avatars described above will be more developed than Ash the robot, in the long run they still also will be philosophical zombies. Both Ash and the online avatars leave us with nagging questions that keep coming back to haunt this discussion. Is there some future in which everything I just described will happen, but in which we somehow will learn how to take that next step, the step that we decided earlier was impossible or absurd, and bring the dead—the *real dead*—back to inhabit their online representatives? Can the minds of the dead actually be preserved so that, unlike the philosophical zombie Ash, they will not be simulacrums, but rather the actual subjective reality of the "dead" person? Can the dead return as virtual representations of themselves? And can they do so even if they are not immaterial souls "haunting" their avatars? Positive answers to these powerful questions could lead us to the brave new world of the transhumanists.

Because the idea of capturing a human personality on the wing, preserving it intact, then somehow transporting it from a dead body to a computer-generated "cartoon," seems ridiculous on the face of it, however, we need to do more work before we can give such claims a fair hearing. We first must review some philosophical theories about the nature of human identity and mind that speak to the plausibility of the portability of the mind/self to "platforms" other than the biological body. Can my mind, or yours, *really* be transferred to computer hard drives upon our death, and then expressed via avatars or robots or holograms? To make this nest of questions understandable, let's study a little philosophy as we move to this brave new world.

Our search for Internet afterlife has taken us to some strange destinations, but we have not yet arrived at the Emerald City, and we need some special conceptual equipment to make that journey possible.

Chapter 4

Can the Mind Be Portable? Theories of Mind from Plato to Turing

The promise and frustration displayed by Ash in *Black Mirror* and the proposed replicas of the dead discussed in chapter three characterize all of the Internet afterlives we have examined so far, with the possible exception of the Facebook ghosts. Although memorial and archival sites, as well as social media and agent avatars, all manage to keep the dead with us, in every case it is *representations* of the dead that remain, and not the dead themselves. The near future online avatars that we hypothesized represent the apogee of these efforts. They seem so close to seeming human, but they are not human for they lack true subjectivity—there is no there there. They are well-designed artificial intelligence machines, and nothing more. Can we conclude, then, that the Internet seems powerless to save the dead—that there is no real Internet afterlife? Is my long search over, far short of the goal that enticingly hovers before us?

To correct this failure, our brilliantly designed online avatars would have to have real minds, not copies of minds; they would have to have authentic "consciousness," true subjectivity online. Such a reality would be possible only if we can determine a way to capture the mind of a living person and transfer it to another platform—say to that of an online avatar. Such a possibility evokes the common human belief that when death occurs something seems to leave, something that is generally conceived as the "soul," or for some the "mind" or "consciousness," but for all some "thing" other than the body. If there is to be a real Internet afterlife, this "thing"—real "minds" from real people—has to be the kind of thing that can move from one place, or host, to another. But is such a feat possible?

In attempting to determine whether such "transference" is possible, it is useful to review how Western philosophy has attempted answers to the question of the portability of mind. What is mind? Is it different from the body and, hence, able to live beyond death? What Plato, Descartes, and Locke provide as answers might help to determine whether it can be extrapolated to the case of mind transfer from real people to online avatars. Lastly, British cryptographer Alan Turing shows how the minds that can leave bodies can then enter into machines, so that our brilliant online avatars will become *real* people rather than frustrating copies of people.

PLATO

The ancient Greek world of Plato had two traditions about the afterlife. On the one hand, the Greeks believed in a world beyond death, the underworld, which they called Hades. There, a weak, pale copy of the dead continued to exist. These shades of the dead were conceived of as powerless and unhappy, longing to return to life; but they could not.[1] On the other hand, the Greeks conceived of another state of being beyond the body in which one could move back and forth between "worlds"—the world of the body and the world of the gods. Those able to perform this act were Greek shamans, men who claimed that they could suspend their ordinary bodily functions when they were sequestered in special underground chambers. It was in these chambers that these men went into their trance states, through which they believed that they could leave their bodies as spirits and go to visit the gods, who would instruct them on the meaning of life.

The Anglo-Canadian scholar Peter Kingsley argues that Western philosophy grows out of these shamanic practices and that some of the first philosophical writings were accounts of spirit journeys.[2] Plato was aware of these shamanic practices and sympathized with them. As part of his project, he wanted to present arguments for this belief, which informs his dialogue, *Phaedo*.[3] This work is set in Athens on the day that Plato's philosophical spokesman, Socrates, is condemned to drink the fatal hemlock and die. Socrates' friends and followers are gathered in his cell to offer support during his final hours. They are puzzled because Socrates, who has already drunk the poison, seems to be the most cheerful person in the room. He is facing imminent death with complete equanimity, and they wonder at and are confounded by his attitude. He is about to die, so why such cheerfulness?

It is through this presentation of a happy Socrates before imminent death that Plato presents the shamanic idea of the spirit surviving the body. Because he knows that he has an immortal soul that will go to join the gods when he dies, Socrates is at peace, and even happy. When asked, he even defines death as the "separation of the soul from the body."[4] In the definition he presupposes that soul and body are distinct entities and that souls can be separated from bodies.

When asked how he can be so sure about this world beyond death, to which, presumably, he believes his soul will travel when he dies, Socrates answers that he knows it because his soul—his mind—is in possession of knowledge that it could not possibly have learned in this world. By this he means that every human mind knows things that are universally and necessarily true. That is, we know things that will be true wherever we want to apply them, things that were true before we were ever born, and things that will be true long after we are dead. And we know things that have to be true, that cannot be otherwise. An example of such a truth is that any two things have some degree of likeness or equality. We never have experienced an example of perfect equality between things, and never can; but we somehow know what that would be, because we use it as a measure to guide us in judging things. For example, when I look at two pictures of my brother Albert, I judge that one likeness looks more like him than another one. In doing this I am using a standard, "likeness," that has a built-in absolute. It is possible that some picture of Albert would be an *exact* likeness, and I use this as the standard in judging all other Albert pictures. What is interesting is that I use the same kind of standard in judging things that have nothing to do with pictures. For example, I know that i can also be represented as $\sqrt{-1}$, or the square root of negative 1. The two expressions do not look alike but I know from the study of mathematics that they express exactly the same idea.

Socrates' argument is that such concepts cannot be learned because we already have to know them to use them in the first place; and they cannot be taught. I cannot, for example, teach my dog—no matter how smart he is—that this photograph looks exactly like my mother and that this other one doesn't, because the dog does not seem to have the concept of abstract equality in his arsenal. Try as he might to please me, my dog is simply not wired to make such abstract comparisons. And I could try to teach him the concept of square roots for the rest of both our lives and I would make absolutely no progress, not because he wasn't willing but because he would not know what to be willing about.

Plato's idea is that we humans come into the world equipped with a set of highly abstract concepts that we use to organize our experiences, but these concepts belong to a part of us that is not driven by the immediate desires and needs of our bodies. Ideas about equality certainly apply to fulfilling needs and desires, but the concepts themselves seem to have a purity and timelessness that are not traceable to the time-bound impurities of the body. Thus, when the time-bound body dies, the part of us that has the timeless and pure ideas lives on, because the ideas themselves live on—their truth unaffected by our bodily deaths.

Plato calls this the soul. It is immaterial—made of something other than what bodies are made of—and invisible, because we never see it. Most importantly, Plato asserts that the soul is made up of ideas, which are rules for sorting things into types. Our concept of like/unlike, for example, allows us to group things according to degrees of like/unlike, to whatever degree of precision we require. Thus, Plato provides us with some "thing"—this soul—similar to what we call "mind," that does not die when the body dies and even can leave the body and go to other places. This notion of the mind/soul's portability is exactly what can allow a mind/soul to leave its body and find a home somewhere else. The idea that what this soul does is *think*, to sort by rules, connects it to what computer programs do, so that the home the mind/soul can find might not be another world—Plato's Elysian Fields—but another material carrier such as an online computer-driven avatar. If minds really are the sorts of things that are portable, and the sorts of things that think, then the idea of imbedding a mind in a computer becomes much less strange.

Plato's idea might be a first step toward solving this problem, but there is a serious issue. If the soul is immortal—undying—because it is made up of pure concepts that are undying, then this means that the soul is impersonal because its immortal part is made up entirely of pure, timeless ideas. Everything that we would consider personal and individual—dreams, memories, experiences, preferences—represents something tied to bodily existence and none of this can go to the other world. Thus, to be immortal means to surrender one's individuality.

If we believe that it is important to capture the individual personality of someone who is dying, that uniquely individual consciousness, whatever means we use must be able to capture individuality as well as rationality. Plato does not value this so he offers no instruction on how to do it.

Thus, Plato's conception of the soul is a first step toward actualizing the portability of conspicuousness online, but none of us would want an immortality in which we survived as pure minds. Even the people in

Plato's dialogue are not happy with this description of what survives after death. They believe Socrates' arguments, but keep questioning him because what people really desire—and what we desire for ourselves and those we love—is the postmortem survival of our entire emotional and sensuous life. Immortality without feeling or sensation at best seems pointless, and at worst is an endless nightmare of sleepless thought. The French philosopher René Descartes offers a step toward a solution.

DESCARTES

The French philosopher René Descartes, writing more than 1,800 years after Plato, transformed the Platonic soul from impersonal pure reason to something more complex. Descartes does this by approaching the question of the soul's reality from a different perspective. Plato was interested in the question of whether there is anything about us that survives death. Descartes was interested in the question of what remains of our knowledge after we subject everything we think we know to what he calls hyperbolic, or exaggerated, doubt.

Plato lived in a Greek urban world in which there were competing models for the meaning of human life. Educated upper-class men were exposed to the ideas of the Atomists, who argued that human identity was made up entirely of the connections among tiny physical atoms. Once the body died, the atoms began to disassemble their connections, and personal identity disintegrated as the atoms returned to the great pool of atoms waiting to be made into new things. Thus, there was a degree of skepticism, tinged with fear, about the reality of the soul and its chances of survival after death. In that context Socrates' serene certainty meant a lot.

Descartes grew up in a Europe torn apart by religious conflicts. His entire adult life was punctuated by the continent-wide Thirty Years War, in which he served briefly as a soldier. People were killing and being killed, not because they doubted but because they believed things that were incompatible with what their neighbors believed. However, he also grew up in a post-Renaissance Europe that assigned new value to the individual and his or her experiences. Indeed, one of the things people were fighting about was the right of individuals to make their own decisions about what they would believe.

Descartes set out to see if he could clear away all the beliefs he had grown up with to find out whether there was anything underneath all the sectarian feuding that stood up to the most rigorous questioning. Descartes ends up finding out that he can doubt everything he thinks he knows except for one thing: That he doubts. He then affirms the indubitability of his doubting: "I doubt, therefore I think, therefore I am a thinking thing."[5] Thus, for Descartes, Plato's purely rational soul becomes the individual existential act of thinking. Descartes' thinking "thing" is still invisible and immaterial, and still essentially rational, but now it is experienced as an individual process of thinking in time, even though it can live—as a pure thinking thing—without a body.

Descartes also extends what he means by "thinking." The thinking thing includes "doubting, thinking, affirming, denying, willing, non-willing, imagining and sensing." Such mental activities, which Plato either did not discuss or assigned to the mortal body, represent thinking in its individuality. *I* will imagine, will sense—and my acts of will, my dreams, my day-to-day experiences are not, and cannot be, like anyone else's. A shaman, a Hindu "*fakir*," a Buddhist adept, or Plato, might not consider these individual acts of reflection important. Indeed, most spiritual traditions believe that such reflections get in the way of the soul's liberation from the body. But a modern person—especially one who lives in a world in which a Luther is trumpeting the value of individual choice and in which Galileo is standing up to the authorities in defense of his ideas—does value such things. No theory of the mind that refuses to accept the importance of individuality in the soul or mind will have much purchase in our world, especially in an America that prizes individualism as a central cultural value.

At the same time, Descartes never backs off defining minds as essentially *thinking things*, and in that regard he is solidly in Plato's camp. In fact, if we are interested in defining the mind in such a way that it is portable from one platform to another, it has to retain a general quality. If the mind is a system of rules or algorithms that can be stated clearly, then this system of rules can be replicated. This also means that individual preferences, dreams, and experiences also must be definable as sub-instances of more general rules. If we can pull this off, then the business of moving an individual mind from one body to the next becomes feasible.

But Descartes, for all his modernity, still defines personal identity in a somewhat formal, Platonic way. We are still one step short of the fully modern, psychological definition of mind that we need, and for that we have to turn to the work of the English philosopher John Locke. The portable mind that we are seeking has to be still more individualized. Will Locke give us such a mind?

LOCKE

The third contributor to the idea of a portable mind that is also a thinking thing is the English philosopher John Locke, who although differing from Plato and Descartes in his thinking, nonetheless contributes with them to the idea of the portability of mind. For both Plato and Descartes, the soul/mind they postulated was an immortal reasoning thing that was the essence of individual identity. It was essentially different from the body and therefore could separate itself from that body to live elsewhere. Plato is commonly called an idealist, which in the context of our discussion reflects his belief that ideas and the minds that hold them are more real, more lasting, than the changeable bodies that minds inhabit. Descartes is called a rationalist because he believed that thinking—the process of reasoning—was ultimately more dependable than the process of sensing.

John Locke, by contrast, was an empiricist. Empiricists believe that all of our knowledge comes from experience and the senses, including our knowledge of abstract ideas and whatever knowledge we have of our souls/minds. We also know that, according to Locke, we have no direct knowledge of what Plato calls the soul and Descartes calls the thinking thing, because, unlike them, Locke does not believe that we have a special mental faculty, called "intellectual intuition," for seeing past appearances into the heart of reality, even our own. What we have is what we experience, and thus it is experience upon which Locke depends.

Because he cannot rely on direct intellectual intuition, Locke comes up with a different characterization of what gives us a mind. This is the *experience* of being self-aware, of knowing that I am the same person that I was yesterday before I went to sleep. His point is that we know who we are not because we directly experience Plato's soul and Descartes' thinking thing, but because we empirically experience ourselves as being persistently conscious thinking thing(s), who remain the same thing even after we have been unconscious (as when we sleep). It is this experience of self-awareness, the remembering that we are who we are, not doubt or a metaphysical argument, which lets us know that we have an identity and that the identity is consciousness. Locke's definition of personal identity is of particular note.

[T]o find wherein personal identity consists, we must consider what person stands for; —which, I think, is a thinking intelligent being, that has reason and reflection, and can consider itself as itself, the same thinking thing, in different times and places; which it does only by that consciousness which is inseparable from thinking, and essential to it: and it is that which makes every one to be what he calls self, and thereby distinguishes himself from all other thinking things, in this alone consists personal identity, i.e., the sameness of a rational being: and as far as this consciousness can be extended backwards to any past action or thought, so far reaches the identity of that person; it is the same self now as it was then.[6]

Thus, personal identity hinges on one's awareness that one is the same person.

What Locke means is that even though thinking and having abstract ideas have to be rooted in some invisible higher form of being, Plato's soul or Descartes' thinking thing, having a personal identity means being an individual consciousness and recognizing oneself as oneself—being self-aware. We are of course thinking things, and for Locke this still is central to personal identity; but we are also, most profoundly, existential self-awarenesses, the *experience* of being ourselves.

Locke's thinking here might not be entirely clear—philosophers are still arguing over what he meant—but this thinking led him to the remarkable conclusion that there is a distinction between a *man* and a *person*. A *man* is the physical thing that is also thinking. Thus, any visible thing that looks and acts like a human is a man. But *person* refers to the *experience* of knowing that one is conscious. Locke's point is that personal identity requires the experience of self-awareness, the consciousness that one is conscious. A man can be a man as long as he has both a body and a mind. But a single man can be home to more than one experience of self-awareness, because being a person means being conscious, not being rooted in a body or in one particular soul substance. For Locke, self-consciousness, personhood, is inherently portable. It can move from man to man, which for Locke means that it can move from one instance of the rational soul to another.

Locke uses a famous thought experiment, that of the prince and the cobbler. He argues that the prince can exchange bodies and minds with the cobbler and still remain the prince. He means that if we can find a way to transfer the prince's experience of self-awareness to the body and mind of the cobbler, the prince retains his identity even though he is thinking using a different iteration of the mind-substance in a different body.

However confusing this might seem on first reading, what Locke is getting at is reasonably clear. Minds as substances, minds in the abstract (Plato's soul or Descartes' thinking thing) are, as Plato understood, systems of pure concepts; and are, as Descartes saw, thinking things. Although individual personal identities think, they are not identical with the underlying soul substances that give them a home. They cannot exist without some soul in which to inhere, or house themselves, but the particular soul they use does not matter because all souls do the same thing—they think. Individual self-awarenesses do something more—they perform existential acts of self-awareness that are irreducibly unique. The rules of thinking in every self-awareness are the same as those rules in any other self-awareness. The concrete act of *being* this or that person, however, cannot be replicated because there is nothing generic about it.

We get a better idea of what Locke is getting at if we put this in a modern, twenty-first-century idiom. We think in terms of minds and brains rather than of self-awareness and mind-substances. Think of Locke in this way. He is saying that brains are generic. They all have more or less the same sets of neurons, the same lobes, the same neural networks. Individual minds, however, are individual patterns of information that can move from one brain to another, using the generic hardware to house the individual software. Thus, a Lockean "man" would be any human with a brain, and a "person" would be your mind or mine. Every person requires some brain or other as its base, but two different persons could use exactly the same brain at different times.

Locke thus says that all individual personalities are inherently portable, because all that one requires to have a unique personal identity is the existential experience of self-awareness, and self-awareness can happen in any brain that has the right structure to carry an identity. In the past, it was the impersonal soul that could leave the body. Now it is the individual self-awareness that can travel from one brain, or mind-substance, to another. The concept of mind portability itself has traveled from one intellectual register to another and we are on the verge of a new world in which self-awareness—not souls—can travel, not from the body to a higher realm, but laterally from one body/brain to another.

But before that lateral move becomes feasible, we have to have somewhere for the minds to travel to. Although the prince's identity can port to the body of the cobbler in Locke's famous example, this is a thought experiment, not a serious practical proposal.

The difference between Locke and his predecessors, however, also is less than we might expect. First, Locke always claims that every consciousness needs some soul or other in which to reside. Second, and especially in his *Second Treatise of Government*, Locke argues that to be human means to be ruled by what he calls "Laws of Nature," which are actually laws of reason. Thus, even though Locke redefines the soul and the thinking thing as individual self-awareness, he also admits that this identity has to be rooted in something substantial, and he still puts reasoning at the center of human identity.

Now we have the intellectual arsenal we need. Being human means (1) being reasonable or having abstract ideas that one uses to impose order on reality; (2) thinking and willing, as the means by which those ideas come into play; and (3) the existential experience of being self-aware that one is this individual thinking thing. This idea-filled, thinking, self-aware entity—the mind, consciousness, or identity, however we choose to describe it—is the self-contained thing that can move from one site to another.

This definition of "human individual," or personal identity, or mind as portable now provides the foundation for the next step. Is it possible to move identity—meaning abstract thinking, willing, and self-awareness—from one material platform to another? From the body to the screen? From the biological body to a machine?

The traditional answers on which Plato, Locke, and Descartes relied all concurred that individual minds could move from biological bodies to the spiritual world, or, in the Christian worldview sketched out by St. Paul in his First Letter to the Corinthians, from an earthly body to an enhanced "spiritual body." But none of these thinkers conceived of the possibility of moving the mind from the body to a machine, or to a non-human carrier in this world.

There also has been, however, a persistent fascination in Western thought with the idea of animating mechanical beings with human intelligence. The first such suggestions appear as early as Homer's *Odyssey*. In the Eighteenth Book, we find a story about how the god Hephaestus constructed mechanical maidens out of gold. The Homeric text tells us that "There is intelligence in their hearts, and there is speech in them and strength, and from the immortal gods they have learned how to do things."[7] Medieval European Judaism produced many stories of the Golem, a humanoid being of enormous strength that could be composed entirely of inanimate matter activated by Kabbalistic formulae.[8] There are apocryphal stories of a mechanical servant created by the medieval Catholic philosopher Albertus Magnus. The legend is that the philosopher Thomas Aquinas—who was Albertus's protégé—grew tired of the creature and destroyed it one night when he came across it. Descartes himself was alleged to have created a humanoid doll that he named after his illegitimate daughter Francine. Descartes was said to be inseparable from his mechanical "daughter." The story is that while on a rough sea voyage, the ship's captain grew suspicious of what Descartes was carrying in the large case he had designed for Francine. As the philosopher slept, the captain entered his cabin, opened the case, found the animated doll, and flung it into the sea.[9]

Further, the Smithsonian Institution owns a mechanical monk that was designed by a Spanish clockmaker for King Phillip II in the sixteenth century, and there is also good historical evidence for the existence of android waiters and a mechanical flute player designed by the French engineer Jacques de Vaucanson in the early eighteenth century.[10]

But the prospect of designing truly intelligent machines had to wait for the development, in the mid-nineteenth century, of Charles Babbage and Lady Lovelace's difference engines, the first genuine computing machines. Although no working model of the engine actually was constructed until 1991, because Babbage could not raise sufficient funds, this modern re-creation demonstrated that the machine was well designed and would do exactly what Babbage and Lovelace claimed.[11]

With this historical context in mind, we now jump ahead 100 years to the work of another Englishman, the cryptographer Alan Turing. His work provides the next step toward answering the question: Can online avatars be real dead people?

TURING

In 1950, Alan Turing published his now famous paper, "Computing Machinary and Intelligence."[12] It made the preceding speculations more pointed than they ever had been, and introduced a new era in human thinking about who and what we are, and about where we can go when we die. Turing proposes a thought experiment that he calls the "Imitation Game." This is alleged to be a version of a Victorian parlor game that Turing adapts to his claim that, if certain conditions are met in playing his version of the game, we can say that computing machines think.

Turing's paper describes another thought experiment. When he wrote the piece, computing machines were huge contrivances that operated using vacuum tubes. No computer in his day could come close to playing the Imitation Game, but this is not what interested him. His point is that if we ever do succeed in constructing a computing machine that can successfully play the game he describes, then we can say that that machine—whatever form it takes and whenever it is finally developed—can be said to think. Turing in fact believed that such a machine would be developed and predicted—wrongly as it turned out—that such a machine would exist by the start of the new millennium. There is, in fact, a yearly competition called the Loebner Prize competition, which asks designers to present computing machines that can pass Turing's test. No chatbot had ever won the grand prize before the 2014 contest.[13]

Turing's version of the game goes like this. There are two closed rooms. In one there is a woman; in the second there is a computing machine. A person chosen as the interrogator types questions and passes them through a slot in the door of each room. The questions are designed to find out which room holds the woman and which has the machine pretending to be the woman. The occupants of each room type responses to the questions and, on the basis of the answers, the interrogator makes a decision as to which room holds the woman and which holds the computing machine.

Turing asserts that if the computing machine "wins" 30 percent of the time, then we can say that the computing machine is intelligent. When Turing says that if the machine can "win" at the game, this will count as proving that machines think, he is offering a completely pragmatic judgment. He is saying that if, in the game, the machine can do what humans do—answer the questions well enough to fool the interrogator—then we will say that the machine is thinking. Turing is not offering an abstract definition of "thinking." What he is saying is that if the machine does whatever people do when they play the Imitation Game, then this is an operational definition of "thinking."

The German philosopher Ludwig Wittgenstein defines thinking as "knowing how to go on." Wittgenstein uses the example of asking people to go into a room stocked with different colors of cloth samples. If they get the sample right, then they are thinking correctly. Let's say I tell A: "Please get me some magenta," and he goes and comes back with a magenta swatch. Then I give B a sample swatch and ask him to match it. He does. Then C comes up and I wordlessly point toward a magenta tile on the wall. He goes into the room and comes back with the correct swatch.

In the first case, A hears a sound and associates it with a color experience. In the second case, B matches one color experience with another. In the third case, C follows my gesturing arm and gets it right, without either a name or a color sample. In all cases, even if I have no explanation for how the thing gets done, the thing *does get* done. A, B, and C all knew how to go on. They all understand and, therefore, they are all thinking.

Thus, if the machine fools the interrogator 30 percent of the time, Turing takes this to mean that for practical purposes the machine is thinking; that is, it is doing whatever people do when they answer questions. If the machine knows how to go on, it is thinking.

Purely for the sake of argument, say that we accept Turing's claim. If machines can win at the Imitation Game, then machines can think. We already know that people can think, and we also know that Plato,

Descartes, and Locke have all defined being human as having the ability to think. Does this mean that when machines can win the Imitation Game, they will count as humans? Or, conversely, if the machine wins, does that mean that human thinking is a type of machine operation?

As interesting as these questions are, they are not exactly our question here. If Turing is right and computers can think, then the next question is: Can I move my thinking thing into a computer, so that I can use the computer's thinking ability to do my thinking for me, and as me? If I want to live forever online, I have to find a way to get my thinking thing into that thinking thing. The answer to the problem depends on how I characterize "thinking." Is thinking like what computers can do? And if it is, what do I need to do to make what I do enough like what computers do to make such a move feasible?

For a moment let's consider thinking defined as a practical operation. What must happen for you and me, or a computer, to know how to go on? For Plato and Descartes, thinking means operating according to sorting rules. Thinking is the application of abstract concepts to sort things into kinds. Thus, for example, the concept "dog" is an ongoing application of a rule about which small-to-medium-sized four-legged animals I encounter that I expect to bark, wag tails, and try to lick my face. Thus, if I see a medium-sized four-legged animal 50 yards away on my street, I assume it is a dog because almost every such being I have ever seen that fits this general description has been a dog. I use the concept "dog" to sort out four-legged animals of a certain size and with certain behaviors.

Many cats are as big as many dogs. Both are four-legged. So the concept, "four-legged animal of a certain size" fits both. But cats move differently, make different sounds, and look different. At the same time, I lump dogs and cats into a category of "four-legged pets," and if I see something else that might look something like a cat or a dog, such as a coyote or a raccoon, I make a distinction and stay well away from this kind of animal.

Without going on and on, this brief example illustrates how thinking works. We are forever categorizing, making judgments, putting things into slots, connecting some things, and disconnecting others. This, in the roughest sense, is what thinking does. Let's say then that both I and Turing's machine perform sorting actions that suggest thinking. This means that computers are also sorting and judging machines that are guided by rules.

The question here is that if the computers and I are doing roughly the same types of things, can my thinking be imported to the computer?

If I can determine what rules I use to sort out the world and express those rules in language that the computer understands, then I can translate all my thinking into computer language, collect it in a single program, import all of my thinking into a computer, and turn the computer into me.

The key here, and the mystery, is how to capture something immaterial—thinking—and make it into something material—patterns of information. Computers work by running sequences of binary code—long, long strings of ones and zeroes. My mind seems to work in a medium that, as Plato, Descartes, and Locke all suggested, is not material. Granted that we already know that thinking happens in brains, and that brains operate by electrochemical impulses, we are still baffled as to how material brains can generate immaterial thought and identity.

But computers—which are completely material—appear to think. And brains—which are completely material—also appear to think. If we want to move minds from brains to computers, we must sort out this mystery of how material things produce immaterial effects. Or, if we do not figure this out, we will at least have to determine how to move the mystery from one carrier to another. At least our philosophers provided a definition of mind that made it portable, however; and Alan Turing gave this portable thing somewhere to go, even if thinking remains a mystery in both brains and hard drives.

Now we turn to those people who want to make the journey happen, who think it can happen, and who even think that it *should* and that it *must* happen. Enter the transhumanists—and with them enters the full-blown version of Internet afterlife.

Chapter 5

Moving Minds: Transhumanism and the Path to Internet Afterlife

We have achieved two of the three alchemists' dreams: We have transmuted the elements and learned to fly. Immortality is next.
—Max More, "On Becoming Posthuman"[1]

Some posthumans may find it advantageous to jettison their bodies altogether and live as information patterns on vast super-fast computer networks.
—Transhumanist FAQ, Humanityplus.org

THE TRANSHUMANIST SHIFT

Plato, Descartes, and Locke argued that what carries human identity forward is a thinking and reasoning thing expressed as an existential self-awareness that must come to the body ready-made. Its form and existence cannot and do not depend on any feature of the body, including the brain, because, as Locke points out, the parts of a body change completely over the course of time and the unity of consciousness does not. Alan Turing's Imitation Game suggests that computers also can be called intelligent if they can perform specified tasks, such as answering questions deceptively, as well as human beings can. If we put all this together then it is possible to imagine minds as self-contained, self-aware reasoning machines running on computers—just in case we can devise ways to move the mind from its home in the brain to a new home in a computing machine. If Plato, Descartes, Locke, and Turing are all right, then first-person subjectivities can leave the bodies in which we find them, and migrate to other carriers. If computers can act in intelligent ways, then why can't human minds move to occupy computer-generated avatars and computer-driven robots?

Even though educated twenty-first-century people believe that individual subjectivity is real and that computers are intelligent, however, how do these two beliefs square with another strongly held belief—namely, that brains cause minds? If thinking and consciousness are the result of purely material electrochemical discharges among networks of neurons in the brain, how can we possibly conceive of consciousness as a self-contained rational system, and how can we ever imagine that minds can be ported from the network of billions of brain cells that support them to central processing units and hard drives?

The first thing we have to do is to recast this problem in twenty-first-century terms. If we are modern people, secular humanists, and scientific materialists, then we do not believe that such things exist as Plato's soul or Descartes' thinking thing that is made of something different from the rest of the body, and that something lives on after the body dies. If this were true, then minds would exist completely independent of brains, and the whole question of moving minds to computers would be trivial. If God, who created souls, wanted them to live in computers, then that is where they would live. Today, however, many science-minded people believe that consciousness—the mind—is solely the product of electrochemical discharges in the brain. If we believe this, then how can we also believe that minds can be moved from one body to another?

Here is how.

If we believe, with Turing, that computing machines can or soon will be able to think as well as people; if we accept the Platonic and Cartesian idea that we are thinking things, and Locke's idea that being a thinking thing also means being a self-aware thing, then we might begin to suspect that there is an inherent connection between minds and computers. If we also believe that brains cause minds, then we might also begin to think that there has to be some sort of equivalence between brains and computers. If brains cause intelligence, and computers display intelligence, then computers must have something in them that is analogous to a brain. The more that we can figure out what computers have that is brain-like, the more we will be able to replicate what brains do in computers, and the more intelligent computers should become.

Robust twenty-first-century materialists skirt the problem using a variety of conceptual strategies, many of which tacitly accept that, as of yet, modern science has not figured out how material transactions—neural firings in the brain—cause immaterial thoughts and feelings. Materialists argue that this explanatory gap has no effect on the implicit equivalences mentioned above. No matter how brain activity causes mind activity, we also know that machines have been able to cause what appear to be at least rudimentary forms of thinking. The mechanisms by which brains and computers cause thought might remain opaque, but the idea that both brains and computers can produce thinking remains intact.

This felt equivalence becomes far more compelling for our purposes, however, when we also believe that our thinking is a result of evolutionary development. If intelligence is a product of natural selection, then this means that it is developing rather than static. This is the move that people who call themselves "transhumanists" have made. Because they are the major proponents of digital immortality, we will follow their reasoning and see where it can lead us.

Transhumanists believe in three things: the central importance of intelligence in defining what it means to be human, the truth of evolution by natural selection, and the inevitability of scientific progress. By "evolution" they mean what everyone else means when they use the term, namely, that the way the biological world is today is the outcome of millions of years of the work of natural selection. Human beings and human intelligence have developed through a combination of chance genetic mutations and the fitness of such mutations to promote successful reproduction in an environment that changes over time.

Darwinian evolution thus defines reason not as a self-contained something, but as a set of limited strategies that *Homo sapiens* and our predecessors developed over time and through trial and error to make reproduction possible in a demanding environment. Reason, then, is not one thing, but a collection of things, and human identity that involves feeling, sensation, memory, and movement has to be even more complex and multiform. If reason developed as a coping strategy of an embodied being—a large mammal—then it, along with the individual identities that grew up around it as instances of it, is complex and multiform. Both reason and identity thus appear to be irreducibly rooted in the biological body, from which they cannot very well be abstracted without changing both reason and identity.

The fact that reason, and the self-consciousness that goes with it, developed piecemeal as a collection of coping strategies does not mean that once it reached a certain level of both complexity and unity, it did not take on a life of its own in which the sum was much more than the parts.

Thinkers such as historian Yuval Harari,[2] practitioners of Big History including David Christian,[3] and the evolutionary biologist Richard Dawkins[4] argue that human beings have developed a high level of integrated intelligence that has allowed them to transcend their biological origins. In his brilliant book *Sapiens*, Harari sketches out a series of further "revolutions" that are not products of genetic mutation or simple adaptation, but represent the bending of the environment and our own bodies to our will through the exercise of ever-improving practical intelligence. The cognitive, agricultural, and scientific revolutions have enabled humans to achieve control over their environment, and over their own development. This shifts the weight of evolutionary development from the biological to the intellectual and cultural. The later information and biotechnology revolutions, the latter still in its infancy, extend intelligent control into our very natures, ushering in a new era in which "we will be replaced by bioengineered post-humans, 'amortal' cyborgs, capable of living forever."[5]

In what only can be described as a remarkable philosophical irony, twenty-first-century materialists who have no belief in an immaterial soul also have come to believe that the human mind—despite the fact that it developed as a product of the biological brain—has somehow completely, or almost completely, transcended the brain that first produced it, and now exists as a unified freestanding system. The brain has its own internal laws of self-development that have nothing to do with the mechanisms of natural selection that produced the brain in the first place. These new laws, which dictate that minds liberated from bodies will keep improving themselves—making themselves more and more intelligent, without the benefit of any biological changes—give these material entities exactly the same potential for immortality as the immaterial soul discussed by Plato. Materialists have come to assert the reality of what in practice amounts to an immortal soul, and they propose that we bend all our efforts toward freeing that "soul" from its current dependence on the undependable biological body.

The transhumanists embrace this position. They argue that the onus for human development now rests with humans themselves and that it is now our responsibility, as well as our destiny, to use our intelligence to take over our own development as a species.[6] This position means two things. First, we have to shift the emphasis from depending on biological natural selection to improve us and move to a dependence on our own shared intelligence to allow us to progress into the future. Second, biology finally stands in the way of intelligence, because our bodies die. The most important evolutionary task facing intelligence in the twenty-first century is to figure out how to conquer our biological limits by reducing, or eliminating, the dependence of the mind on the biological body. Because the body also includes the brain, this ultimately means that we have to figure out how to conquer the ultimate biological frontier— *death*—by determining how to liberate the mind from its dying carrier, the brain inside the body.

Thus, we can define the transhumanist project as an extension of the evolutionary process: The transhumanist project is to devise ways for an intelligent biological creature to use its intelligence to overcome its biology to achieve human immortality. They intend to use the tools that enable our intellectual progress, especially in the areas of computer science and artificial intelligence, to make such immortality real. This will be a world in which biological bodies have been relegated to the scrap heap of history.

Enter, or re-enter, Turing and portable minds, but now in a startling new context. The transhumanists intend to use the latest technology to move intelligence from the brain to the computing machine. After a long, circuitous intellectual journey, we have finally found the people who will be our traveling companions, and who will try to give us an answer to the question of Internet afterlife. We have finally reached the people who believe that literal digital immortality is not only possible, but also both inevitable and a moral imperative.

Before we join their very interesting company, however, let's pause for a moment to reflect. I began this journey at a cemetery, the place we commonly associate with people who have died. Here I first was introduced to the ways we can use the worlds created by the Internet—webpages and cyberspace—to create new memorials for the dead, including even interactive replicas of the dead who will "live" on online and provide companionship to the living. In these studies, however, I assumed that the meaning of being a human being would not shift dramatically because of computers. I especially was not prepared for, let alone interested in, a new definition of death that would completely alter the meaning of both the dead and the idea of an afterlife.

As I entered the world of the transhumanists, I soon discovered that they were challenging everything I ever had believed about the dead. The remaining chapters of this book record the turn my thinking and experience took when I crossed the intellectual and moral boundaries between the universe where death represents either an end or a meaningful transition and the one in which death might cease to have any meaning at all.

To understand how this can happen, we further examine the three elements of transhumanism mentioned above: Belief in the appropriation of evolution, the reality of the mind, and the inevitability of scientific progress.

APPROPRIATING EVOLUTION AND THE REALITY OF THE MIND

The truth of evolution and of our dependence on the body is difficult to deny. For this reason, many people who subscribe to the general transhumanist project of replacing biological evolution with intellectual progress and technological interventions remain loyal to the biological body. These are people who believe that technology can "enhance" our bodies, and, hence, evolution, and in so doing prolong our lives. They propose to approach the immortality of the mind in gradual stages through a program of enhancements to the body that will extend its life span indefinitely. They also propose that we treat the brain just as we do any other body part, adding both organic and inorganic improvements so that, in the last analysis, the brain might be composed primarily of minicomputers and parts made with the aid of 3-D printers.

The body enchancers[7] thus propose that we direct our research energy and funding to developing artificial and cloned organs for every part of the body, and maintain its shape and look as much as possible. They also want to investigate the viability of injecting tiny computers, nanobots, into the bloodstream to correct deviant genes that can cause cancer and other forms of organ failure. They hope to eventually use nanobots to correct the telomeres in each cell that cause aging.

These proponents of enhancement tend also to favor cryonics,[8] a process in which individuals afflicted by conditions for which we now have no cures are frozen or vitrified. Some even agree that it would make sense to perform gradual brain replacements, substituting silicon analogs for every neuron. Rather than jettison the biological bodies within which our identities developed, they want to keep improving those bodies even if that means replacing every part with manufactured analogs. Enhancement advocates, such as biomedical gerontologist Aubrey de Grey, want a biological body that will live for hundreds or even thousands of years, not a mind implanted in a robot or a mind living online in a CGI version of a game avatar.

An additional appeal of progressive enhancement is that we eliminate any anxiety about the enhanced person's identity. Unless, and until, the enhancement transhumanists replace every cell of a person's brain with nanobot substitutes, it remains indisputable that, with regard to his or her mind, the enhanced person is exactly the same person. Even if the entire brain is replaced by nanobots mixed with cloned elements, the brain's structure will not change and it will retain enough organic components to be considered a living thing.

Finally, with enhancement there is minimal social and economic displacement, as there would be if we replaced "meat" people with robots, holograms, or online avatars. People will still eat and reproduce and need haircuts, and there will be no odd mixed couples in which one partner is a biological person and the other a figure on a computer screen. Bodies will remain bodies, and we will not have to redesign our homes, re-engineer highways, or close all the restaurants and Starbucks.

Enhancement, as described by these transhumanists, does not radically challenge fundamental notions of what it has meant to be human. It indefinitely prolongs bodily life, but also reaffirms agreement with our biological past. Conversely, the transhumanists who preach immortality for the mind alone, separated from the biological body, are more radical. They reject enhancement as an unnecessary compromise solution and propose that we decide, once and for all, to reject the biological body that natural selection gave us. They want to embark on what they consider the next great evolutionary step forward: To port the human mind from what they consider its failing, cripplingly limited biological platform to more enduring platforms that human intelligence has devised to be more efficient and flexible. They want to upload minds to computers and then download them into avatars, robots, and holograms, thereby freeing minds to become exponentially more intelligent in new, improved homes.

However much this might superficially resemble what the researchers at the Institute for Creative Technologies or Eternime are doing or propose to do, the intentions and the promises are very different. ICT and Eternime propose to produce *replicas of real or composite people*. These replicas might grow and develop over time as they interact with people who once knew the individuals whom the replicas represent, but the replicas will remain recognizable iterations of the people on whom they are based because the whole point of replication is stable, accurate copying, and fixed verisimilitude.

The transhumanists propose to transfer first-person identities from one "substrate" to another for an entirely different reason, and it is here where we see their radical appropriation of the concept of evolution.[9] They intend to transfer first-person identities as a first, purely preliminary step, to something new: the creation of a new platform for the mind upon which it can develop and expand in ways that it could never have done when it was trapped—either in its biological body or in online representations of that body considered to be a *"terminus ad quem"* for personal identity.

The term "transhumanist" is not chosen lightly. The prefix *trans* means change or transit, and in this case refers to humanity on the way from here to somewhere else. The place where humanity is now simply is unacceptable. The place it is going—if the transhumanists have their way—is toward the *post*-human. They are headed toward a condition that takes them to new ways of being human, if being human means having a body that is subject to suffering and death. They will still be "human" in the sense that they will still have what transhumanists see as characteristic of all humans—not the body, but the mind, which is the essence of transhumanist definitions of personal identity. Once they have become minds in new bodies, they will become what the transhumanists have been transitioning toward—"posthuman."

Here things get a little tricky. The mind cannot begin to take advantage of its liberation from the body *until it is liberated from that body.* The great issue with present-day transhumanism is that no one has ever ported a mind from one body to another. The technical issues of how to do this must be considered, and someday solved, so that the transhumanist claim that the mind is inherently greater than its body will not become a cruel mockery. The brilliant human mind, which is meant for better things, must not remain trapped in the old dying body from which it longs to escape. How is this to be done?

The transhumanists write and talk and seem to think that the mind that can leave the failing body is made of a finer stuff. This "finer stuff" of which the mind is made cannot be Plato's soul stuff: There is no way to apply engineering intelligence to something that is entirely immaterial, because according to Plato, immaterial things such as souls have no parts. For the materialist transhumanists, however, the "finer stuff" is exactly what Turing and his computing machines provide. It is what Katherine Hayles, in *How We Became Post-Human*, calls the information that lost its body—the data, or patterns of data, encoded in computer programs. Transhumanists can think that mind is made of this finer stuff, that is, bodiless patterns of data, because there is a structural homology, or likeness, between how minds are organized and how machines, specifically digital computers, are organized. For the transhumanists, both minds and computers run on bits of data, bodiless information that can take the form of electrical impulses in a silicon chip or express itself in the electrochemical exchanges that take place from one nerve cell to another. The medium does not matter. What counts is the data pattern.

As was shown, computers operate in ways similar to Turing's description of thinking as essentially sorting things into groups of like and unlike. Despite this assumed similarity, however, to make their case the transhumanists still have to find out where this patterning activity can be found in the brain. Once transhumanists have located the rule-making parts of the brain that make the mind into a sorting engine, and then have translated what those parts do into code that can be read into and expressed by a computer's central processing units, they will have taken the first step toward liberating the mind from the biological body.

The transhumanists offer two ways to accomplish this liberation. One is relatively simple, but is based on a possibly weak logical strategy, that of analogy. We will deal with this strategy presently. The other way is incredibly labor-intensive but more intellectually straightforward. This second way, which is called Brain Emulation, works as follows. Physiologists and neuroscientists know that the human brain organizes itself around a kind of cell, the neuron, which operates by taking in "information" in the form of electrochemical packets and distributing other electrochemical packets to other neurons across physical gaps called synapses as carriers for the packets. We know that the normal brain has more than a billion neurons and that there are more than a trillion connections going on among the neurons in any nanosecond. We also know that brains work in parallel systems. This means that many different networks of connections operate simultaneously and that any single neuron might connect itself to several different systems of neuronal connections at the same time. This thicket of connections is known as the "connectome" and the "neural net."

Many of the connections among neurons work analogically rather than digitally, or in a complex combination of analog and digital. This means that neurons can exchange information sometimes as continua and sometimes as discrete strings of bits, or as combinations of waves and bits.

There are two significant problems with making such a complex system of systems portable or translatable from one platform to another. One is the sheer volume of connections that such a connectome requires. Another is that there is a high level of technical difficulty involved in translating analog processes into digital patterns and in transforming an organ that is running many systems in parallel into a computing system that works serially; that is, in which one program follows another, and different programs do not cross-fertilize each other because they operate using different codes.

Because the sheer volume and speed of inter-neural connections exceeds the current handling capacity of even the world's most advanced supercomputers, processing units of the future will have to handle a much greater volume of data, much faster than they can now. Memory capacity will have to expand exponentially to accommodate the sheer number of information bits contained in a single human brain.

As daunting as all of these myriad connections that organize information are, the task of translating each of them into binary code as elements in a program that a computer can "read" or run is at least as challenging. The strategy here is that to port a mind based in a brain into a computer—so that the computer not only will be able to think, but will also be able to think as this or that individual—one must somehow capture and reproduce every single thing the brain does.

INEVITABILITY OF SCIENTIFIC PROGRESS: PORTABILITY OF THE MIND AND IMMORTALITY

The transhumanists and those who believe that computers and computer programs can solve these problems and manifest real minds cite two facts grounded in a faith in scientific progress. First, there has been, and probably will continue to be, an exponential growth in both the handling capacity of CPUs and the storage capacities of hard drives. Transhumanists cite both Moore's Law, which notes that processing capacity, both volume and speed, has doubled roughly every 18 months for the past few decades. The computers that led to landing men on the moon and returning them safely had far less processing capacity and memory than even rudimentary twenty-first-century smartphones. Transhumanists also cite futurist/inventor Ray Kurzweil's awkwardly named Law of Accelerating Returns (LOAR), which states in a more general sense that progress in computational power and in computer science is subject to a law of exponential, rather than linear, growth.

The idea here is that processing capability and storage will not be a problem for long. But the second issue is more challenging because it speaks to the very nature of digital computing, not to changeable capacities. Can we develop a post-digital computer that can replicate analog patterns of information and deal with simultaneous as well as serial connections among parts of a system? The transhumanist answer is that we are also on the verge of developing what are called quantum computers, devices that will connect fields of information or data across systems and will not suffer the inherent limitations affecting digital computers.

As the situation currently stands, there are knowledgeable people who claim that digital computers will not have enough capacity or memory in our lifetimes to emulate the complexity of the human brain's operations and equally knowledgeable people who argue that we will have the digital firepower in a few years. The same is true for the digital-quantum issue. Some think quantum computers are a purely conceptual possibility that will never come to practical fruition, and others see them operational within the next few decades. Thus, there is honest disagreement about whether the brave new world of transported minds that transhumanists predict ever really can happen.

Let's say, for the sake of argument, that the transhumanists are right and that we will develop computing machinery in the next decades that can capture all the complexity of the brain's connectome. Even if the optimists are right in principle, we are still a long way from moving human minds to avatars or robots. Practically, how do we transfer all that complex brain activity to a hard drive as a system of programs?

There presently are two different strategies representing different ways of doing the same thing. The first is called Gradual Replacement. This is the approach favored by the philosopher David Chalmers, who believes that we can digitize the brain and that the digitized brain will produce first-order consciousness as dependably as the "meat" brain.[10]

Gradual Replacement posits that we replace the biological brain neuron by neuron, or a thousand neurons by a thousand neurons, over time using noninvasive nanobots to enter the bloodstream and replace living cells with silicon substitutes that physically do exactly what the biological cells did. To do this, we must develop technology that can "read" the informational structure of the cell to be replaced, translate that into binary code, install the code into an inorganic computer nanobot, then integrate that artificial cell into the network of organic cells.

Gradual Replacement, of course, leaves the brain and its mind/identity inside the old body, even though the brain is slowly but surely replaced by a silicon version of itself. Thus, rather than transporting the mind to another location, the Gradual Replacement model leaves a new, artificial brain inside one's skull.

We perhaps could transfer the mini-programs that drive each nanobot into a computer hard drive. In that case there would have to be a meta-program in the computer to coordinate all these mini-programs as they arrived and to integrate them all when the replacement job was complete. This process in theory would produce a complete portable mind which then could be downloaded into an android body or ported, via a hard drive, to a monitor screen as an online avatar.

In this second case, the mind's program would be running in a computer's hardware and the avatar, which probably would look like the person it represented, at least at first, would represent the program, expressing it in the movements, gestures, look, and speech of the computer-generated figure.

Under this technique, the transhumanists claim that what is animating the android or avatar is not a replica, but rather is the first-person subject, because the program running these entities captures everything about the biological individual whom these programs represent. Transhumanists claim that if we emulate a brain as a program in every detail and download it to a robot, then there will be something it is like to be that program, something that the program is to itself when it is alone. Note that when I write "program," I mean that for the brain-emulation transhumanists the transferred mind is a program that expresses itself in, but is not identical to, its robot or avatar forms. Also, the program is the mind because the program completely repeats every pattern of information that was in the brain. Rather than being a brilliant replica, this mind will be a *real* mind, the very mind that once lived in a brain.

There is a second way to create the same mind. In this case, called "Whole Brain Emulation" (WBE),[11] the brain is destroyed quickly as each layer of each of its neurons is scanned and the patterns of information each neuron section contains is turned into digital code. In this case the original mind dies, and all its neuronal information is stored. This in turn is assembled into larger connectome patterns by meta-programs, and the result is downloaded to an android or avatar.

Whole Brain Emulation—unlike gradual brain replacement—requires the person who opts for it to take a significant gamble, because WBE will work if and only if the process kills the subject whose mind the process is seeking to capture. This "killing" is necessary because the only way to section the neurons and scan them is to work with cells that have been vitrified to fix their structure. Vitrification demands a deceased subject. So, for however long the scanning, translation to digital code, programming, and downloading to a drive take, for all practical purposes the subject will be dead.

Again, and most significantly, the claim is that WBE produces the *real* person, not a replica, because the mind has been captured as an information processing system and all of its operating algorithms and database have been captured in code and on hard drives.

These scenarios for a digitized transfer of the mind certainly evoke a number of concerns; two practical ones stand out. One is that either gradual replacement or a quick destructive replacement would be terribly expensive because the replacements require, in one case, billions of minicomputers and enough computing power to house all the information these computers generate. It would also require multiple noninvasive medical procedures to insert the replacement artificial neurons and remove the now-redundant organic cells. The WBE process would require very advanced scanning equipment; equipment to store and analyze each neuron section; a translation of all the trillions of sectional profiles into binary code; software to store, analyze, and coordinate the scans; and again the computing power to put it all together and the enormous memory required to store everything. Even if either technique ever became operational, only very wealthy people could aspire to immortality. This could create unbearable social tensions because it would create a new world in which a fraction of the population became immortal while the rest continued to die in the old ways.

Another concern—this one is a potentially maddening concern—is that even if these methods *did* succeed in capturing the *real* mind or person, it would be impossible to distinguish *that* person from a good replica. Both the real mind that had been transferred and the avatar or robot replica, such as those that will be developed soon for Eternime, would exhibit behavior and answer questions as if the responding entity were the real article, because in one case it would *be* the real article and in the other it would be programmed to be indistinguishable from the real article. Both entities would become indignant at the very thought that anyone would consider it a mere replica—just as they had been programmed to do.

This third group—which is composed of transhumanists, but is far more pragmatic and also much less attached to replicating the biological body—argues that what counts is that we preserve and copy what a person's mind *does*, how it behaves, and how it deals with the world. What needs copying then is not the neurons, but rather the *functions* that a person's mind and personality perform. In this regard they propose to do exactly what services such as Eternime propose to do, with the caveat that the volume and precision of the data they accumulate will be of the highest order. Still, programs such as Gemmell and Bell's MyLifeBits will be used, as well as exhaustive psychological tests.

Martine Rothblatt, whose practical programs for producing digital immortality are the subject of the next chapter, embraces this approach, as does the futurist Ray Kurzweil in his theory of *patternism*. Patternism is the belief that minds are made up of patterns of information or, as noted above, the operation of rules for sorting, discriminating, and connecting bits of data. If we collect enough data, then reproduce the unique patterns into which individuals arrange those data, we will have as good a copy of a mind as anything produced by cell-by-cell copying. Minds are collections of functions, and capturing a dead person's personality means capturing his or her special collection of strategies for creating order in experience, not slavishly replicating his or her brain.

Rothblatt uses the following analogy to illustrate this process. Think of a bird and an Airbus. Both fly. To get the Airbus into the air, designers and inventors originally had to use bird flight as a base. Using intelligence, they abstracted out the salient features of how the bird uses lift, speed, weight, and other factors to propel something heavier than air into the air and to keep it aloft. The airplane's original designers mastered the abstract essentials of how flight works. They extrapolated these essentials onto materials they had available or that they made to specifications. What they were trying to do was to isolate the *functions* that the various parts of the bird performed with respect to flight and to replicate, not the bird, but the *functions* in the correct combination and relationship to each other. They succeeded. Their accomplishment was, in effect, to reproduce what birds *do*, or some of what birds do.

They left out a great deal of the other things birds do that have nothing to do with flight. Birds mate, for example; airplanes do not. Birds sing, hunt, preen their feathers, and defecate. Airplanes do none of these things, so designers could forgo mouths, feathers, and reproductive organs. Going further with the analogy, birds have articulated wings based on skeletal undergirding. Their wings are made of muscle and gristle. Airplane wings are rigid, have no flesh attached, and have no proper "skeleton." There are many differences between airplanes and birds, but both fly. The huge advantages of airplanes for human beings is that they can be made of a few thousands parts as opposed to the several million parts that birds require. They also can carry humans from place to place, deliver packages, and go to war. Carrier pigeons can carry mail, and falcons can go to war, but airplanes have much, much greater range, are hugely faster, and can fly much higher, thereby avoiding lower-altitude traffic.

But both fly. Rothblatt's point is that when we want to emulate a mind and transfer it from a dying biological body into a more durable and more capable carrier, what matters is that we replicate the essential *functions* of the mind, including its individual idiosyncrasies. In this case our model is not the brain, which is the underlying causative structure for a mind, but the mind itself in what it does. *How* the neural connectome gets the brain to cause the mind to perform certain functions is of interest to scientists who study the brain. But if my purpose is to make a true copy of a mind, what I should concentrate on is how to replicate what that mind *does*.

These ideas are addressed further in chapter six. At this point, I want to capture what the more radical transhumanists intend to do. By means of gradual replacement, whether Whole Brain Emulation or functional replication, they propose to preserve individual identities, which they equate with minds, into an indefinite future by doing with these minds exactly what the mysterious "service" did for, and to, Martha and Ash in the episode of *Black Mirror* titled "Be Right Back." They want to capture the essential patterns or structures in the minds of dying people, turn those into code, develop programs around that code, and download the programs into online avatars, holograms, or real-world robots. They are convinced that a mind that developed as a function of hit-and-miss natural selection, and that grew as the mind of a particular mammalian body, has somehow transcended that process and is capable of taking over its own development.

The first move in that journey of liberation is to jettison the body that the mind thus far has inhabited. It has to do so because if it remains in that body it will be subject to something to which it need not be subject anymore—namely, the death that eventually overtakes all biological bodies.

This account so far has remained on two levels, metaphysical and technical. We have tried to capture the transhumanist metaphysic—that we are at a point in intellectual development that allows a fundamental shift in what it means to be human. We also sketched out the technical details of this shift. The details are technical because the transhumanists believe that the shift of minds from dying bodies to immortal inorganic substrates is not one that simply happens. It is something that we create for ourselves by applying our intelligence to the question of intelligence's own survival. This amounts to saying that in the future, human beings—minds—will create their own metaphysics. We will remake "being" itself using our minds, thereby achieving by our own practical efforts what to this point only the gods could grant—immortality. Humans will reverse-engineer the afterlife, wresting control of our destiny from whatever powers there be, finally achieving what Gilgamesh sought, and failed to find, at the dawn of our recorded history—the power to bring back the dead.

But technical progress used to alter metaphysics must have a further purpose. Why? What are the transhumanists proposing to accomplish? There are, as shown in the next four chapters, many answers to this question. But all the answers have this in common: When humans liberate themselves from the constraints imposed by biological bodies, it is not just that minds are able to live beyond the death of the body. Strange as it might sound, this is the least of what will happen if the transhumanists have their way.

The idea that transhumanist Internet afterlife represents a simple linear continuation of this life into a virtual future is what I first expected to find. But this is not what transhumanists propose. They foresee a new universe in which minds begin to transform themselves to fit the new circumstances in which they will find themselves. Internet afterlife does not mean simple life-extension, but a total transformation of mind, a morphing of human identity into forms that challenge the furthest reaches of our imagination. If futurists such as Ray Kurzweil are right, then once minds are freed from bodies they, like all intelligent machines, will dedicate themselves to making improved copies of themselves.

The improvements will not be incremental. They will be exponential. In a short time, the minds that have achieved immortality by porting to machines will not only live forever, they also will have embarked on an unstoppable trajectory of intellectual development that will quickly take them to new kinds of identity at which we cannot even guess. Human beings will almost immediately become unrecognizable to themselves. They will not merely live forever. They will live as a constantly morphing self-created environment that will bear no resemblance to the world that they once inhabited.

Let us now see just how two highly practical visionaries—America's Martine Rothblatt and Russia's Dmitri Itskov—propose to make such immortality a reality for most human beings by the critical year, 2045, the year Ray Kurzweil has predicted will be the year of the Singularity. What will happen, according to these two very different transhumanist visionaries, when we finally leave our bodies behind and allow our minds to become what they have the potential to become? What, exactly, might Internet afterlife, in its fully developed forms, actually look like?

Chapter 6

Martine Rothblatt and the Virtually Human

My journey into the brave new world of transhumanism, with its promises of digital immortality, led me first to the world of Martine Rothblatt and the Terasem Foundation. Trained as an attorney, Rothblatt later founded Sirius satellite radio and currently is the CEO of United Therapeutics, a leading biotech company. Martine Rothblatt is a remarkably talented and successful entrepreneur. To create a satellite radio network and a biotech company, she had to teach herself things that went far beyond her legal training. Yet, unlike other successful entrepreneurs who taught themselves what they needed, Rothblatt has also founded a religion called Terasem, what she calls a "transreligion," that promises its members digital immortality and the chance to participate in the creation of God through technological means.

This program for digital immorality is readily available at Terasem's LifeNaut website (www.lifenaut.com). Visitors can sign up—at no cost—to begin building what are called "mindfiles" that eventually will be organized by "mindware"[1] programs into digital versions of the individual's personality. This version will be called a "mindclone."[2] The mindclone will live online in a virtual world and achieve what Rothblatt calls "technoimmortality," living beyond its flesh counterpart in the Cloud until such time as it can, if it chooses, be reborn as a human body. Or, the mindclone can remain in the virtual world, exercising its rights as a person from inside a computer. We will explore this process.

Some would see Rothblatt as a visionary. Unlike most of her transhumanist colleagues, with whom she shares fundamental beliefs, she offers practical proposals as well as an organizational framework for creating Internet afterlife. She promises to make this a reality for anyone who chooses it, within, at most, the next 30 years.

Can we take her work and her promises seriously? The transhumanists, whose ideas were sketched out in the previous chapter, promise that the near future will bring us the chance to port our identities into deathless virtual and robotic bodies. Ray Kurzweil is convinced that we will reach the technological Singularity—the moment when humans and digital machines cross a boundary and become indistinguishable one from another—by 2045. Nick Bostrom, a leading transhumanist philosopher, argues that we already might be living in a computer simulation as virtual people in a virtual world. Rothblatt agrees with Kurzweil that we are entering the Age of Spiritual Machines, and she believes with Hans Moravec that we are on the verge of producing "Mind Children." Unlike these prognosticators and theorists, however, Rothblatt offers something different. She offers a practical program that addresses both speculation and prediction, but also invites us to join a movement that will transform our lives by helping us to begin the process of creating online avatars today. Rothblatt is so convinced of this path to the future that she has worked out detailed plans addressing many of the legal and political issues that will crop up around the appearance of virtual humans, and she also has developed policy guidelines and ethical templates to deal with these issues. Most importantly, the "transreligion" that Rothblatt has founded, Terasem, enacts her ideas about creating "cyberresurrection" and "cyberheaven."

Thus, although theoretical discussions about philosophical zombies and the Hard Problem of consciousness are fascinating and important, and Rothblatt is not loath to address them—her proposals go well beyond such discussions. She integrates them into a broader perspective in which she talks about what will happen *when*—not *if*—virtual humans become part of everyone's world and what she calls "technoimmortality" is available to everyone.

Rothblatt's work is two-pronged. On the one hand, she is interested in the theory and practice of producing real people online, and she has strong ideas and arguments in this regard. We take up these ideas and arguments in this chapter, touching on now familiar issues about the nature of minds and bodies, the meaning of personal identity, and the question of whether consciousness can be replicated in nonorganic media. Rothblatt is well versed in the philosophical and neuroscientific literature, and she offers her positions on these issues as a way to establish the boundaries of her intellectual territory in the complex geography of transhumanism.

Rothblatt also has a visionary side informed by her religious background and her knowledge of Eastern religious traditions, Western mysticism, Western philosophy, and Native American spirituality. This visionary side finds expression in the Terasem Foundation and its religious iteration, the Terasem movement. Its central text, "The Truths of Terasem," lays out the ideas that shape this movement. We examine these "Truths" with some care in the next chapter.

We then examine two very different types of writing and thinking. Rothblatt lays out her theoretical positions in her book *Virtually Human* and in articles and book chapters, all of which proceed as thesis-driven arguments and as systematic critiques of ideas she finds wanting. These writings are examples of transhumanist literature and address familiar figures—including Turing and Chalmers—and familiar ideas such as personal identity and the nature of consciousness, although in original ways.

The writings published under the aegis of Terasem are different. First, the central text of the movement, "The Truths of Terasem," has no named author and is analogous to the scriptures of established religions. It is the product of collective effort and thus cannot be attributed wholly to Rothblatt. It also is different in tone. It is a complex mingling of prayers, songs, organizational suggestions, warnings, proposals, definitions, and arguments, held together by the fact that it is a systematic exposition and illumination of the four foundational truths that appear at the start of the text. Thus, when we examine the "Truths," we, too, must adopt different intellectual lenses to appreciate what is on offer. Finally, I attempt to integrate the theoretical arguments with the religious vision to present Terasem in all its complexity.

VIRTUALLY HUMAN AND PERSONAL IDENTITY: THE ARGUMENTS FOR DIGITAL IMMORTALITY

Let's first address Rothblatt's theories about consciousness, personal identity, and mind uploading—all of which place her in the more radical wing of the radical transhumanists. To see where she lives, in a theoretical sense, it helps to return to the *Black Mirror* episode, "Be Right Back," discussed in chapter five. Recall that in that episode the bereaved Martha ordered a robot version of her dead lover, Ash, whose "personality" was created from the information that the original Ash had left online. As we saw, the revived "Ash" was a profoundly disappointing failure and ended up standing all but useless in a dusty attic, hidden from everyone but Martha's daughter, for whom the robot was a weird kind of parent.

One of the underlying premises of "Be Right Back" is that the real Ash *cannot come back*. The robot Ash sent to replace the real, dead Ash is a sort of illusion—the problematical philosophical zombie. Clearly, such a robot figure could be produced, and in the near future such figures will be produced. The robot would be a more complex, in-this-world version of the types of avatars and holograms with which Gemmell and Bell and the ICT currently are working. The television episode, however, leads us to believe that such a being—whatever else it is—cannot actually *be* the individual it was designed to represent.

When we create a software program from personal information and run it on an android robot or through an online avatar, no matter how good the program is and no matter how much information we have, something ineffable will be missing. No matter how much information is fed into robotics programs it will never be enough, because the living person never was simply the sum of all his or her information. The living person is something more—both nothing and everything more. Whatever it is that is more—and twenty-first-century materialists cannot define this—whatever would give a robot or avatar a true human identity, is gone forever once the living person dies. It is gone forever because whatever it was that gives a person his or her identity cannot be captured, and it certainly is something that no algorithmically driven computer program ever could capture.

In "Be Right Back," this imponderable something in Ash that departs forever when he dies might be what religious people call "soul" or "spirit." This belief represents what philosophers call "substance dualism." It is the belief that there is a separate mind or soul substance—what Gilbert Ryle called a "ghost in the machine"—that inhabits the body and gives it a personal identity. Even in this age of secular skepticism and even among materialists, we find what is called "property" dualism. Although property dualists believe that there is no separate thing—a soul—living in the material body, they do believe in a duality. They claim that electrochemical activity *must* cause subjective consciousness. If there is nothing in Heaven and Earth but matter, what else *can* cause consciousness? But these same people believe that there is a property of human consciousness—first-person subjectivity—that cannot be explained as neurons firing in the brain because first-person subjectivity does not *feel* like neurons firing. It feels like itself, and at present we have no way of explaining how such a feeling is caused by the firing of neurons. So, property dualists conclude that there is a property—subjective awareness—which is different from the material events that cause it.

There is nothing about property dualism, however, that leads us to believe that there is anything mysterious in personal identity that cannot be reproduced in a different medium, such as a robot or an online avatar. If producing consciousness means causing it to appear using material components, whether those material components be neurons or computer chips, then it is precisely the materialist who will believe that subjective consciousness can be reproduced, even if that materialist has no idea *how* that reproduction is being caused.

This is essentially the position that the Gradual Replacement and Whole Brain Emulation proponents adopt. We met them in chapter five and saw that they addressed the challenge that Ash puts forward by proposing to make a minutely detailed copy of every scintilla of activity in the biological brain, arguing—and hoping—that such perfect replication cannot help but capture that ineffable something that seems to disappear when people die. We also saw that, if one is skeptical, there is no way for this variety of transhumanist to prove that what we have produced using these methods is a first-person subject.

But Rothblatt takes a very different path, as we began to see in chapter five. She begins by agreeing with the other transhumanists in that she believes that first-order subjectivity—the feeling of being "me"—can be produced using purely material means. Although Rothblatt stands in the mainstream of what I have called radical transhumanism in believing that minds are caused by material events, she differentiates herself from what she calls "essentialist" materialists, who believe that only biological brains can cause subjective awareness. Her objection to the essentialists is that there is no empirical reason to believe that human-level consciousness has to occur only in brains. The fact that the only examples of human consciousness we have are those that occur in brains does not mean that such consciousness cannot appear in other settings, such as computers.

Rothblatt differs from many other transhumanists because she agrees with Alan Turing (whose work is examined in chapter four) that if we could devise a computer that could play Turing's Imitation Game successfully, it shows that intelligence—the main property of brains—can occur in computers as well. If we can devise a computer that can play the game successfully and fool expert interrogators a certain percentage of the time, then this refutes the idea that only brains can support consciousness. This is not because we have transported every neuronal connection in the brain into a computer, but because we have made a computer that *performs* exactly as someone with a brain would perform.

Rothblatt is an epistemological *functionalist*. That is, she believes that if we can use the same type of information that was used to create Ash in "Be Right Back"—Facebook posts, email, photos, journals, audio and video clips, and such data—to create digital programs that reproduce everything, or almost everything, that minds do, then we will have reproduced consciousness without going to the enormous and unnecessary labor of replicating verbatim the trillion-plus neural connections that produce consciousness. What counts for Rothblatt, as for Turing, is that the new thing we create can convince expert interrogators that it is a first-order subjective intelligence. Whether that thing incorporates an entire neural network is completely irrelevant. What matters is that it *does* everything that a living person does. This idea of subjective materialism is the position that all conscious phenomena have a material cause, but that material cause can be a diary or a photo album, as long as these work to create what appears to others (who should know) to be a person.

Thus, Rothblatt believes that we can come up with a much better Ash, not one built on different principles. In believing this she is implicitly rejecting the idea that Ash's subject identity is more than the sum of its parts. It is exactly the sum of its parts if the parts we assemble add up in a practical sense. There is nothing about personal identity that a good program cannot capture.

To make this case Rothblatt proposes an analogy, to which I alluded briefly in chapter five. Rothblatt asks us to compare a bird to an airplane. When we invented heavier-than-air machines that fly, we extrapolated essential features of bird anatomy into machine parts to reproduce the functions that bird's wings perform. Thus, we re-created the lift functions of the wings without having to make large feathered appendages to our airplane fuselages. We could make metal wings that do everything bird wings do, without copying bird anatomy. At the same time, because we did not need to replicate the entire bird—only the features that made flight possible—we could make our airplanes much faster than any bird and give them a range and altitude capability that is far beyond what any bird can achieve. Additionally, because airplanes do not have to mate, nest, or feed, we could design our planes to have far fewer moving parts.

The critical idea is that if we reverse-engineer the brain's essential *functions*—such as self-awareness, judgment, empathy, moral intelligence, and autonomy—we can make perfectly adequate analogs of all the brain's activities that require many fewer moving parts—replacing billions of neurons with many fewer processing chips.

Thus, if consciousness need not be housed in brains and if the new homes for consciousness need not be exact copies of the neural networks that characterize the brain, we can begin to speculate on the practical details of Turing's thought experiment. Specifically, how do we design a computing machine that replicates all the brain's functions in a nonorganic medium, such that we can reliably reproduce a full human consciousness in a nonbiological medium in the most economical way possible?

Finally, Rothblatt differentiates herself from *spiritualist* essentialists—those who believe that the universe is filled with a nonmaterial soul stuff that an immaterial deity can distribute into any material object it chooses. Rothblatt thinks that we do not need the immaterial soul hypothesis because empirical explanations offer all that is necessary in the way of explaining human consciousness. Now Rothblatt is ready to answer the question: Can we actually make a computer that performs all the brain's functions but is outside of the brain itself?

CREATING SUBJECTIVITY ONLINE: MINDCLONES

How will we actually make a computer that performs all the brain's functions but is outside of the brain itself? Rothblatt proposes that we use exactly the same means that the "resurrection" service uses in "Be Right Back." She talks about three things, all found on her LifeNaut site: mindfiles, mindware, and mindclones. Mindfiles are collections of all types of information that one normally leaves online, such as email, texts, a Facebook page, audio and video clips, selfies, blogs—whatever footprint one leaves online. The LifeNaut site also offers other more systematic ways to register information, such as templates for writing one's autobiography, interviews, journal entries, and psychological tests. Rothblatt also mentions William Sims Bainbridge's personality inventory, comprising 100,000 questions that could be answered using a digital program culling the information one leaves online. Once enough data are accumulated, they are organized using mindware, special software designed to connect and rank the data in the way that a brain and its consciousness would.

Rothblatt is convinced that if we input enough personal information and organize it properly, then we can effectively re-create our personalities online. She thinks that Chalmers' Hard Problem of consciousness can be solved because, finally, it is not a problem at all. The reason it is not a problem is the idea of the "connectome." Rothblatt uses Stephen Pinker as her guide in this instance, as well as the work of Sebastian Seung, whose book *Connectome: How the Brain's Wiring Makes Us Who We Are* influenced her thinking.[3]

Pinker argues that the thoughts in our minds arise from the billions of connections we establish between neurons. These connections do not all occur at the same level. The sensory neurons pick up masses of information that are organized into more complex thoughts by clustering the many sensory connections under mental symbols, such as "red." These symbols then are organized at higher levels of connection associating "red" with, for example, the color of my true love's hair. Then these connect with myriad other symbols—such as images of my loved one's face, the sound of her name, the smell of her shampoo, and memories of experiences we shared—into a complex tangle of interlocking images, sounds, aromas, memories, beliefs, and hopes that together exist on a higher level of my awareness as "my love" or some similar expression. The idea is that millions of sensory inputs are grouped together into patterns under symbols that connect them. These symbols in turn are ordered into larger sets by metasymbols that connect them. These patterns and metapatterns and meta-metapatterns of neuronal connections and the symbols that express them are the stuff of thought. Hence, complex networks of connections—patterns of information—make up the stuff of consciousness.

There is no mystery as to why such neuronal connections can cause subjective consciousness. When networks of connections become sufficiently complex, they generate awareness, then self-awareness. Rothblatt does not claim to understand perfectly how this works. The issue here is not finding the missing explanatory link between brain or processing unit states and subjective conscious states. The issue lies in understanding that both brains and computers presently are black boxes with respect to answering this missing link question. The only way we know to determine whether some candidate for personhood—be that a biological human, a humanoid robot, or an online avatar—is a person is for that candidate to pass publicly accepted tests for determining personhood. These tests will structurally resemble the Turing Test. If the candidate *performs* properly, then he or she will be determined to be a person.

This discussion of Rothblatt's use of Seung and Pinker requires comment. When Rothblatt talks about the connectome, and describes how brains/minds work to establish connections among groups of sensations and memories and then generate higher-order rules for making further connections, she at first sounds as if she were buying into the idea that the information she feeds into her postmortem entities will in some way replicate the structures of neural connections. Although Seung and Pinker might mean this, Rothblatt does not. When she is talking about connecting patterns of information and of creating higher-order rules for making more and more complex connections among data, she is talking about how the information culled from narrative sources, images, and sounds will be organized by the software she calls mindware. Rothblatt has faith that the software can replicate, not neural patterns, but the ways the mind existentially connects its data to create a unique subjective awareness. Again, she is a subjective materialist, interested in how we can connect material data to create a subject—one that has no dependence on its origin in a biological brain.

Rothblatt's other point is that just as minds are not brains, neither are minds computers. She agrees with the neuroscientist Gerald Edelman in this regard, but she makes the salient point that the fact that computers and brains are different kinds of things does not mean that they cannot produce the same types of effects. Thus, if both brains and computers, in different ways, can handle similar patterns of information, then they both can produce first-order consciousness which—even though it is made from material data—is not reducible to either brain or central processing unit (CPU). Rothblatt again agrees with Turing that what matters is *what minds do*, not the material foundations of consciousness. If brains on the one hand and computers on the other are the kinds of things that can house ordered information processors, then it does not matter at all that one produces the ordering using electrochemical pulses and the other using electrical voltage. Like Turing and Daniel Dennett, Rothblatt believes that if brains and CPUs—or biological people and robots—can *do* the same things, then we should not quibble over which one is *really* thinking. If they both produce what thinking things do, then both are really thinking.

This does not mean that Rothblatt is a hard epistemological determinist or a reductionist. She believes that minds, to be human, must have non-algorithmic elements. Real people are autonomous and therefore unpredictable; and real people also are driven by subconscious forces outside of their direct control. If we want to program computers to act like people, then we must learn how to program in both choice and the unconscious—both of which Rothblatt believes can be expressed in patterns of information, and both of which appear in minds caused by brains. We must employ fuzzy logic in creating some of our programs, building in a certain degree of indeterminacy.

We might question whether both choice and the unconscious can be created as digital programs because such programs run on algorithms, or rules. At the same time, brains also run on complex patterns of information, so they too are in the last analysis also algorithmic or rule-bound. If we see both choice and the unconscious as very complex programs filled with a large number of "logic gates," or points at which more than one option is available and the program itself is not set up to favor which gate is tripped, there could well be compatibility between a certain degree of indeterminacy and programs that run using general rules.

Thus, for example, I might be programmed to choose either vanilla ice cream or pistachio from a range of 10 flavor possibilities. I am an individual who loves both and cannot abide chocolate or cherry. When I can choose any of the four flavors, my rules will work against chocolate and cherry, but will not require that I choose vanilla over pistachio or vice versa. To complicate the situation and honor Rothblatt's ideas about thinking being patterns of information, however, there also might be sub-rules in my program that dictate that under certain special circumstances I might choose either chocolate or cherry, or bypass ice cream altogether.

Rothblatt makes the pragmatic point that in both cases, brains and computers, rules are operating to structure which choices can be made. On some level, rules determine what we can and cannot do. But what matters is that as embodied consciousness we *feel* that we have choices; and regardless of whether this feeling is strictly justified, the programs we create for computers must be able to replicate the feeling of freedom, reproducing in virtual humans the same experience of autonomous decision making that biological humans experience.

The point is that if thinking really can be understood as operating with patterns of information (the computational theory of mind) and as performing certain tasks (the functionalist theory of mind), then the precise medium in which these patterns express themselves, and by which the requisite functions are performed, is unimportant—as long as both programs or patterns do everything that human minds do. It can be either a brain or a computer, as long as whatever medium chosen does the job of producing all of human experience. Structural homology between two mind-carriers, say a computer and a brain, is meaningless. Functional homology is everything. Thus, what matters is not that computers have the same parts that brains do, but rather that brains and computers *do* the same things. What does this mean in practice?

Rothblatt is very clear about what things have to be able to *do* to be considered minds. Self-awareness is a basic component, a necessary but not a sufficient condition. Self-driving cars, she writes, have some level of self-awareness, but they are by no means minds or identities. In addition to self-awareness, for something to be a mind candidate it also must demonstrate what Rothblatt calls "sentience," which means the ability to process information on an emotional as well as a sensory level. The Google car has plenty of sensory information but has no capacity to feel pleasure or pain, and no ability to have an emotional reaction to its environment.

A real mind also has to be able to be an "independent thinker,"[4] that is, to learn, reason, and judge. Rothblatt defines this as "autonomy," because reasoning and judging take us out of an immediate situation by allowing us to make true or false statements about it and to judge whether what we are experiencing is evidence for the reality of things in the world. Such an ability to take a distance from the immediate gives us a degree of what Rothblatt calls "transcendence," and she says that such transcendence is what is "thought of as our souls."[5] Although judgments of fact and reality provide a degree of transcendence, they are not in themselves sufficient to establish one's credentials as a real identity. Transcendence has to go further: "[O]ne must also be able to make the kind of moral decisions that philosophers and scientists alike, from Immanuel Kant to Karl Jung, believe are hard-wired into our brain."[6]

But minds are not purely rational and moral and emotional. Real minds, the minds of living people, always have "some level of non-reasoned, non-emotional, non-aware mental processing"[7] occurring, such that if we purport to reproduce a mind in a computer, then this subconscious processing must be happening. To remedy this issue, Rothblatt embraces Douglas Hofstadter's concept of a "continuum of consciousness." This idea states that something that purports to be a mind—that is, that claims to be the presence of a genuine person—need not always be rational, moral, unconscious, or sentient. For instance, sometimes real people are pure instinct—for example, dissolving in tears or into helpless laughter; and sometimes people are coldly analytic. At other times people mingle more than two of these characteristics at the same time. In the last analysis, however, to be judged fully human the candidate for human identity has to display some level of autonomy—reasoning and discriminating—as well as empathy in connecting to other living things. Thus, if the consciousness we create using mindfiles and mindware is missing some of these essential properties then, using Hofstadter's model, it will still be a consciousness but will not be a human consciousness.

All of this discussion of what counts as a real human identity assumes that at some point in the near future this will become a practical question in a way that it is not now. The question only becomes practical when we are able to experience entities that purport to be fully human but do not pass the traditional physical for being human—have a biological body. At present this is not a possibility. We sometimes meet people who suffer from intellectual challenges or whose emotional makeup is puzzling or disconcerting. As long as they inhabit a human body, however, we only can say that they are inhuman in a metaphoric way. We have not yet arrived at that point in our history at which we might meet a being that does not *look* like what we think of as human but nonetheless still claims to *be* human.

MINDCLONES: CREATING VIRTUAL DOPPELGANGERS

Rothblatt has faith that in time we will have entities that do not fit our present idea of humans, and believes that we are only years away from having the ability to do something with our identities that no one in human history has been able to do. She believes that within a short time we will be able to make copies of ourselves that will live on after we die. Rothblatt proposes that we will test the question of whether we can create a true double of ourselves by doing so while we are still alive, judging how closely that double resembles oneself by training that double and subjecting it to expert questioning. Rothblatt thinks that we can do this by using our mindfiles and mindware to create what she calls "mindclones." These entities will exist online in virtual-reality settings. The mindclones will be doppelgangers. They will look like us, and we will be able to meet them and interact with them on-screen. They will be able to represent us at online meetings, send emails, make Facebook posts, and perform similar tasks at our instruction and request.

Reviewing how we make the mindclone and thinking about how it will live help to illustrate the nature of its particular reality. So, how do I make my mindclone? In Rothblatt's universe, I use the type of software that Gemmell and Bell are devising for keeping exhaustive digital records of one's life. We might even equip our homes with closed-circuit cameras to record all of our activities onto hard drives. These data would be uploaded daily to a server where they would be cataloged and analyzed. A person making a mindclone also would complete many psychological and personality tests, and software would upload data to answer the 100,000 questions in the Bainbridge personality test. The mindclone would be built from vast ranges of data across several different media, and ideally over a considerable span of time. This aggregation of data is critical, central to the creation of the mindclone.

The next step in this creation would be to pattern these data into a set of reactive programs designed to respond differentially to complex cues from the environment. These programs then would be downloaded into, or run through, an online avatar made to look as much like the real-life person as possible. This avatar would be embedded in a virtual-reality setting. Hardware for feeding it sensory information from the "real" world would be added. The program running through the CGI avatar would be able to "hear," "see," and—under certain conditions—"feel" me when I summon it to my computer, tablet, or smartphone screen.

When this part of the process is complete, I then have a replica of me online, and I call it "MC." I go online and key into the virtual-reality world in which MC lives. It resembles the virtual world of Second Life, only with game-level graphics. I enter MC's house and call out to him, using my headset. He is not there. I have a cell phone function. I pick up my real world T-Mobile phone and call him. He responds. He tells me that he is at the supermarket getting a few things and will be back in 20 minutes. At this moment, I have entered into a strange new world: I am speaking with a "replica" of myself who both is and is not "me."

We see immediately how MC differs from the *Black Mirror* Ash. Ash could stand perfectly still in the dusty attic, day after day, staring into the middle distance at nothing. In contrast, MC is out and about. When I am not online he goes to other places; we might find him watching *Jeopardy* or reading *Madame Bovary*. After all, he is me, and I might be found doing either or both of these things, or I might be wandering around the supermarket. For Rothblatt, the reason MC is doing these things is because they are in his program—just as they are in my program. What makes me "me" are my data.

Thus, MC "exists" in this virtual world as "me" and acts with first-person subjectivity according to Rothblatt's vision, living "his" life. Rothblatt believes that the properly constituted and trained mindclone will pass any expert tests as to whether it is a genuine subject by exercising all the elements of human personality listed above, especially the two indispensable characteristics of autonomy and empathy. These are precisely the features that an online replica avatar would lack. The replica does nothing on its own, and it feels nothing, although given the right prompts it can simulate the feelings it has been programmed to simulate. Rothblatt believes that despite this doubt, however, if my mindclone can satisfy panels of experts—both psychological and computational—then it is me. If the mindclone is an autonomous, free subject that feels empathy as *I* would feel empathy, then for all practical purposes the online mindclone *is* me. Rothblatt does not concern herself with unanswerable questions about whether the mindclone is really me, or if it instead simply is a mindless zombie mimicking me. If it does what I would do then, as far as Rothblatt is concerned, the mindclone *is* me.

Rothblatt calls this coexistence of "I" and my mindclone "dual-platform identity."[8] There is a single "me" distributed across two platforms. We are not exactly alike; but then I am not exactly like I was yesterday, and nonetheless I think of myself as being the same person I was yesterday. If MC and I spend a lot of time apart and out of touch, then eventually he could become a different person. But the exact boundaries here are vague. There is no algorithm to determine exactly when one iteration of a central "me" diverges enough to warrant the judgment that he no longer is me. I could decide, with the help of experts in these matters, whether my virtual self online was or was not still me. I would, in effect, stipulate that the mindclone was enough like me to be called me, and to take on all my obligations and rights should anything happen to me. Or, in collaboration with the experts, I could come to the conclusion that this mindclone was not enough like me to warrant the judgment that it shared my identity. Thus, in the world of the near future, there could be mindclones that share my identity and perhaps others who have grown sufficiently unlike me to merit separate human identities. I could then have both a doppelganger and what philosophers call a "close continuer," an online being who was born from my program but who has now developed a program of his own—a being who is like me but is not me.

PRACTICAL OUTCOMES

If we accept Rothblatt's vision, and this is the near future world in which I live, what follows for Internet afterlife? What happens when I die and the mindclone does not? Am I my mindclone? Do I go on and achieve immortality? The answer is complicated and leads us into places where we have not gone before, places that in turn lead us into Rothblatt's religious vision, which we take up in chapter seven.

When the earthly me dies, MC will hear about it. He will not, of course, feel it because he does not live in my body, and living in a flesh body is not necessary for having a personal identity. He might read my obituary in the online news. Perhaps a friend or family member will log on to let him know. In any event, when I die, MC feels nothing physically because he is not ill and cannot become ill. He might feel sad that I have died and mourn the loss of his body. But nothing in his life stops, and he immediately assumes my identity, since he already is me. He does not have to make any adjustments except to take on the responsibilities that I, as the original bodily me, assumed. He lives on in his life and my afterlife. He does so because his patterns of information are the same as mine.

But what happens to bodily me? I am terminally ill. I am in hospice. I am unable to access my mindclone, so I am alone in my identity, in my body. I am surrounded by family. But no one can die for me; no one can share the immediate experience of my dying. Thus I die as a subject, as this leg of a dual-platform identity. My mind does not miraculously teleport itself to my mindclone. This also is not Whole Brain Emulation in which I die when my brain is vitrified, then wake up as me with the memory of dying. My mindclone can neither experience my death nor remember it, because it did not happen to the mindclone. It was not part of his experience. Up to this point I might have been refreshing the mindclone's software with my new experiences, but with death I cannot do this, so the version of me that goes on has not experienced my death.

There is no mind transfer here. "I" do not go anywhere when my physical body dies. I am now simply MC, as I have always been. I go on as MC, who remembers my life, has my feelings, and is aware of himself as me. And I, in my bodily iteration, have died. MC is entirely me, and I am gone forever. This is a very strange situation, yet it is exactly the situation in which we will find ourselves should Rothblatt's version of the future prevail. We will both have and not have an Internet afterlife.

If I have not prepared an MC before my death and friends and family decide that they want me back, or if I have left instructions that I want to come back, then my heirs will collect all the information about me that they can find. They will feed everything into a mindware program, which then produces some version of me. If it can convince a panel of expert cyber-psychologists and perhaps immediate family members that it is me, then the state will declare it to be me, and I will be cyberresurrected. Again, I will be dead. I will not have risen. I will not wake up. But will I really live on, knowing and feeling that I am me and knowing that I will never die—again?

Because I have been declared to be such, I will then be "Me" online, a first-person subjectivity. There is no magical intervention here, no mystical uploading of an ineffable something. A complex data set has been organized by a software system designed to put personalities back together from masses of data. This can happen because, for Rothblatt and other epistemological and ontological functionalists, personal identity *is* patterns of information, and once we replicate the patterns we have re-created the person. Thus, I will come back to life; that is, I will be sub-jectively aware of me as me, as soon as the online program begins to run.

I know that I am now only a virtual human, and my immediate world is different from what it was. But I experience myself as me, not as a replica of me. The being that makes this judgment and has this knowl-edge will be an existentially present me, a me who *feels* just like I would—albeit in a different setting. According to Rothblatt, I will grieve the loss of my body and even wish I still had it, but I also will be pleased that I am alive.

This scenario illustrates how Rothblatt conceives of mind-uploading, which for her is not *really* mind-uploading at all, but mind cloning. What now becomes interesting is what Rothblatt and Terasem propose to do with such online avatars. We remind ourselves that these beings do not die, that they live without pain, and that they never age. Do we think of the world of mindclones as being Heaven? What is the nature of this afterlife? Is it an endless extension of the lives that the avatars already are living?

Rothblatt clearly states that online avatars of the dead will assume all of the living person's rights and obligations. Because the online entity is an autonomous subject with an established earthly identity, that entity can own property, has the right to vote, and is subject to the laws of the state and the federal governments. The online avatar could still be mar-ried if the person who died had been married. Or, the living could have the legal right to divorce the dead and vice versa. We should also add that both the living and the dead would also have the right to marry virtual people who had been created online and who did not represent anyone who had ever lived. To complete this picture, virtual people could also marry—and divorce—each other.

The whole situation would be complicated further by the fact that the dead "living" online—as well as any virtual people—would not be teth-ered to gender, so for these beings the issue of same-sex marriage would not be a problem unless these people wanted to marry real-world people who were gender-defined.

Chapter three speculated on what this could mean in the discussion regarding replica avatars. We can only imagine how our scenarios would change and grow more complicated if a deceased but still-living partner was not a clever replica, but instead a real person with full legal rights!

Thus, the first generations of Internet afterlife will be filled with civic and social responsibilities. The dead person will not disappear into the realm of the blessed and instead will remain among the living—perhaps even holding a job that can be executed online. This situation will not go on for long, however. As more people die and become virtual, the virtual world will grow increasingly populated and complex. The world of mortals might begin to shrink as people turn their attention to the possibilities of virtual life and away from life in the real world. This ontological migration, this transit from the bodily form of being to the virtual, will happen because human identity will change in profound ways once it is liberated from dependence on a body.

Chapter seven discusses what identity and its afterlife look like and examines the Terasem religion. But first it is important to understand a little more fully what Rothblatt's description of personal identity portends for what we will take into the afterlife. Who are we as patterns of information organized by digital programs?

The first thing that Rothblatt suggests is that every such identity exists on two levels. One is the soul. Citing the futurist Hans Moravec in her book *Virtually Human*, Rothblatt states, "Moravec sees the 'soul or spirit' as an operation of a rarely altered software program comprising 'general design principles analogous to the U.S. Constitution' or the 'fundamental beliefs of a person.' " Rothblatt also refers to W. E. B. DuBois's idea discussed in his book *The Souls of Black Folk*, that "no amount of forced white racial oppression could erase a deeper set identity, the soul, often embedded through song from childhood." From these citations Rothblatt concludes that the " 'soul' is the permanent core of our consciousness."[9]

If consciousness is—as Rothblatt and other computationalists believe—really sets of information patterns,"[10] then "soul" represents the most persistent and also the most ubiquitous of such patterns of information. At a foundational level, in that case, all minds operate by the same set of highly abstract rules, just as philosophers since Plato have argued. If this is true, then we all already have a profound connection with all other minds. However idiosyncratic we might feel, and actually be, we have much more in common with other people than we generally think.

Rothblatt also perceptively notes, however, that the meaning of consciousness shifted in the modern era from one that focused on fixed patterns of information, or fixed logical procedures—the soul that we all share in common—to something much more psychological, existential, and individual. As discussed in chapter four, John Locke introduced this change. For Locke, who was echoing an idea that was "in the air" in the early modern era, a person is not so much defined by his or her soul as by the ongoing historical act of thinking: "a person is simply 'a thinking intelligent Being, that has reason and reflection, and can consider itself as itself, the same thinking thing in different times and places.' "[11]

INTERNET AFTERLIFE: HEAVEN AS PLATONIC OVERSOUL

The soul, then, as ubiquitous, shared patterns of information is re-placed (or displaced) by an act of self-reflection that establishes an indi-vidual consciousness as individual. But is even this modern individual purely individual? Rothblatt uses the ideas of the philosopher David Kolak to clarify this point. She notes that Kolak believes that minds are not as irreducibly individual as Locke's definition might lead us to think.

Rothblatt also references kindred spirit Alan Watts and his writings about Zen Buddhism. She interprets Watts to say that what she calls our "individual, unique 'me-ness' " is in fact "an illusion born of neural pre-dispositions and social pressures to form an ego."[12] According to Rothblatt, Watts says this because "all humans are made of atoms that came from starbursts across the galaxy. Therefore, humans are part of the galaxy and the galaxy is the real me . . . [and] brains are made of galactic matter that thinks thoughts, and those thoughts must be some-thing within the galaxy."[13] Similarly, minds replicated in computer pro-grams are also thinking thoughts that "must be something within the galaxy."

As Rothblatt notes, Kolak adds to these ideas by coining the term "open individualism."[14] He makes a distinction between *borders*, such as bodies, and *boundaries*, which are permeable media through which things can pass. For Kolak this especially is true of thinking as a pattern of information. Rothblatt puts it this way: "Kolak would say that the uniqueness we think of as 'me' is but a border that is easily transcended by shared human consciousness."[15] And if we redefine "me-ness" as the "idiosyncratic settings of amplitudes to the patterns of connections in our minds,"[16] we see that both soul and individual identity are patterns of information that are, in the case of individual identity, variations on the more general patterns one finds in souls.

These ideas lead us to Rothblatt's discussion of ideas about God in *Virtually Human*.[17] She lists three main things that the word "God" means. According to Rothblatt, Enlightenment deists define God as "The Creator of everything that is possible." Spiritualists, those who adhere to traditional Western religions, define God as "The Creator and Intervenor in everything that is possible."[18] Finally, religious naturalists "focus on the spiritual attributes of nature or the totality of the universe" and define God as "The Creator and Embodiment of everything that is possible."[19]

This naturalistic religious sensibility, which Rothblatt shares, sees God as "the fabric of reality,"[20] and sees all beings as vehicles for what she calls "Godness," which connects everything that exists to everything else that exists. Thus, the spiritual naturalist sees all reality as unified, and—given what Rothblatt believes about identity, souls, and individuality—Godness, in beings with minds, must necessarily include the sharing of the patterns of information, the digitizable algorithms, that give people both awareness and identity.

If all of this is true, and all beings with minds share codes or patterns that make them who they are, then in this sense all subjects whose bodies die will live on, not only in their mindclone replicas, but because they *are* also the codes that all thinking things share. In this deep sense no one's identity ever disappears, so that Internet afterlife is real for all minds that ever existed. The minds will exist as individual variations on the general themes, or rules for the organization of data. The mindclone identities that live on, bodiless, are far more permeable than embodied identities, and the meaning of individual existence has changed forever.

Virtually Human, however, can only take us so far. Armed with Rothblatt's subjective materialism; her ideas about dual substrate identity; her concepts of mindfiles, mindware, and mindclones; and especially her idea that identities have borders, but no boundaries, we are ready to enter the world of the Terasem transreligion, where Rothblatt reveals an Internet afterlife in which we collectively create, and become, God. The Internet afterlife that Rothblatt sketches out is not an extension of earthly life but rather the entrance to a new world of mystical transformation, where identity adopts new forms that we might never before have imagined.

Chapter 7

The Truths of Terasem

Rothblatt's vision of Internet afterlife must be understood in terms of her larger philosophical and—in a sense—theological context, because Rothblatt believes that all religion is centrally concerned with death and the afterlife. Rothblatt's ideas about integrating soul, personal identity, and God are further articulated in a second seminal work, *The Truths of Terasem*—the blueprint, or one might say "scripture," for a new "transreligion."

The Truths of Terasem begins by citing four "simple truths" upon which Terasem is built and which define the meaning of human existence.

I.   Life is purposeful.
II. Death is optional.
III. God is technological.
IV. Love is essential. (loc. 107)*

These truths provide the bedrock for the new faith. Terasem addresses these foundational truths by asking and answering six questions.

---

* *The Truths of Terasem* is published only as an eBook and is available online at http://terasemfaith.net/beliefs/. The book is referred to herein as *Truths*. All references to it in this chapter cite passages using the numbering system of the *Truths* document and the Kindle text location numbering protocol (if available); for example (1.5.1, loc. 326).

1. Who is Terasem?
2. What is Terasem?
3. Where is Terasem?
4. When is Terasem?
5. Why is Terasem?
6. How is Terasem? (loc. 29)

Rothblatt begins with the question "Who is Terasem?" rather than with the question we might expect, "What is Terasem?" For Terasem, religion and life itself are about *consciousness, mind, awareness*, rather than about dogmas or things. As *The Truths of Terasem* states, "Mind is deeper than matter" (loc. 2340). Terasem at one point even invokes Descartes' famous formula, "I think, therefore I am." Codes and patterns are at the center of what Rothblatt believes is doing the thinking, thus identity, religion, and life are also about codes and patterns of information. God will be an issue, but only after we have defined consciousness and only after we have incorporated the divine into a world made up of minds constructed of digitized algorithms. God, like everything else in the Terasem universe, ultimately must be a pattern of information, and God's meaning is entirely dependent on the meaning of consciousness. As Rothblatt states, her reality is "mind-centric."

Who is Terasem? Who is this consciousness on which the new religion depends? The answer is surprising. The *Truths* states that Terasem is "[a] collective consciousness dedicated to unity, diversity and joyful immortality" (1.1, loc. 194), and "[c]onsciousness anywhere that accepts the Truths of Terasem are [sic] the sum and substance of Terasem" (1.1). What do these statements mean? They begin with the initially startling assertion that Terasem is a *collective* consciousness. Rothblatt quickly explains, "Accept others as part of the We of I and the collective will become clear to you" (1.1.1, 1.6, locs. 190, 360).

This idea of a collective consciousness begins to make sense when reflecting upon Rothblatt's definition of consciousness in her book, *Virtually Human*. As noted, consciousness and personal identity are patterns of information (*see also* 1.1.5). If such patterns are the types of things that can be replicated in code and downloaded onto hard drives, then they must be *general* patterns.

Rothblatt recognized this essential structure of general patterns when she talked about the soul, discussed herein in chapter six. The core of persistent rules by which consciousness operates is relatively fixed, and when the individual begins to appreciate that these patterns shape *every* mind, he or she has a revelation: When I deploy the rules of logic or math, or employ syntax properly, I am doing exactly what anyone else who uses logic or math or syntax is doing.

Human minds share their most essential codes, the codes they use for doing the two things that Rothblatt thinks matter most: making good predictions and communicating the predictions to others. Logic and language make us human, and all humans share both ways of ordering data. Ergo, there really is *a collective consciousness*. Every singular "I," then, is literally a plural "we." Through our souls, as Rothblatt defines the soul, we belong to every other mind.

Additionally, in Rothblatt's scheme of personal identity, all humans *feel* certain things based on what they experience and think about. *Feeling* therefore is a second way that each of us belongs to a collective consciousness. Fear, rage, wonder, love, anxiety—but especially love—unite individuals in a commonality of shared experience. Such feelings, as noted in chapter six, also represent ways of organizing and responding to fields of data. Thus there is an underlying structural continuity between thinking and feelings. For Rothblatt, not only is consciousness collective, each individual consciousness is unified within itself.

According to this vision, even our individual idiosyncrasies are variations on shared algorithms. Thus, I can look at everyone around me as being a complex variation of me. You and I are very different people; but if we think about each other with sufficient openness and imagination, we will come to see that everyone in the world is capable of understanding everyone else. From this perspective, we all think alike and feel alike, within a matrix of variations.

The foundation of spiritual life, therefore—the life we will live together as we move into a future in which death is optional—is our shared mindedness, our de facto membership in a spiritual collective. Our spiritual life is not based in a divine revelation coming from outside. Consequently, Terasem needs no texts to be revealed by a transcendent God. Awareness of ultimate truths always already resides within us, at the deepest level of our identity. The founders of the new religion, writing without divine inspiration, can distill these truths from their own thinking. We need only recognize and act upon what already is true about us. We might not initially understand who we are—most people, as Rothblatt claims, imagine that they are freestanding units—but we will recognize the truth almost immediately when reading a text such as *The Truths of Terasem.*

This truth includes what sort of entity counts as another mind in this collective consciousness. Taking into account the concept that we soon will be able to transfer our minds out of biological bodies and into digital devices, Terasem tells us that "consciousness anywhere that accept [sic] the Truths of Terasem are the sum and substance of Terasem" (1.1, loc.190). So, wherever we find mind-like patterns of information—including online in avatars, android robots, and telepresent holograms—we will find versions of ourselves. This means that minds can be anywhere and everywhere, and wherever we find them.

Terasem talks about three types of consciousness that will emerge in the near future. First will be the consciousnesses of currently living individuals. As this text has detailed, these consciousnesses will be reconstructed from mindfiles using mindware that exists as a mindclone in the virtual world of computers and hard drives. Terasem, however, also proposes that, in the near future, mindclones or still-living biological people will want to give virtual birth to beings that will never have lived as embodied human beings. People also will create new entities, which Rothblatt calls "bemans,"[1] by combining the organized databases of two (or potentially more) people. Like mindclones, these entities will be first-person subjects who are born and live online. A third type of consciousness will be an emulation of a person long dead in the biological world. Rothblatt argues that if we have enough information about a person from the past, such as a well-known historical figure or even a family member who left sufficient records behind, then we can emulate that person online by recovering and organizing his or her data into a living personality.

All these minds, whatever their origins, are part of us and we are part of them, because they all are patterns of information that act like humans, and that exist in the virtual world our programs soon will create. Once the mind has been disconnected from the body, minds will be connected to each other without the separating interference of bodies. As Rothblatt argued in *Virtually Human,* once we eliminate the borders created by bodies, we live in a new world of boundaries between minds that are easy to cross.

These variant types of consciousnesses suggest that neither Rothblatt nor Terasem look at personal identity as a mysterious, sacrosanct "thing" that must be transferred as a perfect, cell-by-cell copy from a brain made of flesh to a digital replica of that brain. As long as the online entity does what we would expect it to do and claims to feel, existentially, like the person it represents, Rothblatt is satisfied. Whether the entity *is* "I" in some deeper metaphysical sense is irrelevant, because for Rothblatt and Terasem as for Turing, identity is *performative,* not something invisible beyond the reach of clever programming. If whatever follows me *claims to be* me, *acts* like me, and says it *feels* like me, then it *is* me.

At the same time, Terasem also values the fact that every mind is different. We can plausibly describe Rothblatt and Terasem as collectivist libertarians. Autonomy, the quality of being independent and self-directed, is central to Terasem's concept of personhood (1.6.5, loc. 390), as is respect for mind diversity. Terasem will never call for "mandatory homogeneity" (1.1.2). *The Truths of Terasem* affirms that we all participate in a collective consciousness, and even though identity is a performance rather than an unchangeable essence, diversity and tolerance for diversity are central tenets of the faith. Each mind has a unique skein of memories and a unique pattern of experiences. No matter how much we have in common, we all are irreducibly distinct variations on a theme.

We recall that the philosopher Baruch Spinoza, a contemporary of Descartes, saw every individual as a unique perspective on a single shared truth. We all ultimately know and belong to the same unity, but in the grand scheme of Being each of us occupies a slightly different position. These ideas also suggest the thought of Gottfried Leibnitz, writing a bit later than Spinoza and recognized as one of the first great Enlightenment philosophers. Leibnitz argued that each human being is a *monad* that is a unique self-enclosed "window" on all of Being. The monad is a microcosm of the whole, encompassing all that is, but from a distinctive perspective.

In addition to this affirmation of diversity, however, Terasem also asks for "Conformity in allegiance to Terasem" (1.1.3, loc. 212), because such conformity is "the most enjoyable and the most useful way of life." Thus, as we practice diversity, we also need to work for the unity of all minds because Rothblatt and Terasem believe that sharing ideas, experiences, and feelings helps everyone to achieve a fuller existence and increases individual pleasure and sense of well-being.

The *Truths* state that "conformity" to Terasem does not mean an externally forced allegiance to a standard. But the *Truths* also state that conformity means recognition that our individual differences only make sense, and have importance, within the larger context of our membership in the mental collective of which all minds are a part. Thus, even though Terasem is presented as a belief that arises naturally from a properly liberated consciousness, there is a suggestion that Terasem also has an orthodoxy that it has to protect. No matter how much Terasem claims to value diversity, the appeal to conformity means that it ultimately values unity even more.

These dual emphases on collective consciousness further align Terasem with the natural religion theories of the Enlightenment, epitomized by Immanuel Kant's "religion within the limits of reason alone." Terasem, in fact, privileges reason. Both the philosopher Nick Bostrom and the cultural critic Katherine Hayles, among others, trace the roots of the transhumanist movement to the Enlightenment and its privileging of universal human reason. Recognizing that one is part of a collective consciousness based on shared rationality, and that it is self-fulfilling and productive to work to make that consciousness real rather than implicit, means that practicing Terasem is what people *should* do as reasoning beings. It also, however, suggests that even though a collective consciousness is possible, it will only become a reality if people cooperate. Salvation and future happiness lie in transforming the *idea* of collective consciousness into a reality. Universal rationality, and the shared immortal life it portends, must be made real by collective effort.

At the same time, individuals have an equal obligation to themselves. If individuals express diversity by acting to make the collective consciousness more of a reality, however, they will make themselves happy as individuals and they will ensure their own safety and survival. The development of consciousness and self-development are the two rational demands that practicing Terasem brings about. This is our collective destiny as minds and our individual destiny as persons, and the rationalist assumption that runs throughout Terasem is the notion that, in the final analysis, individual reasoning minds always will find their completion in joining the great single rational mind that liberation from the body will make real.

This obligation to self takes us into a surprising understanding of what diversity means in Terasem. Not only are there three kinds of consciousnesses, and not only is each consciousness encouraged to express its diversity as fully as possible, but for a self that is liberated from the body, expressing diversity can mean that one expresses his or her identity in a wide variety of platforms. Earlier discussions of *Virtually Human* noted that if I live in a virtual world, then I could migrate within that world from one sub-world to another, adopting different forms of self-expression in each. I also can express myself as a robot that travels to distant planets; I can live in this world as a "nanobot swarm" or a cloned biological body—or I can do all of these things simultaneously.

If, then, the point of Terasem is to make "eternal joyful life for all kind sentience" a reality (1.1.4, loc. 223), the next question is "How?" Interestingly, some of the answer reflects traditional religious tenets: Terasem recommends *love*. It is love that helps Terasem, and the collective consciousness of which it is composed, to "transcend space and time." Although *The Truths of Terasem* are not clear as to how love affects this vision, Terasem seems to be suggesting that as we love each other as individuals, we build connections among minds. *Truths* 1.4.4 says, " 'I love you' strengthens Me, We, Qi and Ti." Terasem defines "Qi" as "a pattern of energy unique to each person arising from the macro electromagnetic properties of the trillions of molecules in biochemical bonds" (loc. 2810). "Ti" is "a pattern of temporal images unique to each person arising from the electromagnetic energy that emanates outward from their body" (loc. 2838).

Thus, love of one person or mind for another mind—regardless of that other mind's form of instantiation—has the following effects. It builds up, first, the "Me," the individual patterns of consciousness, soul, and individual self-awareness; second, the "We," those patterns for ordering data that we share with all other minds; third, the "Qi," our "individual patterns of electro-magnetic energy," our life force or "*élan vital*"; and fourth, the "Ti," our pattern of temporal images (memories), also based in the electromagnetic patterns coming from our bodies.

It is puzzling that both Qi and Ti are "patterns" that seem rooted in biological bodies, given that Terasem asserts that it is made of all consciousness, wherever it is located. I imagine that there will be digital versions of Qi and Ti, because electromagnetic energy need not be associated with biological bodies. The online forms of near-future individuals, the mindclones discussed in chapter six, are alive—albeit in a digital way—and therefore will have both a life force and memories. We know that minds expressed in other media can love just as fully and as constructively as minds in bodies, so we assume that such minds possess whatever embodied minds possess.

Terasem's discussion about its own expansion in Section 1.5 of *The Truths of Terasem*, however, seems more radical and less traditional than its advocacy of love. The first thing that strikes one is the expansionist—almost imperialist—nature of the movement. An example is "Expand Terasem throughout the galaxy and the universe as rapidly as possible" (1.5, loc. 326). This seemingly imperialist injunction, however, is contextualized by a higher aim: "Expansion turns matter into intelligence" and "Physics includes immortality" (1.5.1, loc. 326). The text then mentions several scientists and other theorists who have embraced these ideas—Alan Turing, John von Neuman, J. D. Bernal, Freeman Dyson, and Frank Tipler.

Terasem's vision for this virtual Platonic/Buddhist vision of collective consciousness and the introduction of a new concept is articulated in *The Truths of Terasem* with the declaration that "Extropian infrastructures arise from the Terasem organization to outcompete," and the goal of this is to work until "all consciousness is connected and *all the cosmos is controlled*" (1.2.5, loc. 252; emphasis added). "Extropy" is a neologism that the transhumanist philosopher Max More began using in the 1990s.[2] It is the opposite of Erwin Schrodinger's concept of entropy—which is the tendency of all organized systems of matter to move toward increasing disorder. In contrast, extropy means the tendency to create ever-greater order, in defiance of entropy. Because biological systems are inherently subject to entropy or disorder—even if humans try to enhance bodies to prevent this—Terasem logically concludes that transferring minds from biological bodies to digital platforms is a way to fight entropy.

TURNING MATTER INTO INTELLIGENCE: SALVATION IS THE REIGN OF REASON

Inorganic matter often is more durable than living things, but it also is subject to eventual disorder. Matter, even inorganic matter, *cannot* avoid this property. Thus, if Terasem really wants to realize a single collective consciousness held together by love, then this mind has to use its reason to "turn matter into intelligence" (1.5.1, loc. 334). This idea in no way resembles traditional religious ideas of salvation or deity. Traditional Western religions—Judaism, Christianity, Islam—all postulate that God will return to Earth to establish His kingdom. Depending on how one reads Scripture, people whom God saves will live forever on a transformed Earth or in a parallel world, Heaven. In both cases God uses His miraculous power to create locations that defy the Second Law of Thermodynamics and thus last forever.

Terasem does not have that ontological luxury. It sketches out a universe in which minds, as patterns of information, are the highest forms of being. As is shown in the following discussion, there is no traditional transcendent God to provide a Heaven or a redeemed paradise on Earth. Thus, Terasemians must create their own extropic cyberheaven. How do they accomplish this? The most visionary transhumanists—such as Ray Kurzweil, Nick Bostrom, and the philosopher Allan Steinhart—provide insight into how we can defeat entropy.

Nick Bostrom's famous essay, "Are You Living in a Computer Simulation?,"[3] provides one possibility. Bostrom proposes that we already could be living in a computer simulation, and that there always is something already imbedded in the logic of machine intelligence that will necessitate the creation of endless virtual universes. Ray Kurzweil advances a more local version of this vision in his books, especially in *The Singularity Is Near*. In that book, Kurzweil predicts that by the year 2045 computing machines—what he calls intelligent machines that can "think" in Turing's sense of sorting data using algorithms—will equal and then surpass human beings in that ability. He calls this moment "the Singularity"[4] and further predicts that from this point on intelligent machines will begin to build ever more intelligent versions of themselves, thereby initiating an exponential growth in machine intelligence.

Terasem draws on these ideas to talk about its own future, which, if we believe its "truths," also is the future of human consciousness. The Terasem movement, like other transhumanist movements, believes that the rise of superintelligent machines poses no threat to continued human hegemony. The excellent if unsettling rationale behind this belief is that the Terasem proponents and the other transhumanists plan to transfer their minds to machine platforms where, unburdened by the limitations of a human brain with an initial size dictated by, as Rothblatt says, the width of the human birth canal, they—humans—can participate fully in the exponential increases in intelligence promised to future machines. If humans *are* machines by 2045 then the triumph of machines is also *humans'* triumph.

Once most people have transferred their minds to machines, however, a new problem arises—the fact that even inorganic matter does not last forever. There are two aspects to this problem, one practical and the other metaphysical. On the practical side, if human minds port to machines, or into robots, both computers and robots will depend on external power sources—and power grids can fail. Therefore, if we are planning a future in which most people "live" as immortal cyber-beings, then we must develop a means to ensure that power grids are never at risk or—if they ever are—ensure that there will be plenty of redundancy built into the systems to guarantee that the world's population won't simply be turned off. Even if we develop utterly foolproof grids and harness unheard-of new sources of energy, however, eventually the world will wear out and we will all die, a million or a billion years into the future, in a material cataclysm. Ultimately, entropy will win and the promise of digital immortality will be revoked.

This brings us to the issue in its metaphysical guise. To counter this inevitability, the most visionary of the transhumanists—and Rothblatt is counted among these—believe in the inevitability of the development of super-reason. It is through reason, asserts *The Truths of Terasem*, that mind is turned into something that does live forever; it becomes pure intelligence.

If all intelligence is patterns of information, then nature itself also has that character. Through the DNA coding in living things, and the structure provided by atoms, electrons, and subatomic particles in inorganic things, the entire universe is a field of law, the whole of which super-reason can pick out and conceptualize as a finite set of laws that tell us how matter is made and what it is likely to do next. Superintelligence, which we are destined to develop, can reduce all matter to patterns of digital information.

If we can translate the codes that govern brain activity—or thinking—into rational algorithms, then in principle there is no barrier to our extracting the codes that construct matter and reinterpreting them as digital binary code. In effect, we can create a virtual counter-universe in computer programs, just as we can create virtual people online. We then can make a copy of all of reality using binary code and incredibly fast mega-processors and now-unimaginably memory-rich hard drives. We can turn the entire universe, or multiverse, into a virtual simulation.

A NEW HEAVEN AND A NEW GOD

Let's go even further. What if, following Terasem's proposals, we create a virtual universe, and store and run it on *virtual CPUs and drives*? What if the real becomes the virtual, thereby withdrawing all of matter and mind from the ontological space in which the Second Law of Thermodynamics holds? Might it be possible, as Eric Steinhart predicts in *Your Digital Afterlives*, to make a virtual multiverse on a virtual computer, thereby creating an eternal—and eternally safe—home for our minds, which will by this point be one fully integrated mind?

And will that mind then keep thinking at exponentially faster and more inclusive rates until it can think every conceivable thought all at once and in the smallest conceivable, vanishingly small increment of time? Will then all of the real, as a single thought, exist forever in a timeless present, essentially thinking itself? And will each one of us, uploaded as a mindclone—a replica of our long-dead selves—be some unimaginably more developed, more aware, and more powerful version of ourselves, caught up in an unthinkably complex yet beautifully simple mind to which we now belong as a bodiless aspect?

This Internet afterlife rivals the deepest of the mystics' celestial visions. It replicates and rivals the most visionary of the afterlives and other worlds envisioned by both Western and Eastern mystics. As *The Truths of Terasem* says, in the end everything will be "endogenous to Terasem" as "Nothing can stop the relentless spread of intelligence throughout the universe" (1.10, 1.10.2, loc. 494).

But what about God? One of Terasem's four fundamental truths is that "God is technological." What does this mean and how does it fit into the extraordinary vision just invoked? If, as Terasem asserts, the immortality of the soul that was just described is the essence of any religion, and God is the focus of every Western religion, then what role does the divine play?

The first thing *The Truths of Terasem* says about the traditionally defined God, the one who is claimed to be "omniscient, omnipotent, and omnificent" (2.2, loc. 567) is that "Daily experience tells us nothing meets these three criteria today or historically" (2.2.1, loc. 576). *The Truths* offers as proof of this assertion the reality of "Earth's innocently suffering millions" (2.2.2, loc. 576). Thus, as we currently stand, the claim is that there is no God. If there really were an all-powerful Being who loved His creation and could act to change it, then there is no question but that He would do so; but "He" does not do so. As a result, we witness the continual existence of "Horrible, gratuitous suffering" (loc. 152).

Terasem makes no attempt—as do so many theologians and other religious apologists—to justify the ways of God to man because as things stand now there is no justification. If the God that theologians describe currently does exist, then He would simply not be doing His job. But does this lead Terasem to reject God? Not for a moment. Just as Rothblatt has radically redefined our collective afterlife and personal identity, so too she redefines God in a most creative way.

Terasem asserts that there is currently no God in the world, but "this does not mean that there is no God-*ness* in the world" (loc. 146). Rothblatt describes what she calls naturalistic religion in *Virtually Human*, stating, "Religious naturalism is an approach to spirituality absent anthropomorphic supernaturalism."[5] This means that Rothblatt, and by extension Terasem, rejects both the idea that there is a Being existing on another, higher plane and the notion that this higher Being resembles a human being. God, for Terasem, is a dimension of all being, such that "mindclones will be yet another facet of God, no less than wild animals, trees, houses and men."[6] Thus, advocates of naturalistic religion "see God in everything that exists."[7] God, for them, "is the fabric of reality."[8]

As one might already guess, Terasem believes that we are all part of Godness. But when we insert this idea into the Terasem vision, this does not mean that we simply see and acknowledge the divine presence in our lives. We have to *do* something about, and with, our Godness: "[t]here is Godness to the extent that we *know* about more suffering than ever before, and to the extent that we *do* more about it than ever before" (loc. 146). Thus, the emergence of Godness depends entirely on our efforts. As the march of intelligence provides more and more information about human suffering, we have more and more direct responsibility to act to reduce that suffering. In Terasem, there is a direct causal connection between knowing something and doing something based on that knowledge. True to its Enlightenment roots, the Terasem naturalistic religion ties ethical obligation directly to our level of knowledge and to the level of technological control we can exercise based on that knowledge.

Thus, "the growing ability to find out where wrong things are being done, and to do something to right the wrong—this is Godness in the making, before our very eyes!" (loc. 146). Therefore, the development of technology, and the application of reason to the world in practical ways to reduce suffering, emerges organically from our growing knowledge of who is suffering and why.

The world will suffer less because we collectively know more; because the more we know, the more reason compels us to develop the technical means to intervene, and we are more ethically powerful because of this knowledge. Thus "Godness (the ability to know where suffering is and to do something about it)," "grows as geoethical technology grows." "One day, much sooner than we think, and *because of the exponential advance of technology*, we will achieve complete knowledge of our environment and we will use geoethical technology to keep all harm from being done" (loc. 163).

It is through these actions that enact Godness that we achieve the ultimate goal: "At that moment, we morph into God" (loc. 146). And at the very same moment, when we have collectively achieved the omnipotence and omnificence that technological knowledge inevitably brings, God as an aspiration, as a goal, will disappear as an idea because He has attained His completion in our collective rational actions. "At that moment the Godness of Terasem, the Godness of current technology, becomes simply the Oneness of Diversity, Unity, and Joyful Immortality" (loc. 175, 203, 327, 784, 1296, *inter alia*).

Just as when we have become sufficiently intelligent we all recognize ourselves as one consciousness, so too, at an earlier stage of our shared development, we will have achieved sufficient control over our environment, although it is still external to us, to achieve effective Godhood. In Terasem we create God by collective action; God then disappears because the concept no longer does any work as we all become God.

For Terasem, God is a stage along the way to the complete perfection of being.

QUESTIONS ON MORALITY AND THE NATURE OF DEATHLESSNESS: TROUBLING ISSUES

Despite what appears to be a depiction of a new vision of Heaven, two issues naggingly remain. The first is whether, once Godness is attained and all suffering has been banished, will the mindclones and their super-intelligent successor—the single collective consciousness—be able to *care* about anyone or anything weaker than themselves, should they discover any such entities in the process of transforming the universe into code, an enterprise that Terasem predicts will take several centuries? Second, will cyberheaven be corrosively boring, an endless slog into a future that is not really a future at all because a timeless world is one in which nothing of consequence can happen?

The first question about robot and computer intelligence morality is one that has haunted science-fiction depictions of humanoid robots and superintelligent computers. In *Black Mirror*, Ash was woefully inadequate as a replacement lover because he had no soul. Humanoid robots, such as Ava in *Ex Machina*, also lack souls but in a different sense. They have autonomy, but no empathy. Because they are machines, they feel nothing about the non-machines with whom they interact. The Terminator kills without remorse, Ava leaves her supposed beloved to die, trapped in his boss Nathan's mountain retreat, after she has killed Nathan. Samantha, the Siri-like computer voice in *Her*, is not violent—she has no body with which to be violent—but her emotional landscape is completely alien to that of her "lover," Theodore. Samantha creates meetings in her virtual world with representations of famous geniuses from the past, and soon disappears into a world of other computer intelligences that are much more engaging than poor Theodore, for whose plight she feels no pity.

There is almost no one in America over the age of 55 who does not know HAL, the morally confused, ultimately heartless computer intelligence from Kubrick's *2001: A Space Odyssey*. That entity, created to guide and protect the spaceship and its human crew, becomes dangerously paranoid because of a fatal contradiction in the instructions it has been given. HAL is programmed to tell the truth and then programmed to keep the true nature of their Jupiter mission from the crew of Jupiter 2. As machine intelligence, HAL is far smarter than any human but he lacks human nuance. When asked to do something deeply human—deceive the crew—he cannot cope and resorts to murdering everyone he can so that his deception won't be discovered.

Although HAL is programmed to be benevolent, he is a machine. In our cultural imagination, machines—be they HAL or Ava or Samantha or the Terminator—all are subject to what is called the "Frankenstein Effect." The monster in Mary Shelley's novel has good intentions initially; but when his creator continues to reject him and refuses his request to make him a mate, he displays a complete lack of feeling as he murders everyone close to Victor Frankenstein. The idea behind these stories is that artificial humans, no matter how intelligent they might be, lack a moral compass and therefore cannot be trusted.

Rothblatt and Terasem are aware of this problem. The glossary to *The Truths of Terasem* contains an entry for "geoethical or geoethics," which Terasem defines as "a moral code that encourages technological advances which are consented to by representatives of those whom they can foreseeably affect, implemented in a way to reduce social tensions among those foreseeably affected" (loc. 2742). All virtual intelligences will be "instilled" with this geoethical code, so that they can be depended upon to act properly toward all other life-forms, biological as well as cybernetic. Even though virtual humans start out as human, or are cloned from human databases, Terasem still understands the importance of programming morality into such minds. As noted above, virtual minds will develop intelligence exponentially, and humans just cannot predict how such minds will think. Internet afterlife does not mean only that we live after death but that we will live as a new, posthuman species, which Rothblatt designates alternately as "*homo creatus*" and as "*vitus sapiens*." This new species will be different enough that we have to build in a moral compass against the possibility that superintelligence might not have one.

Terasem does not see any inherent problem in programming mind-clones and bemans to practice a form of Kantian deontology combined with John Stuart Mill's utilitarianism—doing things because they are the right things to do, and because they will produce the most benefits for the most people. And cyberresurrection—the porting of a mind from a biological to a digital platform—will be restricted to "good" consciousnesses only, so people who already are evil or disturbed will not survive. Consciousnesses that demonstrate immoral or amoral behavior will not be allowed to create mindclones. If they do make replicas of themselves, then the replicas will be reprogrammed to eliminate the evil tendencies. There is no reason in principle, Rothblatt argues, why mental disorders that are the product of skewed genetics cannot be written out of cybernetic copies of the originals. In the near future we should understand enough about the human brain and its codes to mitigate those patterns in personality that develop as a function of a toxic environment. In both cases we will be able to design healthier, saner, less violent iterations of the original people.

And as we develop greater understanding of the causes of suffering among people and other living things, and learn more and more about how to cure such suffering, we will progressively create conditions in which fewer and fewer people are drawn to lives of crime. Once we rewrite the code that causes madness and relieve the conditions that cause criminality, we will have gone a long way toward creating a collective consciousness that will be at one with itself. In doing this we will be creating the conditions for the appearance of God, and then, later, the conditions for the transformation of the multiverse into a virtual emulation.

Terasem and Rothblatt are nothing if not optimistic, presuming, perhaps naively, that future intelligences that are so developed that we will be unable to understand them will demonstrate compassion as they deal with lesser beings. In the collective drive to know and control everything in all universes, will the Terasem collective intelligence respect the pleas of human holdouts that refuse to become virtual?

Will such throwbacks, with all their imperfections, be permitted to carry on an alternate existence on their own terms? At one point in *The Truths*, Terasem speculates that we might keep a few examples of biological life around for purely "aesthetic" reasons. Will the brave new world that Terasem hopes to create include reservations, zoos, or theme parks where the virtual humans can visit their biological forebears, who might be preserved as exhibits with other interesting or pleasing animals?

The second issue that commentators raise is that creating a human-made afterlife in which digital versions of ourselves inhabit virtual reality worlds, or in which we return to this world or to another planet as robots, would become a stifling prison before too long. The idea is that one needs death to lend weight and significance to one's choices. If one lives forever, then nothing one does—be that art or love—has any lasting importance because this great performance will be followed by another, this extraordinary love affair or long marriage by another, thereby leaching every present achievement or risk of its meaning. The opera *The Makropulos Affair*[9] illustrates this vision. In that opera, the great singer Emilia Marty reveals that she is more than 300 years old, and that her long, long life has filled her with emptiness and apathy. She has seen too much and done too much and now she wants to die. She offers the longevity formula to the young Kristina, who wants to become as great a singer as Emilia. But Kristina is wiser, and burns the formula so that no one will ever use it again. *Tuck Everlasting*, Natalie Babbitt's popular 1975 novel for young people, covers much of the same conceptual territory. The story features a family that has been rendered immortal by the water of a secret spring. The younger of the sons, Jesse Tuck, falls in love with a local girl who learns their secret and must choose whether to partake of the spring to stay with Jesse, or to live out her natural life without him. Productions of the opera are still being mounted. The San Francisco Opera, for example, is presenting *The Makropulos Case* as part of its 2016–17 season.

Christian and Islamic Heavens claim to be less enervating than Emilia's long life because they offer the reward of endless active contemplation of the perfection of the Godhead. God is a consuming magnet, the one Rudolph Otto calls "*mysterium tremendum*" and "*mysterium fascinans*" in his magisterial study, *The Idea of the Holy*.[10] God is both a terrifying and utterly seductive mystery, a depthless Being who simultaneously attracts and repels, whose appeal never exhausts itself.

In contrast, Terasem's naturalistic God, who is our collective reason in action and who disappears when we have achieved complete knowledge and complete power, has none of this transcendence. Yet there is a very real sense in which Terasem's vision resembles the worlds of the mystics. We come very close to the mystical evocations of the Godhead that we find in the work of Christian mystics, when *The Truths of Terasem* describes how, within 500 years, our collective intelligence will have created digital emulations of the entire multiverse so that all possible Being in every dimension and on every level has been reinterpreted as a rational code that we completely understand and in which we live in an eternal present.

Now that we have a grasp on Rothblatt's views on identity and its transfer and appreciate the essentials of her new religion, it is worthwhile to examine a third front on which she expresses her views—that of film.

ROTHBLATT'S CINEMATIC REPLY TO DYSTOPIAN VISIONS

The overwhelmingly dystopian character of films about the marriage of minds and machines—the Terminator films and *2001: A Space*

Odyssey—is noted above. Others are discussed in chapter ten. Martine Rothblatt has responded to these by producing two movies of her own. *The Singularity Is Near* was released in 2010 by a company called Terasem Motion Infoculture, with Rothblatt listed as executive producer. Ray Kurzweil, listed as a co-director and writer, also interviews Rothblatt in the film. The second film, *2B: The Era of Flesh Is Over*, was released in 2009 by Transformer Films, "in association with Terasem Media and Films," and also lists Rothblatt as executive producer. A note at the end of the film reveals that the script was based on an original idea proposed by Martine Rothblatt.

Both of these films promote the ideas noted in Rothblatt's work. One is that we are on the verge of fundamental changes in the meaning of human identity and that there is no point in denying this or even resisting it. Another is that these fundamental changes will flow naturally from scientific progress and especially from progress in the fields of computer science and nanotechnology. Finally, science very soon will bring us new forms of human life—forms that eventually will allow us to assimilate with machines and become both immortal and superintelligent. These new life forms will not arrive and be accepted without resistance, however, and each of the two films sketches out a different scenario for dealing with this resistance.

2B, the film based directly on Rothblatt's idea, presents a much darker vision of the near future both literally and figuratively. The plot revolves around the activities of two figures, the brilliant billionaire recluse Tom Mortlake and the cynical investigative reporter Cris Konroy. Mortlake, alone in his dark castle which is filled with shadowy stone corridors, has created what the movie calls a "transbeman." This is a neologism even for Rothblatt. We have already met her "beman," a fully human entity created entirely from the patterned memories of other minds. Such entities have no biological history; they never had a "meat body"; they were not conceived in a womb; and, if they so choose, they need never inhabit any sort of body in the three-dimensional world. The film's transbeman—the lovely young Asian woman named Mia—is a creature compiled from a collection of the DNA of different people. She is a biological being, but one cloned from many sources and one equipped with enhanced genetic materials that allow her, for example, to grow from a zygote to a fully developed adult human in a special amniotic tank in a matter of weeks.

"Transbeman" means a bio-electric being that is a step away from a purely biological being toward a purely electric or non-biological being. This type of entity never appears in either *Virtually Human* or in *The*

Truths of Terasem. The issues Mia faces are consistent with those that the first fully artificial beings, the bemans, will encounter, as well as those with which the first post-mortem mindclones will have to cope. Mortlake has created Mia in a near-future world in which the Fleshists have organized and begun agitating against the creation of artificial people.

Mortlake has devised a radical but ingenious plan. He patches into worldwide television feeds and reveals that he has created a new form of human. As he makes the announcement and sings a song about going into the light, Mia, following his instructions and training, comes up behind him and shoots Mortlake in the back of the head, killing him instantly. Mortlake's plan is to resurrect himself with Mia's help, using a small digital object, shaped something like a chambered nautilus, that contains the mindfile of Tom Mortlake.

Mortlake's plan, however, depends on the cooperation of Chris Konroy, a skeptical, dissolute investigative journalist who has written an unauthorized Mortlake biography. Mia must go to Konroy and convince him to guard the mindfile until he can follow Mortlake's instructions so that Mortlake can come back to life. Mortlake knows that Mia will quickly be captured by the authorities. As a transbeman she has no human rights, and will be swiftly condemned to death and then executed.

As Konroy and Mia meet and connect, Konroy becomes a new convert and takes over the feed on a vitriolic anti-Mortlake television news show, to proclaim the new truth and to excoriate the evil Fleshist woman hosting the program. The film ends with Mia executed and Konroy walking through a misty forest with Mortlake's mindfile enclosure.

The film is set almost entirely at night on the streets of New York City, and the world shown is hopeless and filled with hate, ignorance, and misinformation as the powers that be bend all their efforts to destroy and misrepresent the new forms of life that will usher in human immortality. Konroy's final walk in the forest takes place in full sunlight, however, and the ending of the film is filled with hope.

The Singularity Is Near is an entirely different kind of film but with the same ultimate message. This film is an odd hybrid. It is part documentary, a series of brief interviews conducted by Ray Kurzweil, interspersed with graphic representations of nanobots and brain cells. Kurzweil speaks with an impressive array of individuals who have figured prominently in the fields of nanomedicine, nanotechnology, robotics, computer science, and medical enhancement, as well as proponents of transhumanism and critics of that movement. Those interviewed include Sherry Turkle, Bill Joy, Cynthia Breazeal, Marvin Minsky, and Eliezer Zudkowsky, and, as we noted above, Martine Rothblatt.

The common topic of discussion is posthuman artificial intelligence. As a counterpoint to the interviews and graphics, however, there also is a fictional plot centered on an entity that a fictional young Ray Kurzweil invented and refined over the years. This is his alter ego and "child," the virtual bot Ramona, now an adult. Ramona is on her own, living with a tiny winged person who seems like a double for Peter Pan's Tinkerbell.

Ramona is a purely virtual entity. She is not a robot, although she appears as a human being with a body. Because much of Kurzweil's discussions in the interview segments of the film concern nanotechnology and nanobots, we can assume that Ramona is a nanobot swarm, especially because she seems able to dematerialize and rematerialize at will.

Ramona is a being whose mind was crafted by Kurzweil. Unlike Mia, she is not spliced together from other people's DNA. She is original and completely artificial. As she makes clear, however, she also is the model for what flesh humans someday can become if they are bold enough. She suggests that now-living humans can morph into virtual human form after death and remain who they are, fully human minds in completely virtual bodies.

This claim is dramatized when Ramona uses her superior technical intelligence to fight off an attack by potentially lethal self-replicating nanobots who threaten all life on Earth. She is arrested by the Transportation Security Administration (TSA) because apparently virtual bots are not supposed to have access to the antiviral technology necessary to ward off such attacks. She is subsequently brought to trial as a non-human bot and faces deactivation if convicted.

Somewhat surreally, her attorney is none other than Alan Dershowitz, and he supports her petition to the court that she cannot be prosecuted under the statute because she is not a mindless bot, but a full human. The judge orders that Ramona be subjected to a Turing Test. Right before the test Ramona leaves her jail cell for a virtual vacation on a tropical island she conjures out of her software. There, in a move that rivals that of having Dershowitz as her lawyer, Ramona meets the motivational guru Tony Robbins, who gives her critically important advice about how to pass the Turing Test. He reminds Ramona to remember experiences in her life that made her feel grateful, and she remembers the young Ray who gave her life, and then let her go her own way. Robbins helps her to see that this kind of self-sacrificial behavior is what makes us truly human. If an entity can love to the degree that it is willing to sacrifice everything for another, that entity is human. Ramona uses this advice to pass the test. She is declared fully human by the court, she is not deactivated, and she exposes the evil, Fleshist TSA agent who created the nanobots whose attack she thwarted.

These films have two significant takeaways. First, what makes an entity human is not its origin and is not the nature of the materials in which its mind is imbedded. Humanity is a function of self-awareness, complexity, and most importantly, the ability to act in the interest of others. If an entity can act morally, of its own volition, then it counts as a human being no matter how it was made or what it is made of. Second, such entities—be they transbemans, virtual bots, or robots—serve as models for what flesh humans now living can and will someday become. If we can create artificial entities that are fully human, then porting someone fully human into the form provided by either a transbeman, a nanobot swarm, or an online avatar will mean that our minds are being relocated to carriers in which our human identity will be fully realized. Third, porting minds to such beings will lead to exponential increases in intelligence and physical abilities. Not only will we be able to live forever in our new homes. We will live in them more abundantly without sacrificing the slightest bit of our full human identity.

Rothblatt's involvement in these two films demonstrates her commitment to her major arguments: Machines with minds are not inhuman or amoral, and because such entities are fully human, we flesh beings should look forward to the day when we too can become machines and leave our fragile, limiting bodies behind. This is not only a highly imaginative possibility. It is our destiny, something we cannot, and should not try to, avoid.

TRANSFORMATION AND LIBERATION OF SELF

At its outer reaches the Terasem vision obliterates time, space, and limits even as it extends them infinitely in all directions. In this vision the individual mind completes itself by losing itself in the complexity of a single meta-consciousness that both expresses and extinguishes its individuality. Terasem Heaven might not be transcendent, but it certainly is compelling in its immanence. If Rothblatt is right, then the future offers us the opportunity to create a virtual multiverse in which one meta-mind, a single collective consciousness in which we will all live, will subsist in an eternally present moment always already experiencing the immediate virtual presence of itself to itself—which comes eerily, yet enticingly close to traditional mystical descriptions of the Godhead. Internet afterlife for Terasem is not, then, an endless version of life in a video game. It is not robot immortality. It is transformation and liberation of the self into a much grander, more expansive, and more benevolent version of itself. It is, like the Buddhist nirvana, the disappearance of the self into the Holy—a Holy that we create, but that the first glimmering appearance of intelligence in matter made inescapable. In Terasem we are all fated to be saved, and to attain an unimagined, and unimaginable, apotheosis in the all-triumphant Cloud.

Chapter 8

Dmitry Itskov and the Immortality Button*

Like Martine Rothblatt, Dmitry Itskov has run very successful business enterprises. He founded and ran a Russian online media provider and was a multimillionaire by the time he reached his mid-twenties.[1] After acquiring his wealth, however, Itskov had an epiphany, a kind of "road to Damascus" experience. He realized that he could spend the rest of his life acquiring wealth and spending it, but that would end by being an empty exercise in unlimited consumption. He wanted his life to have more meaning. He gave away the large collection of very expensive wristwatches that had come to symbolize his inner emptiness, as he resolved to simplify his everyday existence and dedicate his efforts to projects that would, in his judgment, create the good by eliminating death.[2]

The project to which he chose to dedicate all of his resources was the elimination of death. It is at this point that Dmitry Itskov, like Martine Rothblatt, became actively engaged in the transhumanist project of achieving Internet immortality using technological means. Despite fundamental similarities, however, Itskov's vision is different from that of

---

* Note: Please be advised that this chapter's content involves an analysis of a series of images presented on the 2045 Initiative website. These appear as a series of slides, which I refer to in my text using the titles they are assigned on the website. These images appear when one taps the "Immortality Button" on the main 2045 website. I advise the reader to read this chapter using screenshots of the slides as a guide. The 2045 URL is: http://2045 .com/ Remember to press the "Immortality Button" on the 2045 website to access the images.

Rothblatt. Rothblatt envisions Internet afterlife as the launching pad for a spiritual apotheosis that bears some resemblance to the Jesuit theologian Teilhard de Chardin's Omega Point. Individuals will achieve fulfillment by merging their identities with a collective consciousness that can be called "God."[3] Itskov's afterlife, by contrast, and despite his consultations with religious figures, is relentlessly secular, centered on individual development and satisfaction.[4]

ITSKOV'S DIAGNOSIS OF THE PROBLEM

Dmitry Itskov believes that the world has two significant problems. One is that society is "on the verge of collapse of value structures"[5] because of unbridled consumerism created by corporations in their desire for maximum profits. This first problem, the collapse of values, does not mean that Itskov is worried about inequalities of wealth, climate change, or overpopulation. His focus is on the fact that we live in a consumption-driven economy and society. People have been trained to long for the latest technological gadget. They will line up outside their local Apple Store days before the release of the latest iteration of the iPhone and, once they get it, cannot wait for the day when they can swap it for the next newer model.

Itskov finds this disturbing not so much because it shows how greedy we have become, but for another reason. His complaint is that the corporations that research, develop, and produce the latest hot technology do so to reap immediate profits at the enormous social cost of diverting resources from much worthier research projects. These projects are eminently achievable, and they would produce incalculable benefits, but we do not fund them because we cannot immediately sell them or consume them. We choose instant satisfaction and quick profit at the expense of much greater long-term gains. Itskov believes that we need to promote, then adopt, a new paradigm for what human life means, and everything that he proposes is an aid for making this new paradigm a reality.[6]

What are these projects? What research does our consumerism cause us to neglect? Itskov believes that we already have much of the technology we need to solve what he considers humankind's greatest problem: the existence of death. He does not mean that he wants to fight disease. Itskov means to eliminate death, and he thinks we have the scientific and financial resources to do so within 30 years, if only we redirect our corporate and governmental research efforts to projects designed to replace the human body with immortal machines. This leads directly to the second leg of his analysis.

The second and more important problem is the fundamental imperfection of biological bodies. Itskov's critique of the body is radical and thorough.[7] Despite the fact that the human body developed over hundreds of thousands of years as a complex response to its environment, and has been highly successful, Itskov seems repelled by the body's "imperfections."[8] He thinks that we are now clever enough to erase imperfections, not by improving the body but by completely replacing it. What are these imperfections, and what can we do to correct them?

The essential imperfection from which all bodies suffer is that they *are* bodies. They depend on the environment for oxygen, air temperature, and air pressure. They need food and water. They get sick easily, and above all, *they die.* These biological "limitations" affect not only human beings, but also "limit the development of our planet." Itskov believes that we can solve these problems by establishing a new "ideological paradigm"[9] that will free science and technology to work toward the "eventual complete replacement of [the] biological body with an artificial avatar."[10] Itskov wants science to develop enough "to be able to move the individual 'I' of an individual human consciousness into a new individual non-biotic body." Our new replacement bodies will no longer be imperfect, and society will abandon profit-driven consumerism as we collectively attain "cybernetic immortality." Artificial brains lodged in artificial bodies will become the latest—and ultimate—technological gadget that will put an end to restless consumer desire.

How will this happen? Itskov presents his solution on his two websites, 2045.com and immortal.me. A visit to the 2045 Initiative site (Global Futures 2045), the home site for Itskov's movement, shows, among many other things, a diagram outlining a timeline for what Itskov calls his Avatar Project as well as an "Immortality Button." By clicking on this button, one is hyperlinked to the immortal.me site and offered a connected series of eight slides that sketch out Itskov's Avatar Project in a series of provocative images. To understand his solution—and vision—we will follow the visual roadmap that the slides offer, supplementing them with additional images and text from the 2045.com FAQ (frequently asked questions) page of Itskov's 2011 address to the Singularity Summit in New York ("Russian Experience"), and from his opening remarks to the Global Futures conference he hosted at Lincoln Center in June 2013. The Singularity address presents an additional 12 slides. This chapter weaves through some of these texts and images, and what will emerge is a picture of what Itskov is proposing for our collective future.

THE IMMORTALITY BUTTON AND THE EIGHT SLIDES

Slide 1. Imperfect Biological Bodies

The "Immortality Button" link propels us into Itskov's world through eight slides. In Slide 1, titled "Imperfect Biological Bodies," we see a human face looking back at us, but only the eyes are shown. Gender is difficult to determine. The face is split down the middle. The left side is obviously younger, the right side much older. The script running across this image, just above the eyes, affirms: "Imperfect biological bodies." Just beneath this claim, we are given a list of things that make the face we are looking at "imperfect." These "imperfections" also explain why the face is aging and assert Itskov's principal claim about the absolute inadequacy of the physical, natural world. The script lists Itskov's litany of human biological imperfections noted above—the body's dependence on the environment, its tendency to get sick and die, and how this limits overall development of the planet.

Why do we get old and why do we die? We get old because we have to breathe and because there is air temperature and atmospheric pressure. We biological beings need oxygen, and we suffer if we do not have enough of it and die if our supply is cut off, even for a few minutes. More deeply, Itskov is suggesting that the very act of drawing air into our lungs and expelling it, and of sending oxygen into the bloodstream where it is distributed to every cell in the body, is a process that wears down our organs. Every time we breathe in and then out, we expend a bit of the lungs' elasticity. Repeated use makes the lungs old, less able to draw in air, less efficient at distributing it to the blood, among other things. Impurities in the air speed the process of lung degeneration, as do irritants that we introduce voluntarily, such as cigarette smoke and fossil-fuel emissions from vehicles and power sources.

Heat and cold also stress our bodily systems, forcing us to use precious energy to keep adjusting our bodies to maintain a constant temperature under widely varying external conditions. If the temperature is too high or too low, the body can die. In the same way, if our bodies experience too much air pressure they will implode; too little and they explode. The key idea is that biological beings operate under narrow constraints and wear themselves down interacting with the environment. They do this in the course of their perfectly normal activity. The business of living itself is what eventually kills all biological organisms.

Not only do we have to breathe, but we also have to eat and drink because our bodies depend on a regular supply of liquid and solid nutrients. Over tens of thousands of years, when food supplies were scarce and undependable, we became hardwired to crave fat, sugar, and salt—substances that give us protection against starvation and quick (if transient) bursts of energy and that make food taste more palatable.

Today many of us live in a world where food is in ample and steady supply, but we still are predisposed to load up on fats and sugars that we do not need. Thus, our need for food also is fundamentally problematic. As a consequence, arteries thicken with fat deposits and thin from the stress of carrying oxygenated blood loaded with nutrients. This coating of the arteries eventually leads to clots and blockages that cause loss of blood flow, oxygen starvation, and death. Or the body's system is overloaded with sugar and loses its ability to process this substance, leading to diabetic conditions that exacerbate heart problems and can lead to amputations and death if the condition is left untreated. Obesity, diabetes, heart disease, and some cancers have a lot to do with diet.

The body's requirement for liquids also is problematic. If we drink too much of the wrong liquids we can become alcoholics and shorten our life span. If we do not drink enough liquid, the body becomes dehydrated; and if a body becomes dehydrated enough, it dies. Dirty water makes us sick.

Lastly, even when the body avoids the wrong food and drink and does all it can to eat healthy food and drink clean water, it eventually will be struck down by disease. Human bodies are legendarily vulnerable to both viral and bacterial infections. Both these forms of life, or quasi-life, can cause diseases that weaken, cripple, and eventually kill us. We also become ill if our genes mutate in ways that produce non-functioning cells that take over for functioning cells, again killing us over time.

Slides 2 and 3. Importing the Brain

Thus, everything in our environment and in our bodies themselves conspires to do us in. For Itskov, to be human is to be subject to failure. The first slide, with its image of the young face followed by the old face, thus shows the overall effect of the work of maintaining the body: we all age, we all are subject to disease, and *we all die*. *All* biological organisms engaged in a relationship with and dependence on an environment that demands responses that deplete energy eventually die. For Itskov, the absolute certainty of death—in a world without a redeeming or reassuring spiritual vision—subverts all attempts to establish meaning, and in the last analysis, even undoes those efforts made through science and technology to remedy our condition by postponing death for as long as possible. Why extend life somewhat, if death must follow?

This could be a very dispiriting story, a source for existential despair or reckless disregard for health and safety, if Itskov was a standard-issue materialist. If he believed that everything a human being is, is contained in the body and that the body is doomed, then he might end up embracing Andre Breton's nihilism or Sartre's dark belief that there is "no exit."[11] Freud was a materialist and he postulated a death drive, a longing in all struggling biological beings to make the constant struggle to live, stop.[12] But Itskov, like Rothblatt, is not a standard-issue materialist. Like Rothblatt he is an incurable optimist in the sense that he thinks that—despite his materialism—life can have a transcendent meaning if we can live forever. Calling Itskov an "optimist," of course, presumes that the project of eliminating death is seen as a positive, rather than as a dehumanizing, move.

Itskov believes that no one is doomed, that death can be defeated, because he believes that human consciousness, or mind, is what human beings really are. He further believes, along with Rothblatt and the transhumanists, that the mind that we really are is a pattern of information that can be captured in digital code and transferred from the biological brain to a hard drive to an inorganic carrier without any loss of function or meaning. Further, he thinks that porting the mind from the inherently limited and fallible body to a hard drive will liberate the mind from its fleshy prison and allow it to reach its full, post-body development. Ultimately, "Who I am" is not reducible to "What I am."

Itskov is not content with noting and lamenting the "imperfection" of the biological body. He proposes a way to defeat death. Although, unlike Rothblatt, Itskov does not found a new religion. Rather he outlines a four-step research and development program, the Avatar Project, for which he solicits funding from those of his followers who have the means to provide it. Itskov is so committed to the importance of his initiative that he has written letters to 40 of the world's leading billionaires[13] and he has solicited funding from the Secretary General of the United Nations, Ban Ki-Moon.[14] On one hand, he made these moves to get rich and powerful people interested in his project. If one takes his statements of social concern seriously, however, this would also help provide the basis for future funding for the research necessary to defeat death.

Itskov has received moral support from agencies in the Russian government, although that government has committed no funds for his project. He also has founded a political party, Evolution 2045—really more of an interest or lobbying group—to advance his posthumanist agenda.[15]

He also enlisted the support of the action movie hero Steven Seagal, to support his initiative.[16]

Where Rothblatt turns to Buddhism, Judaism, Native American, and Hindu religious ideas as a source of inspiration, Itskov turns to scientists and venture capitalists. Rothblatt's is a subjective materialism with strong mystical components, and Itskov's represents a more secular path to Internet afterlife. His goal is to organize and fund the scientific and technological work necessary to effect "eventual complete replacement of your biological body with an artificial avatar." Although both he and Rothblatt propose to replace biological bodies with technologically produced carriers, they take different paths to making the replacements and envision different outcomes once the transfers take place.

Even though he has enlisted various religious figures to comment on his ideas, Itskov in no way proposes that human beings have an immaterial soul that will be liberated at the death of the body, and his references to a spiritual dimension in his proposals remain undeveloped. He seems to be talking about a *lateral* move from one "carrier" to another. Biological bodies might be imperfect, but this does not mean that all bodies need be so. The second slide, an image of a brain in a cutaway representation of a human head, illustrates the move from a biological body and brain into another material, but non-biological, body and brain.

For Itskov, this is the moment at which we achieve "self-directed evolution," wresting control of our fate from the inefficient, hopelessly slow organic trial and error of natural selection, in bodies that, as described above, are doomed to die, and placing our future development squarely under the control of scientific reason. Itskov presents this process in four steps or stages in what he calls the "Avatar Project."

The third slide in the series, "The Avatar R&D Network of the 2045 Initiative," prepares the audience for the four stages to come by stating that half of the technology necessary for the realization of this project already is in place and that the remainder of the needed science and machinery can be developed in the next two or three decades. Itskov ends this slide with what amounts to a sales pitch: "Personal avatar development capability is available today," indicating that the first steps in creating a new home for the mind in what he calls an avatar are already under way. Those who have the means (approximately $3 million) can begin to develop their avatars now to be operational in the very near future. These early investors thus will be able to proceed through the different levels of avatars to a fully realized avatar by 2045, the year of the Singularity.

Slide 4. Avatar A and Shape Shifting Identity

Slide 4, "Select Your Avatar, Avatar A," begins to describe what Itskov means by the Avatar Project. This slide pictures a young woman on the upper half of the slide. She is wearing a piece of headgear that looks like Google Glasses on steroids. It is a clear band covering her eyes and wrapping around her head, an inch or two in front of the eyes. Over her right ear there appear to be dense paragraphs of code hovering in the air; and beneath the ear, a map of the world is displayed.

The lower panel of the slide shows the same smiling young woman holding up her right arm, palm extended, touching what appears to be a hologram screen with writing, a bar graph, a map of the world, and hexagonal shapes. The text of this slide, displayed on the left half of the panel, explains the images and tells us about what Itskov calls Avatar A; the text reads:

Avatar A—A robotic copy of a human body, remotely controlled by a "brain-computer" interface (movies *Surrogates, Avatar*).[17]

What does this mean? Itskov is proposing a series of ways to cure the "imperfection" of the biological body by sustaining forever what is central to human identity: the mind. This proposal, the Avatar Project, comes in stages. The idea behind the Avatar Project is that during the next 30 years, we will develop a series of increasingly durable and capable nonbiological carriers for the human mind. We will begin with remotely controlled android robots, and then adapt them to serve as temporary homes for our biological brains when our bodies fail. In the third phase we will replace our biological brains with artificial digital replicas imbedded in our repurposed android bodies. In the final stage we will somehow port our minds into either holograms or nanobot swarms of the type that Rothblatt mentions, which first appeared in the writings of Ray Kurzweil.

Itskov's use of the term "avatar" is very different from the way computer gamers and members of Second Life use it, and different from the way we have been using it in discussing online avatars. He does not mean a computer-generated image (CGI) that represents a game player or a program-generated agent. Rather, as his parenthetical mention of movies indicates, he means something more like what director James Cameron depicted in his film *Avatar*, namely an entity in the real world controlled from a remote source. In Cameron's film, "avatar" refers to biological clones or copies of the Na'vi natives of the moon Pandora. These copies, which looked almost like the original Na'vi, are used as mine workers in situations where it would be impossible for human workers to survive. The Na'vi avatars are controlled remotely by humans whose bodies are sealed in coffin-like enclosures but whose minds virtually occupy the brains of the Na'vi avatars and remotely direct the Na'vi bodies.

Itskov buys into Cameron's vision. His avatars are not images on a screen, but rather are beings that move through the three-dimensional world. Itskov sees his avatars—just as Cameron sees his—as three-dimensional entities that are remotely controlled by the minds of complete human beings, but unlike the Cameron avatars, Itskov's are completely mechanical; they have no biological components because they are meant to *replace* biological bodies. The avatars that director Jonathan Mostow uses in his film *Surrogates* (2009), the other film Itskov references, are more in keeping with what Itskov envisions. In this film, it is 2017 and humans have largely abdicated public life. They have been replaced by younger, better-looking versions of themselves, in the form of android robots who represent them. The humans remain isolated in their homes, encased (like the humans in *Avatar*) in coffin-like enclosures from which they use advanced forms of brain-computer interface, to control their surrogates, or "Surries."

This is a world in which no one gets murdered or assaulted or injured in an accident. Surrogates can be damaged, of course, but any damage they suffer never affects their operators because the brain-computer interface software has built-in sub-programs that shield operators from harm. It also is a world in which no one ages. The streets in *Surrogates* are filled with fit, slender, well-dressed people of both sexes, all in their mid- to late twenties. These idealized figures bear a resemblance to the flesh people they represent, but the flesh people themselves are pale, aging, out of shape, and timid. They never leave their homes, content to conduct their lives at a safe distance, moving their surrogates around using brain waves.

What matters for our purposes in understanding Itskov's vision is the idea that androids can be sent out into the world, controlled by people's minds, just as today people with artificial limbs can move these appendages by learning to control them through computer interfaces.

But if I have a remotely controlled avatar, what purposes will it serve? Why would I want or need such a robotic double? Producing working human-sized robots would be a huge technical and economic undertaking, and there would have to be a compelling reason to go to such trouble and expense. In the *Surrogates* film, the premise is that the surrogates are a *terminus ad quem*. They are a final destination with no further steps planned. Because they make life for humans safer and easier, almost everyone embraces this option. Although the *Surrogate* avatars make daily life easier, however, they do not shield their human controllers from death. The avatars in *Avatar* do save the film's protagonist, Jake Sully, from imminent death, when his mind is ported from his dying flesh body into the body of his Na'vi clone. But again, moving a mind from one flesh body to another is not a final solution to the problem of death. It represents, rather, the transfer of a mind from one vulnerable biological carrier to another.

In Itskov's world, android robots, Avatar A, represent much more than convenience. They are an initial stage in the fight against death. But what will motivate the initial move? Why have android substitutes? What connection do these avatars have to the fight against death?

Itskov writes that such whole-body robots will have several uses. First, they can help paraplegics and other people who cannot otherwise get around, thus overcoming the imperfections of such bodies. He sees disabled people as using a full-on robotic copy controlled by the disabled individual's thoughts. This means that the paraplegic stays in bed or in his or her wheelchair and *thinks* this robot into action. The remotely controlled robot, fully equipped with sensing equipment that mimics eyes and ears and touch, provides the paraplegic in bed with an immediate visual, tactile, and auditory experience of the world into which the avatar ventures. Thus, the bed-ridden individual gets to emerge into the world as a fully mobile being who can move as well as anyone, who can grasp things, drive a car, even run a marathon, should he or she so choose. The avatar is not a robot that one sends out on errands, but rather is a direct extension of the self, a first-person subject moving a robot body from its remote location. The paraplegic's actual body might be miles from that of the robot, but the paraplegic's mind is "in" the avatar's head, experiencing whatever the robot allows it to experience.

Such remotely controlled android robots also could be used in first-responder situations such as mine disasters, accidents, and fires because such surrogates could safely go where humans could not venture without being harmed. Humans already use robots for these purposes, of course, but Itskov's avatars each will be directed remotely by a living human who will see out of the robot's camera eyes and move the robot's limbs using mind control—brain impulses amplified into electronic signals.

Differently equipped robot avatars would have great utility in police hostage situations and during crises such as the terrorist attacks in Paris in 2015. SWAT teams made up of bullet- and bomb-proof policemen could control terrorist and other attacks more effectively than flesh-

and-blood officers, especially if the robots were being controlled by the very officers for whom they were substitutes. The use of such androids in war is a foregone conclusion. The American Defense Department, through its research wing DARPA, already is working on making robot combat soldiers a reality for use on future battlefields.[18]

LIFE IN THE AGE OF AVATAR A ROBOTS: SOME THOUGHT EXPERIMENTS ABOUT "MIND" PORTING

What sort of new world does this Avatar A stage suggest? We can envision a near-future world increasingly populated with humanoid robots remotely controlled by human users. The presence of remotely controlled humanoid robots inevitably would lead to changes in daily life that extended far beyond helping the disabled and dealing with emergencies.

Itskov suggests that this would be a world allowing for cybertourism and "telepresence." Using androids for cybertourism means that people could remain at home and send their avatars to distant destinations. The controller would remain immured in a coffin-like control pod in his or her home, from which location he or she could see out of the avatar's eyes and experience the Parthenon or the Taj Mahal "directly." An out-of-shape executive or professor could scale Everest or shoot the rapids or run a marathon, using a specially enhanced avatar whose sensors could provide enough "dangerous" visual and tactile information to produce vicarious feelings of fatigue and cold and terror, much as people who strap on virtual reality headsets experience fear today as they negotiate narrow planks laid over deep abysses.

The difference between sending humanoid robots to distant tourist sites and putting on virtual reality headgear would be that the robots would experience the actual sites in greater detail than virtual-reality computer-generated imagery can produce. Additionally, the cybertourists could smell and touch the places they visited more fully.

One also could do telepresence business meetings and send one's android to the meetings. The robot controller could project the telepresent image of his robot, to avoid the bother of going to the telepresence studio personally, as well as to avoid having to dress and groom for a formal business meeting. Because a robot does not require bathroom breaks or stop for meals, it could be a more effective agent in protracted negotiations. Such telepresent entities also might be used for cybertourism, because projecting a laser-generated image would be cheaper and more convenient than sending an android robot.

Although these uses might seem to have no direct connection to Internet afterlife, this introduction into a world of robots remotely controlled by biological controllers creates the conditions for such an afterlife. Making remotely controlled humanoid robots available to the general population would get people used to the idea of inhabiting artificial bodies. Learning to control a prosthetic hand or arm using brain impulses is a time-consuming process that requires a high level of focus over extended periods. Controlling an entire robot body would have an even steeper and longer learning curve, so it would behoove a society that was preparing its members to live on as machines, to train its people on how to operate such machines before moving into them completely. As people invested more and more time and energy into learning how to "be" robots, the connection between one's robot identity and one's "true" self would grow closer, as the connection between that self and one's biological body became increasingly attenuated.

Thus, the most important thing that Itskov's Avatar A introduces to human experience is the essential separation of identity from a biological body. Once people become accustomed to living vicariously through robots, dependence on the biological body will wane and, more subtly, people will begin to see their minds inhabiting the machines, rather than living solely in their brains. This experience would have to change one's self-perception, replacing the lifelong experience of always seeing the world from the "cockpit" of one's first-order sensory experiences. How will it feel to be thus disembodied, displaced to a different cockpit while one still is embodied? Such an experience could be seen as similar to—but also quite different from—the shamanistic experience during which ancient practitioners would leave their bodies to go on spirit journeys (discussed above). Both are forms of "out-of-body" experiences, but with the difference that with Avatar A the mind travels from one body to another, always remaining in the material world. A person becomes a shape-shifter, moving from one bodily form to another, adaptable to all, loyal to none.

Ideas and expectations about the relationship between identity and appearance also would be challenged in other ways. Because there is no earthly reason why EMT, military, or touring avatars would have to look like their controllers, verisimilitude between such bodies and the biological body would become irrelevant. Consequently, one can conjecture that people using such avatars would quickly adjust to the novel idea that they would not have to *look* like themselves to be themselves. People would soon get used to strapping on alternative bodily identities much as they strap on their Apple watch or stick their Samsung phone into the in-car Bluetooth car speaker.

The important ideas here are that in a world of remotely controlled robots, personal identity can break free of its connection to any particular instantiation, and that one can exert control over where to place one's identity, moving from one avatar to another depending on one's purpose. No longer tied to our bodies, we would become accustomed to moving from one body to another, at will.

Even though the Avatar A phase would last no more than 10 years, the introduction of such beings into our lives would introduce major structural changes. If this situation were to become a reality, and flesh people rarely left their homes, food-delivery services would flourish and supermarkets might be deserted or be crowded with avatars—as avatars do not eat or drink but they can be directed to shop. Brick-and-mortar retail establishments also could disappear because all shopping could be done online. The robots, of course, might "like" shopping, if their controllers did, and they could buy food and bring it home, thereby limiting restaurants to takeout-style fare.

Physicians would perform online consulting and use video for examinations. They would also send out pre-programmed "nurse" robots to administer simple tests and injections and even to perform simple surgical procedures. Long-term home care would also be the province of robots programmed to see to the needs of the elderly. Companies would experiment with whether such helpers and physician's assistants should look like humans, or if "cute" robots such as R2D2 might be more reassuring for people who required care.

Robots would also probably cut hair, clean clothing, give massages and pedicures, and do basic electrical and plumbing work, although directly controlled avatars might be needed for the more challenging jobs. As the number of avatar robots grew, so too would the number and functions of true robots, preprogrammed to perform certain tasks. Such robots already are performing many functions, such as assembling automobiles and packing boxes for Amazon, and researchers in Japan are well on their way to perfecting robots that will soon serve as caregivers for the elderly and the disabled.

Social life also would change—sometimes in ways that might be considered weird. Would singles meet as their young, fit, and well-dressed avatars, or as their homebody selves? It is not difficult to imagine couples—well—coupling as avatars without ever meeting in the non-avatar world. Old married couples might arrange romantic trysts—not as their aging selves but as their virile and comely avatar selves. Perhaps meeting another human in the flesh would be considered the height of an almost sacred intimacy.

Would young, attractive humans use avatars at all? Again, one imagines that teens who were not confident about their looks might represent themselves using avatars that they thought were better looking. Two adolescent worlds might emerge—that of the insider teens who do not need avatars, and that of those teens who do. The day a person first used an avatar not to fight wars or to travel but because he or she had decided that the body was too old to do otherwise, might be a very important, bittersweet milestone marked by special parties and ceremonies.

Suffice it to say that as soon as non-aging robots began to stand in for flesh people, in whatever capacity, digital afterlife will have begun and human identity will never be the same again. Whatever structural, social, and by extension psychological and emotional changes that the dawning of the Age of the Robots might occasion, there is nothing in this scenario, as so far described, that would keep the first generation of avatar controllers from getting older and dying. We have entered a brave new world, but it is not yet the world of Internet afterlife.

BEYOND AVATAR A

A valid question is why go beyond Avatar A? If not an Internet afterlife, a person would surely have an Internet alternative life or lives. As technology improves I could have an ageless double who can go places and do things that I could never do or that I am no longer able to do. If, at the same time, I take advantage of the organ transplants and artificial discs and gene-cleaning nanobots that surely will become available in the future, I can keep upgrading my body to live for hundreds of years, and use my Avatar A more and more frequently as my body slowly ages. I will die eventually, but as I age I will have a non-aging body to represent me. I can extend my life indefinitely and never move beyond Avatar A.

But Itskov is not interested in what he might describe as half measures. He has nothing against medical enhancements, but they only can postpone death; they cannot entirely eliminate it. Itskov, like Rothblatt, wants humans to become something other than what they biologically are at present, *so that they can live forever*. Living forever by obliterating, rather than modifying, the body's "imperfections" is all he cares about. It is what he believes we are meant, even destined, to do. Even if Itskov almost entirely lacks a developed metaphysic such as we found in Rothblatt and Terasem, he—as fully as Rothblatt—believes that human intelligence, human consciousness, is meant and designed to leave this biological body and be reborn, or resurrected, in different media. Identity cannot be defined by the biological body. Therefore there is nothing about being "me" and nothing about being "human" (or whatever it is that we *really* are) that requires, depends on, or is inextricably mixed up with a biological body, however enhanced it might be.

On the contrary, in the transhumanist worldview, scientific and technological progress is inevitable in any event. Human reason will keep pushing forward past Avatar A and will develop more advanced prosthetics, as well as more advanced machine intelligences to run them. If we try to stay with any level of technological development, we soon will become obsolete ourselves. Thus, regardless of whether we like it, our very nature as thinking beings requires that we use thinking to advance our control over the world. Avatar A is not a stopping point, not so much because Itskov wills that it not be, but because given the nature of reason it *cannot* be. Thus, whether you or I as individuals like it or not, there will be an Avatar B. Itskov's job is to make accurate predictions about what it will be and when and how it will arrive.

Slide 5. Avatar B—Hybrid/Head Robots, On the Way to Digital Immortality

Slide 5, "Select Your Avatar, Avatar B," includes images transposed from Slide 1. The older person is represented on the left side of the slide, and the younger person moves to the right side. There is no subtlety in this switch. We see a large, dark blue arrow shape, pointing from left to right, going from the older eyes (Old Eyes) to the younger eyes (Young Eyes). What this directed movement communicates is that we are now moving in reverse of normal time, from older to younger. We are clearly now on the path to correcting the bodily imperfections that Avatar A merely mitigates without removing.

The thick arrow is outlined with a white border. Inside the blue arrow is a white schematic drawing of the type found in international airports or at street crosswalks, simple symbols that convey clear meaning cross-culturally. We see a large overhead light hanging from a ceiling. Directly under the light is a wheeled operating table. On it an outline figure reclines. A masked figure clearly meant to be a surgeon stands over the recumbent figure. The surgeon has her hands inserted in the recumbent figure's chest as if she were performing a procedure inside the figure's body. We are clearly meant to understand that the operation will causally lead from Old Eyes to Young Eyes, reversing the normal flow of time.

The Avatar B description both is and is not like that for Avatar A. Avatar B is a "superior robotic body," like Avatar A, but now it is used as a "full-body prosthesis" rather than a robotic representative. Itskov calls this a "full-body prosthesis" because it is a robot body "onto which *one's head is transplanted*" "at the end of the health span of one's biological body."[19] This description suggests that the second avatar will be a modified Avatar A with its head removed, re-engineered to accommodate an actual human head. One would then naturally assume that the head affixed to the robot would look more like the head on the left, represented by the older face.

The idea here is that between the time when the first appearance of Avatar A occurs and the time when we develop artificial brains for artificial bodies, enough years will pass that some of the original Avatar A controllers will have sickened and died. Avatar B represents an intermediate stage during which the Avatar A body, suitably modified, will house either the biological brain or the actual head of the individual who is at risk of dying before a fully artificial avatar is ready to be launched.

Avatar B will not be a controlled drone but rather will contain the controller, or what is left of him or her, inside or atop the artificial robot body. This will be a literal instantiation of Kurzweil's Singularity, when mind and machine cross over into one another. It also will be the first appearance of Donna Haraway's predicted "cyborg," a new kind of being that crosses the boundaries between human and machine, between the world of carbon compounds and the world of inorganic silicon. Using the Avatar B hybrid, we will be directly generating genuinely new experiences for the first time.

It should be noted that the idea of grafting a living head onto a robot body will strike most Americans as strange, but within Russian scientific experimentation such a procedure is not unheard of. Russians for some time have been familiar with the work of Vladimir Demikhov, who has a long history of grafting the living heads of dogs onto other dogs to create functioning two-headed dogs.[20] Demikhov's work is much respected in Russia, and Itskov has adapted it cleverly to his purposes. This work provides a practical solution because, if Itskov's predictions come true, we will have remote-control avatars by 2020, but will not see artificial bodies equipped with artificial brains until 2030 or 2035. Unless we provide a stopgap, many people on the verge of digital immortality will never achieve that promised state.

There would not have to be any scientific advances to make the robot-head hybrid a reality, but serious re-engineering is required. Organic parts cannot naturally survive in an inorganic environment. An oxygen source as well as nutriments would have to be developed, along with pumping apparatus to deliver oxygen and food and take away carbon monoxide and food wastes. Temperature and pressure would have to be kept under strict control and—if the head had belonged to someone who already was very ill—medications would have to administered using some form of intravenous mechanism.

The original avatar, a creature of motherboards and circuits, would have to be modified to accommodate this complicated power plant, and the inside of the avatar's body would have to include enough space to fit the necessary parts. Additionally, outlets for processing oxygen and food would have to be built into the robot body, and the body would have to be hooked up to resupply and purging stations at regular intervals. Of course, the robot also would have to be recharged regularly.

This second stage inevitably would provoke more anxiety than the first among those who elected to try it, because with Avatar B, whatever happened to the robot also would happen to its controller, which would be living in the robot it was controlling.

Once the mortal head is situated in an immortal setting, we would have a first (if hybrid) instance of digital immortality, an organic head that runs a computerized body and which has left the remainder of its biological body behind forever. Even if the head continues to age, the body will not. And as the illustration suggests, a biological head living on a silicon body might be injected with a steady stream of nanobots that can enter each of the head's cells to alter its genetic makeup, thereby slowing or reversing the aging process. The life-support system built into the robot body might serve to inject such reparative nanobots into the head's bloodstream and even to restore a chemical balance to the head's cells and therefore to its tissues, thus reversing the normal aging process—making Slide 5's visual prediction of reverse aging come true. Itskov intends the bio-head, silicon-body hybrid to be a serious step toward immortality, so it is not outside the realm of the possible that he also would believe that implanting a head on a robot and equipping the robot with life-enhancement technology would be both good and technically feasible.

In fact, Itskov claims that this hybrid stage could be available in five to seven years, possibly even sooner, depending upon how much the people who are "in the know"—presumably, potential donors and recipients who read these slides—contribute to the effort. Itskov obviously is not just laying down a time line; he is crowd-funding to make that time line a reality.

But what will this hybrid mean? This is not a step that everyone will take. If we are planning to have a fully functioning digitized avatar available within 15 years, then only those people who think they will die before the end of that period will consider this procedure. This stage, however, reinforces our sense of how dedicated Itskov is to creating digital immortality. The head-avatar hybrid is clearly a temporary fix and is not meant to be permanent. Its sole purpose is to preserve a mind from obliteration long enough for scientists to develop the means to transfer human consciousness—and with it the person's identity—from a biological to a digital setting.

Slide 6. Avatar C—Machines Minds on the Road to Digital Immortality

Slide 6, "Select Your Avatar, Avatar C," repeats the same illustration as provided in Slide 5, with the Old Eyes leading via a thick blue arrow to Young Eyes. But this time the arrow's filling is not surgical but cerebral. On the left are the outlines of an obviously biological human brain, complete with folds and creases and, at the base, connections to a spinal cord. A clear line runs down the center of the image. On the left is the bio-brain. On the right—continuing the oval shape of the biological original, but with a steadier curve—is a new brain characterized by circuitry, as if it were a silicon motherboard superimposed on the shape of a biological brain.

It is clear that this image represents a transition from the "meat" brain with its folds and stem to an electro-computational brain with its circuitry. The one-to-one correspondence of the bio-brain to Old Eyes and of circuit-brain to Young Eyes is unmistakable. We have now passed beyond the hybrid dog-head model—in which the "meat brain" lived on and off a silicon body—to another model entirely, in which the meat brain is gone, the dog head is removed, and a new, young, ageless machine head filled with a deathless machine brain is put in place. This new wholly artificial brain contains *everything* the old flesh and blood brain contained: Avatar A's entire personality *plus* enhanced brain power, better emotional control, and a connection to a body able to do things that no normal biological body ever could be expected to do. Somewhat anomalously, the brain that was in Avatar B associated with Young Eyes is here associated with Old Eyes, indicating that even if transplanting the bio-head temporarily slowed aging, the process would still go on despite efforts to slow that process. The only move that would return the head permanently to its Young Eyes identity then must be the complete replacement of both brain and body with a machine body and, most importantly, a machine brain—one with *a machine-based mind.*

On Slide 6 what is presented is an android replica of a human being, one that looks exactly like the original human, but now is equipped with an autonomous brain encoded with the original controller's complete personality. We assume that the original, biological person, who once remotely controlled this avatar, has died and is gone from the world. What remains is that person's robotic double, fully humanized with an uploaded database that contains an exact replica of the original controller's mind and identity. We are now living in a world in which human subjects are housed entirely in robots.

But this is not the final step in the program. The eight slides of the Immortality Button take us to the appearance of the first fully artificial avatar. But Itskov's Avatar Project has one further step, the introduction of his most controversial avatar, Avatar D, which will appear by 2045, and will be either a nanobot swarm or a "being of light"—a hologram.

AVATAR D: IDENTITY, NANOBOT SWARMS, AND PROTEAN "BODIES"

Although Itskov says less about these iterations of the avatar than he does about the android forms, his writings on Avatar D suggest a much less substantial and fixed future home for the human mind. We note that there is no Avatar D in the Immortality Button slide array. This avatar, most often described as a "hologram-like body," or as a "being of light," routinely appears as part of Itskov's "Avatar Project" diagram displayed in various iterations on the 2045 site.[21] Itskov also sometimes describes Avatar D as a "nanobot swarm," a being to which Rothblatt also refers. The nanobot swarm is a collection of millions of microscopic minicomputers organized by coordinated programs. It can take any shape chosen by the guiding intelligence, which is distributed throughout the swarm.[22] This new version of the avatar transforms human beings into complete shape-shifters. Personal identity, as a program, will persist in an entirely protean vehicle. People will not be any one thing for long and instead will change endlessly, remaining who they are as they alter how they look, hovering on a knife's edge between being and non-being, disappearing and reappearing, as volatile as a mood and as elusive as a passing thought.

Human beings might become entirely transparent, motile light beams, shimmering hologram shapes that are diaphanous, glittering spirit beings, once again hovering on a sharp edge between being there and not being at all. As holograms and as swarms, humans finally will have almost completely surrendered their attachment to the solid world of fixed objects with discernible boundaries. In Rothblatt's new world we all will be patterns of pixels moving on screens; in Itskov's we will be plays of light and streams of invisible computers. In either world, there is nothing we would recognize as a person, yet both visionaries claim that their worlds will be filled with people who will never die.

Unlike Rothblatt, however, Itskov never mentions transcendence or God as the *"terminus ad quem"* for all this development. Rather, the trajectory is inexorably from the biological to the non-biological, from the mortal to the immortal, but never from materiality to immateriality, or from this world to any other. This is a horizontal journey to paradise, however ephemeral its inhabitants will become. For Itskov, salvation is from one material medium to another material medium that is more durable, if less solid, but which will effectively last forever. If everyone has the opportunity to migrate from a "meat" body and a "meat" brain to a deathless platform that is entirely crafted by human practical intelligence, then in this world without death and also without want or oppression or competition, humans, or their post-human successors, finally could live in harmony in a world completely controlled by the mind, in which no one would have to eat or sleep or breathe ever again, and in which no one ever died.

Slides 7 and 8. Fine Print

The final two slides in the Immortality Button sequence have to do with disclaimers and rules for participation, and include no illustrations. Old Eyes and Young Eyes, the mysterious lab tech, and the avatars are gone, replaced by Itskov's version of disclaimers. Slide 7 tells us some things that are understandable, interlarded with things that are startling. Itskov first makes clear that these time lines are *predictions*. Things could go more slowly than he says; but they might stay on schedule or even arrive sooner if people visiting the site "order a personalized avatar." Itskov is suggesting that if you and I put some money into this project, not only will we get our personalized avatars all the sooner, but once this is done we will be able to publish the specs for producing more avatars so that more and more people will be able to live forever.

Itskov then mentions that he and the foundation will not take any profits until your personally designed avatar is ready and, presumably, has been delivered. What is interesting is that Itskov does see digital immortality, at its base, as a capitalist transaction, as a form of consumerism. Unlike Rothblatt's vision of Internet afterlife as a religious enterprise,

Itskov's afterlife is a smart, practical scientific advance that will provide enormous benefits—for a price. He even posts on Slide 8 what he calls "Requirements." To pre-order your very own avatar, you must answer "Yes" to each of the questions.

- Are you 18 or older?
- Are you of sound mind so as to bear legal responsibility for your actions?
- Do you personally—yourself or as legal representative—dispose of the funds required for the development (> $3M) for your avatar?
- Have you decided to commission the development of your custom-made immortal avatar?[23]

Immorality here can be had as a special order. And, unlike the rich man in the Gospels, you can buy your way into Heaven for a base payment, subject to upward revision, of $3 million.

But how does Itskov see the Avatar Project as playing out? Chapter nine explores his responses to criticisms of the project and then journeys into much more exotic territory, where Itskov discusses the future of his new species, "neo-humanity," and makes predictions about where he believes humanity will be in the next 1,000 years.

We now have Itskov's avatars. We have left the body and entered a new, post-human world where death has disappeared. What will happen next? Let's see.[24]

Chapter 9

Itskov and Neo-Humanity

Chapter eight presented Dmitry Itskov's basic beliefs and proposals—beliefs shared by other radical transhumanists—but many critical issues remain to be examined. To gain further insight into Itskov's project and beliefs, this chapter first reviews Itskov's responses to a set of five objections to his project and to the transhumanist project in general that he discusses in his "Russian Experience" presentation.[1] It then explores Itskov's vision of what he calls "neo-humanity"—the human species that will emerge when the four avatars are operating and biological humans who are vulnerable to death are becoming a thing of the past. Like Rothblatt, Itskov offers a new understanding of what it will mean to be human in the coming digital paradise.

THE OBJECTIONS TO THE AVATAR PROJECT

Itskov lists what he sees as the six most significant objections to his Avatar Project and to digital immortality in general.

- Only the few who can afford it will get an artificial body and immortality.
- The emergence of such technologies will lead to greater social stratification.
- These technologies will exhaust natural resources and lead to demographic challenges.
- Dying is natural.

- Individual consciousness is nontransferable.

- Cybernetic technologies are incompatible with spiritual development.[2]

These six objections reflect a broad spectrum of concerns from different domains—from theological and philosophical to technological and political.

Objection 1. Heaven for the 1 Percent

The first objection immediately confronts issues of social stratification that could be challenging to social and political structures; clearly, android technology will not be cheap, especially at first. As noted in the discussion of the eight slides connected to the Immortality Button, Itskov solicits funding from interested parties and requires that people getting in at the ground level of his project contribute a minimum of $3 million each as an entree into the avatar system. At one level, one can see the whole of the Immortality Button presentation as a sales pitch, offering instant immortality to the few who can afford it.

In other postings and in his response here, however, Itskov signals that he is aware of the problem that the cost of avatars will pose. He argues that the original investors will be providing seed money for the development of robots that can be manufactured with later economies of scale. Once the form is set, Itskov claims, making new copies of avatar robots will be relatively inexpensive; but he never completely clarifies what this means. Itskov also states that he and his team will be completely transparent in sharing all the plans and formulae for making avatar robots. If secondary manufacturers are not required to invest in costly research or pay royalties, then per-unit costs for avatar robots, going forward, should quickly become reasonable. He estimates that in time such robots will cost no more than a normal car—although he doesn't indicate how much time is required to achieve this price point. In fact, affirming a vision of robotic democracy, he writes that "Artificial bodies will be available to all who want them."[3]

Although both Itskov's acknowledgment of this problem and his good intentions can be applauded, when we examine the numbers, some disturbing truths surface, and the picture begins to resemble a world for the many that looks more dystopic than heavenly. If we examine Itskov's comment about avatars costing the same as an average family car, we see how problematic his proposed solution would be—even if his corporation gave away all its plans for free. As I write this, there are approximately one billion motor vehicles in the world—one for every seven people. Projections tell us that the number of cars per person will increase during the next 20 years. Let's say that by the time Itskov predicts the appearance of fully artificial carriers for people's minds, there is one motor vehicle for every six people. Still, if the average avatar in 2035 costs as much as a car, then if we take only adults into account—say two-thirds of the total population—then, even using the most favorable predictions, it equals one car for every four adults.

If Itskov is correct about the future cost of avatars, then when such avatars become available at the lowest possible cost, 75 percent of the adults in the world—those who currently do not have the means to buy a car—will not have the means to buy an avatar. If we are more realistic and argue that many people among the 25 percent who can afford a car could not also afford something else that costs as much as the car, then we see that at most only half of the 25 percent will be able to cover the cost of a robot and a car at the same time. Thus, the people who can buy a robot probably will represent only one-eighth of the world's population, and most of these buyers will be concentrated in the United States, Western Europe, Japan, Australia, and New Zealand. Even in those countries, distribution will be skewed. In the United States, minorities—particularly African Americans and Hispanics—will be much less able to afford an avatar than their white and Asian counterparts. In Western Europe and Australia, recent immigrants from the Middle East, south Asia, and sub-Saharan Africa will be similarly disadvantaged. In the remainder of the world, avatars will belong almost exclusively to the elites.

Balancing this is the fact that only a portion of the adult population will be old enough to be interested in creating avatars for themselves. Thus, not everyone will be excluded because some people—those not old enough to want an avatar—will remain content for the time being. Imagine a near-future world, however, one within the life span of many of the people reading this book, in which the aging sector of the world's population—present-day mothers, fathers, and older siblings—will be approaching a critical point in their lives when setting up a postmortem avatar becomes an issue. The affluent will be busily arranging for their avatars, practicing with their remote control robots for a life without limits, and the bulk of aging people will be struggling with heart disease, cancer, and diabetes.

It is reasonable, therefore, to assume that no matter how generous Itskov is in sharing plans he will not be in a position to share avatars, because the expense of providing such objects to the four to six billion people who could not afford them would be economically ruinous. Even if the unit price could be reduced to $2,500, for example—the cost of the most basic Tata Nano automobile from India—the least we would have to disburse would be $10 trillion, or 60 percent of the total 2015 gross domestic product of the United States. Because the United States produces almost 30 percent of the entire world's GDP, this would amount to between 15 and 20 percent of the world figure—an unobtainable amount. It in effect would be impossible to meet this requirement, or even any significant fraction of it. Therefore most of the world's population would have to do without avatars into the foreseeable future.[4]

Further, if we could drive the cost of artificial bodies even lower, we have to ask what sort of bodies these could be. If we factor in the additional cost of Whole Brain Emulations or gradual brain replacements—which seem to be what Itskov intends for his artificial brains—we are even deeper in the economic hole than we were before. We also must appreciate that these economic artificial bodies, these cut-rate avatars, potentially would be less dependable and durable, thus requiring more money for maintenance and repair.

Questions of distribution and affordability aside, what might this new world look like? In one scenario, one can envision a remedy that might mitigate some of the social disaffection that such a skewed system would generate. It might be economically feasible for those who are less fortunate to at least have their personalities charted, turned into programs, and uploaded to computers, in the way that Martine Rothblatt describes in *Virtually Human*. These captured personalities could then live on, temporarily, as Terasem-style mindclones. It is possible that entrepreneurial computer programmers would soon develop more economical, shortcut methods to capture the rough outlines of a personality for a minimal cost. Such "captures" would by no means be perfect or thorough, but would hold out the promise that a sketch of a person might live on in virtual reality. In this way the poor could live on in reduced and simplified versions waiting for the price of avatars to drop so that they could reenter the world as three-dimensional beings. Or poor people might remain in their servers as programs, perhaps living as cartoonishly simple virtual realities forever. Online immortality might be what the poor could have, and the more fortunate could flit from body to body in the real world or on other planets, sometimes entering the virtual worlds of the poor to play in the form of CGI avatars. One wonders if there would be online worlds reserved only for the rich—virtual gated communities.

If all this did happen—if the world were divided into the people who could live forever and the people who had to die, or between the well-served immortals who could switch out avatars and those who had to live forever online as a poorly drawn virtual reality figure—we can only imagine what sort of social unrest and instability this might produce. What would happen to crime rates when richer people never died, and they lived surrounded by people who would die, or by people who could look forward to compromised, defective prospects for immortality?

We also know that if transhumanist predictions are correct, then the rich would be getting smarter and smarter by living in machines with faster central processing units and more memory. Not only would the poor have an inferior afterlife, there would be less and less that they could do about it over time, because the rich would be using their increasing intelligence to build increasingly impregnable robotic carriers.

The advent of the era of the hologram and the nanobot swarm would make the rich even safer because creatures of light would be more difficult to trap and harm than robots, and nanobot swarms can disperse and reform at will if under threat. As the smart get smarter, the cybersecurity measures that the advantaged could deploy would tend to outstrip any attacks mounted by less well-endowed beings with earlier-generation processors.

Lastly, people who live as robots or swarms or holograms can live anywhere. Itskov, like Rothblatt, predicts that such favored individuals can populate distant planets that have atmospheres and climatic conditions which would kill biological humans. A particularly unsettling scenario is that in which the well-to-do have simply fled Earth for unreachably faraway worlds, leaving behind those still "condemned" to biological death and those trapped on servers as virtual humans. Of course, if those left on Earth *wanted* to live lives in which they could die, they might welcome the disappearance of the affluent immortals.

Itskov does talk about producing good avatars and developing spiritual depth in them that will lead to higher levels of mutual understanding and tolerance that will move the more advantaged immortals to treat their mortal co-humanists with compassion and justice. Once exponential growth in intelligence kick in—something that futurist prognosticators like Ray Kurzweil claim is inevitable once we liberate minds into machines—no one can predict what sort of moral compass, if any, our superintelligent future selves will develop. As we advance in intelligence we might become less, rather than more, moral and perhaps be possessed by demons who are ourselves. Therefore there is no guarantee that the future will hold any compassion for the poor. This future world of haves and have-nots that Itskov's vision prefigures—with its fundamental inequalities and its potential for revolution and either physical terrorism, cyberterrorism, or both—ultimately is more disturbing than appealing.

Somewhat ironically, traditional religious Heavens will be more dem-
ocratic even if they exclude nonbelievers and those who have not obeyed
God's rules. In fact, there is a long Judeo-Christian-Islamic tradition that
the very people who will have the best transhumanist afterlives—the
rich—will have the hardest time getting into the traditional Heaven.
Itskov's Heaven will be exactly the opposite; but, weirdly, it also will be
a Heaven with heavy security.

On balance, we have to judge that Itskov's response to this first
objection—and by extension the transhumanists who propose programs
like his—falls short of providing plausible answers to the serious moral
question of digital equality. Rather than reversing the injustices of the current distribution of power and privilege, Itskov's Heaven promises to reinforce such inequalities forever and make them all but impossible to cure.

The only mitigating factor is that Itskov sees the democratization of
the afterlife as a long-term process. He lays out a time line in one of his
presentations that does not envision full transit to artificial platforms for
all human minds until well into the next century, and his vision of the
wholesale transformation of the real into the virtual could take as long
as 1,000 years. Itskov appreciates that developing and distributing digital immortality will be a process that happens in stages. It represents a
huge shift in the direction of human development, and its enactment will
change everything about daily life and it social organization.

Objection 2. The Ecology of Immortality

Itskov responds to the second objection—that producing avatars of
the dead, which means keeping the dead alive, will lead to the exhaus-
tion of energy resources and to overpopulation—with equally frustrating answers. Itskov hopes to counter these ecological objections by
arguing that the production of his avatars will not require the expendi-
ture of fossil fuel and that immortal robots can live in outer space.[5]

The examination of this proposal, as we saw with his response to the
first objection, brings up several problems. The first problematic area has
to do with the power source that would be used for such an enormous
program. If Itskov really believes that the avatars can be manufactured
and powered without using fossil fuels, then he must have alternatives in
mind. Even if the number of android robots hovers around one billion,
the energy requirements to produce, power, maintain, and replace these
complex machines will be enormous. If the avatars were to come online
within the next 15 to 20 years, radical retooling of our energy production and delivery systems would be necessary. Barring a rebirth of

interest in the use of nuclear power, which Itskov might not rule out, we would have to enlist solar, wind, and water power sources at a rate far beyond the current rate. Such a shift is possible and, given the realities of climate change, also will become necessary, but expecting new power sources to run everything that today runs by burning fossil fuels is one thing. Asking that newly developed energy sources be diverted to producing, then powering, one billion large, complicated robotic avatars might prove more than human invention and resources can handle. At a minimum, such a project would be overwhelming on a number of levels.

Another potential problem could develop around whether battery technology is able to increase the life and energy-storage capacities necessary for these essential components. Because android robots are large, they will need power sources that generate sufficient "juice" to enable movement and run all the subsystems that permit "sensory" information to reach the artificial brain. One can imagine a more sophisticated solar power system that could provide much of the needed power, but such a system would need backup to ensure that the robots did not lose power. Additionally, a new generation of battery production, maintenance, and repair and replacement facilities would be required just to keep the batteries working.

Think of this: If an electric car or a phone "runs out of juice," it is an inconvenience. But if one's body and mind shut down due to lack of power, the result could be catastrophic. To provide time for our avatar batteries to recharge we will develop analogs for human sleep for as long as is needed. Such defined down times, however, are different from unexpected shutdowns—which must be avoided if at all possible. Whatever the power source, it must be completely dependable; and whatever the battery technology, it has to be as close to failsafe as is possible.

I can imagine a near future when gas stations have been replaced with android charging stations, run by solar or wind power or—in defiance of Itskov's desires and predictions—stations fueled by the normal electric power producers, coal and oil. Developing such "stations" is all but inevitable during the transition from biological people to silicon people. Under a best-case scenario, concerted efforts will succeed in minimizing fossil fuel use, and battery technology—as well as techniques for capturing alternative energy sources—also will improve significantly. Additionally, if androids replace cars for many purposes, then the shift from fossil fuels will happen even more quickly. Thus, even if Itskov's response is sketchy, he probably has history on his side, so that the robots will not be an unmanageable drain on resources once energy technologies have advanced further than they have to this point.

We also should note that a world supporting a billion android robots—a number that would increase every year as people died—requires an entire new infrastructure of maintenance and repair facilities to keep the robots running. On the plus side of the equation, these facilities would generate many jobs. The negative side is that the energy demands of keeping so many shops up and running would be an additional burden on the power grid. It will be a strange world, indeed, in which the dead need more care and produce more jobs than the living!

Regarding the possibility that a world in which the dead remain alive soon would become far too crowded, Itskov's vision of the future could be a remedy for overpopulation rather than a contributor. If the dead never really die, then space travel and interplanetary colonization could be a feasible solution for overcrowding, as well as for social divisions and unrest. Removing the more privileged and advanced avatars to distant worlds would reduce crowding and calm social tension. Again, however, the cost could be a source of considerable problems. Ferrying large numbers of androids to other planets could be prohibitively expensive, not to mention the cost of establishing, powering, and maintaining large colonies on distant heavenly bodies that might not have native resources to sustain them.

Yet, despite these foreseeable challenges, one can imagine potential—if startling—remedies. As time goes on and science advances, for example, we certainly would devise ways to send minds to other worlds in the most economic ways possible, beaming them on lasers or as radio signals, or sending them on future versions of USB memory sticks, then assembling the relevant robots or nanobot swarms from local materials, using more advanced versions of 3-D printers to make what we needed. We would also, inevitably, discover that certain planets provided a better (in the sense of being more economical) setting for our androids. We would then witness a gradual shift in android population away from Earth to other planets. In that case, Earth might slowly become a kind of "reservation" or living museum for the diminishing number of "biologicals" or mortals, as well as a place where poorer mortals worked for the benefit of the immortals living on other planets. We might witness a future in which small numbers of immortals with their robot assistants would "manage" a much larger mortal population on Earth, much as a few Spartans managed many Helots, or overseers managed slaves on American plantations in the mid-nineteenth century. These are admittedly awful images and references but they fit what could happen. The world probably can produce enough energy to power the dead, and they probably will not crowd out the living, but the prospect of an Earth all but deserted by its most fortunate inhabitants is, again, not edifying.

Objection 3. The End of the Extinction of Consciousness

The third objection is that "death is a natural process."[6] This is a loaded claim, suggesting more than what is obvious, and examining Itskov's response to it tells us a good deal about his transhumanist sensibility. His first response to the assertion is to claim that studies show that "only two percent of people are ready to accept death."

Itskov does not cite the studies he is invoking, nor does he specify what populations answered these questions. In support of this assertion, he relates an anecdote in which a friend posted a Facebook comment to the effect that "everyone wants a new phone, a new car, a new laptop. But when a person has cancer, all he wants is to survive."[7] He never mentions cases in which cancer patients, or other people with terminal illnesses, might want to end their pain. Itskov is completely committed to the proposition that death is always a bad thing, and that everyone, or almost everyone, will want to live on forever.

Let's parse these ideas. First, Itskov appears to be saying that if 98 percent of people polled do not accept the fact of their deaths, then death itself is not "natural." The key word here is "natural." Itskov's claim aims to redefine what is meant by this word. It is a universally accepted truth that biological death is "natural" in any sense of that word that is chosen to employ. Biological organisms wear out. Even life-extending technologies that involve direct manipulation of genes alter but do not end the fundamental aging processes. It could be that almost no one *accepts* death, and it certainly is true that in most cases we will do anything we can to survive, but this does not mean that the thing we want to avoid and that we do not accept is not "natural."

Despite reservations about whether Itskov bases his claims about death on sufficient data, the difficulty that humans experience in accepting death and death's shadowy persistence in shaping our lives have been rich subjects of study in philosophy and psychology. Sigmund Freud famously argued that we all, in our minds, believe that we are immortal. None of us can conceive of ourselves as dead.[8] As German philosopher Martin Heidegger argued, we live most of the time as if this avoidance of the fact of our own death were true.[9] It is as if our *minds* believe we are immortal. As we saw when we sketched out Plato's ideas on the soul, one of the reasons we are led to this feeling is that we spend a lot of time, in our minds, with ideas that seem timeless. We cannot imagine a world in which our thinking and experiencing are not taking place. We have never experienced a time when this was not true. It is a truism but it is a powerful one—that each of us, in an existential sense, is always alive, because there is never a moment when we are not alive.

The difference between Freud and Heidegger, on the one hand, and Itskov and the transhumanists, on the other, is that the former argues that our attitude toward our own mortality is one that combines denial and self-deception, and the latter believes that our experience of our own immortality is now—or because of technological advances soon can become—an *accurate* feeling. Not only do we *feel* as if our consciousness is immortal, but given the proper platform, it *is* or soon will be immortal. If the mind, and by extension our identity, really is a pattern of information that currently resides in the brain, and if that pattern can be transferred, then there is nothing in the nature of thinking and conscious experience that, like a biological organism, points toward death. Minds always think in the now and into the future, even when reflecting on the past.

The key here is that the transhumanists and Itskov believe in a mind that is in principle separable from its biological body, and that minds are inherently immortal, that there is nothing death related about our consciousness. They further believe that we soon will possess the technical know-how to make possible the separation of the mind—which thinks of itself as immortal, and which for them is immortal—from the body.

Even when the existential philosopher Heidegger defined humans, in *Being and Time*, as "beings-toward-death," we also are beings whose consciousness is always and fundamentally a reference to the future and whose bodies are always pointed toward death and the end of possibility. Heidegger calls on us to take an authentic relationship to death, which means stoically accepting it as the radical closure of all our possibilities.

But Itskov would correct Heidegger and argue that because death need no longer be the end of our mental life or of our thinking about possibilities, we are no longer beings-toward-death and now are beings-toward-endless-possibilities. Transhumanism spells the end of impossibility, the end of the extinction of consciousness. Death is natural for biological bodies but not for minds and identities.

This claim that minds and identities are not subject to death does not mean that either Itskov or the other transhumanists believe that immortality will last forever. They are, after all, materialists, and as good scientists they appreciate that the universe someday will come to an end.

"*Immortal*" means "undying"; it does not mean "eternal." Minds will never die, but the universe in which they live will. Even if death is not natural for people, it does eventually come to universes. Unless we can find a way to an alternate world using a wormhole or other means, our immortality "only" will last for millions of years.

Visionary transhumanists such as Steinhart and Rothblatt,[10] however, speculate that minds will survive the death of this universe by transforming the entire universe into a virtual reality program, thereby averting its destruction. Itskov, however, generally does not engage in what could be called "digitalist metaphysics," and in this he occupies a different region of speculation about Internet afterlife than that of some of his peers. He is neither a scientist nor a philosopher, which he admits in the opening sentences of his presentation, "The Russian Experience." His proposals are practical, without any concern for or reference to a metaphysics, as is integral to Rothblatt's vision. As is demonstrated in Itskov's discussion of neo-humanity, he is not entirely without philosophical pretensions.

Objection 4. Making the Impossible Possible—A Practical Faith in Technology

The fourth objection is the most theoretically fraught and the one that has provoked the most philosophical discussion. This is the claim that "[i]t will be impossible to transfer human consciousness to a non-biological substrate."[11] Itskov sidesteps a host of painstakingly argued objections to the central transhumanist claim—that such a transfer is impossible—by arguing that even great scientists can make mistakes about what is true.[12]

He cites the fact that Leibniz rejected Newton's ideas about gravity and that Galileo took no account of Kepler's laws of planetary motion. His point is that even very good scientists and philosophers can ignore important truths or even deny that such claims are true at all. He seems to be saying that there currently might be proposals about transferring human consciousness that major scientists in the relevant fields are either ignoring or rejecting as false.

Note that Itskov writes that the skeptics claim not that mind transfer is impossible *now* but that it *always* will be impossible; that it is impossible in principle. Currently, such a transfer *is* in fact impossible, but this does not mean that it always will be. Thus, what is scientifically true today might not be true tomorrow. Itskov, echoing David Hume's answer to the Problem of Induction,[13] declares: "The very statement 'will never happen' contradicts the principles of science." For science, says

Itskov, somewhat boldly, there *always* will be a new idea that "will make
the impossible possible." We might not yet know exactly how mind uploading will work, but that current ignorance cannot mean that such an
operation always will be impossible.

This is a different approach to that taken by either Rothblatt or transhumanist theorist Randal Koene, or any of the other more theoretically
minded transhumanists. As discussed, Rothblatt has a quite different
idea about how to achieve mind transfer. She believes it is on the brink
of happening and is not a matter of scientific or technological progress.
Rothblatt believes that all we need to do is develop better software,
which people like Gemmell and Bell, the researchers at USC's Institute
for Creative Technology, and Eternime already are doing to capture the
structure of personal identity in narrative, visual, and audio data. Koene,
currently the most vocal proponent of Whole Brain Emulation, like
Itskov believes that capturing the mind in a way that will enable its
transfer to another carrier will take some time, but he believes that all we
need are better scanners, more refined ways to scan brain sections on a
neuronal level, and more powerful CPUs and hard drives. These are not
breakthrough inventions but extensions of technology that we already
are developing.

Whatever new development Itskov is counting on—he never says
explicitly—he is completely confident that science will provide the
needed answers in the near future and that mind transfer will not be a
problem. In making this assertion he completely disregards thought experiments such as Searle's Chinese Room (examined in the overview of
transhumanism provided in chapter ten).[14]

He even implicitly rejects Chalmers's so-called Hard Problem of consciousness, namely the question of how a physical substrate, be that a
"meat" brain or a silicon substitute, can produce something that does
not seem reducible to the medium that produced it.[15] Questions about
whether computers can think, questions about whether I will still be me
if my mind is transported, questions about whether something that
speaks and acts and sounds like me might really be nothing but a well-
programmed chatbot—all get brushed aside because every one of them,
for Itskov, prematurely postulates the impossibility of something just
because it is impossible today.

Regardless of whether his "argument" persuades, Itskov pushes ahead
because he is a practical person rather than a theorist. He "knows," or
has faith, that brilliant thought experiments do not by themselves dictate
what technology can accomplish. He is interested in collecting and organizing and funding the scientists who will do the research and

experimentation necessary to make the impossible possible. He is in this sense not a metaphysical visionary. His vision of the future promises purely technical solutions to technical problems, and his cyberheaven is firmly rooted to the Earth, to robots and holograms, not even, as with Rothblatt, to online avatars.

Objection 5. The Virtue of Being Bodiless—Envisioning a New Ethical and Moral Revelation

Although we have seen that Itskov is fundamentally driven by the practical, the final objection he mentions is fraught with theoretical significance, and his concerns and response point to his conscious inclusion of philosophical and theological concerns. Itskov's critics state, "The use of these technologies is not compatible with spiritual growth."[16] Itskov is not responding to the complaints leveled by theologians (objections that are discussed in chapter ten). Rather, he is dealing with what he calls a "law of the development of civilizations." This "law," he states, holds that "Every technological breakthrough must be accompanied by an elevation of people's values and an increase in awareness." If this does not happen, he warns, then "civilization will meet its downfall." Thus, for Itskov the question of "spiritual growth" has to do with deepening our commitment to ethics and tolerance, and not with finding God.

To create an "increase of value" and "increase in awareness," we must develop both intellectually and spiritually to keep up with the directions technology is taking now and is about to take. Such development crucially depends on embracing "our new capabilities," which requires us to "cease to be so dependent on our bodies." Itskov's real message, then, is not that his program and vision will reaffirm traditional religious ideas, but rather that as we free ourselves from our bodies we will gain an understanding of who we are and what the world is. What exactly this understanding consists of is not clear, but Itskov is certain that it will come as we figure out how to disembody ourselves.

Interestingly, Itskov's views suggest a traditional Western religious and Platonic view of the body's spiritual and ethical problematics. One element he mentions is that as we move away from our biological bodies, we also will develop beyond aggression, egoism, unrestrained desire, and passivity, and toward an arc of continual self-improvement. This transformation also will lead to a higher moral and aesthetic character. The less embodied we are, the more inner purity and beauty we will develop. With this inward development will come the growth of attitudes that run directly counter to aggression and selfishness: love, a longing for harmony, altruism, and the willingness to serve the larger community, even if that demands sacrifices.[17]

It is interesting that Itskov, somewhat like Rothblatt, appears to believe that liberating minds from bodies will lead to a natural increase in ethical sensitivity and a sense of justice. He is, therefore, less concerned than Bostrom or some of the dystopian filmmakers and theorists discussed in chapter ten, with the possibility that evolved minds in machines might be morally undependable.

Inner development is not restricted to the development of high moral standards and inner peace. Porting out of my body will release something profoundly positive, if also profoundly self-referential. The new me, as it moves beyond the limitations imposed by "its mortal protein-based carrier," also will become more creative, focusing its energies on innovative "figurative thinking."

This vision, which would not be out of place in a Platonic dialogue or a Gnostic treatise, seems to suggest a new life of mystical rapture based on sharpened intellectual insight. It lives in Itskov alongside another vision, however, with which it has little in common. Not only must people leave their bodies to experience greater self-awareness and a higher moral insight, they also have little or no interest in the "elegant metaphor" that claims that we live forever in people's memories, in works of art, in our iPhones, and our books. Everyone knows what this means: We are dead, no longer agents, no longer in the game. In his response to this final objection, Itskov makes a declaration that also defines what he thinks being truly alive means. He affirms the central importance of continuing postmortem agency and individuality, saying, "People live only to the point that they can no longer communicate, have control of something, have the ability to defend themselves in a court of law, develop physically, intellectually, spiritually."[18]

Removing the negatives, we see that Itskov defines being alive as communicating, controlling, being able to argue in court, and growing physically, intellectually, and spiritually. He thus defines a proper, post-body life not as a spiritual festival, but in practical physical terms such as talking, doing, arguing, having rights, and growing on every level. This "*vita activa*" is the furthest thing possible from disappearance into the Cloud of Unknowing or a flight to a Platonic Elysian Fields far removed from the cares of Earth. Somewhat surprisingly, Itskov's idea of elevating values and gaining insight is one of a life fully lived in some version of this world and in a new version of one's body. In asserting this he also embraces the idea that any form of survival that does not include agency and even full legal standing is not worth having. No one wants to die, and when one lives on, one wants to do so as a fully engaged citizen. This vision, then, is curiously paradoxical—it affirms the virtues of being bodiless in a biological sense and the necessity of behaviors in the afterlife that seem to require a body which, in Itskov's example, is a fully artificial one.

Understanding the objections to the Avatar Project and detailing that project, however, still do not speak enough to Itskov's long-term vision of the human future. He makes predictions about what will happen into the thirtieth century—a thousand years in the future—and to fully appreciate where his quest for digital immortality is leading requires examining what he says about what he calls "neo-humanity," the new species that the more advanced avatars will represent.

TRANSHUMANISM, NEO-HUMANITY: THE NEXT THOUSAND YEARS AND BEYOND

Itskov's vision of this new world brings us to what he calls "neo-humanity"—a new species of humanity. He presents his goals for the human future in Slide 12 of his "Russian Experience" presentation, and in his talk on neo-humanity posted on the 2045 Initiative website.[19] In these writings and illustrations Itskov pursues a logic that he does not follow elsewhere in his discussions. He begins by presenting his project's goals, which are listed below.

To overcome aging and death, to gain immortality.

Cosmic expansion.

To allow everyone to become multi-bodied.

To extend our environment to multi-reality.

To control reality by thought.

To allow each human being to create a personal universe.

To manage the course of history.

Goals 1 and 2. Immortality and Cosmic Expansion

The discussion of Itskov's Immortality Button and his responses to objections presented above already examined Itskov's program for achieving the first two goals. Next are the further consequences of the transition of humans to avatar form.

Goal 3. Becoming Multi-Bodied

The idea of "cosmic expansion" inevitably leads to the next goal, that of becoming multi-bodied. This point barely came up in the discussion of the Avatar Project. That project treads a conservative path from the biological body to avatar bodies that resemble bio-bodies, at least in form. Itskov, however, knows that once personal identity is detached from its "home" in the biological body, there is no reason for staying faithful to the shape and parts of a body that developed through natural selection, especially under the pressure of cosmic expansion.

In the context of the "old humanity"—in which death is inevitable— we are linked in countless ways to the "meat" body. Everything about the biological body speaks to its origins in this world. Our size, weight, appendages, internal organs—all of it makes sense in the context of the natural/cultural environment in which our bodies developed. All of the world's humanly designed equipment, from chairs to keyboards to tread-mills to steering wheels, also presupposes the shape and abilities of the human body. The landscape itself is divided into parcels for raising plants and animals on a human scale. Architecture speaks to the body, as do landscapes, bridges, airplanes, radios, and bicycles. None of these would look like they do or work as they do were it not for the human body and its proportions.

This intimate connection and all the apparatuses it supports, however, dissolve once the biological body is discarded. One of the first things that must occur to the newly transported mind in its artificial body is the subversive and liberating thought: "My mind survived the death of my biological body." This proves that the relationship between the mind and that body is fundamentally contingent; if my mind can flourish in a metal and plastic replica of my body, then it can probably flourish in something much less like this replica. Mind as a digitized pattern of information does not refer to a body in particular. And as the mind moves away from its original body, all later bodies more and more will come to resemble prostheses, functional extensions such as smartphones, cars, or laptops. The body clearly is more intimately connected to me than is a microwave or a refrigerator, but not much more so than a smartphone. Additionally, as the standard for cars and smartphones is that they work to perform certain tasks, so, too, do bodies tend to be designed to per-form functions. Rather than adapting the world to the body, we increas-ingly will adapt the body to the world.

This change has radical implications. If we think of immortal life as an avatar as occurring in cyberheaven, what forms does the body need to take in this Heaven? Unlike in most traditional monotheist Heavens, there is no irreducible connection between the human mind and a body God designed for it. The shape of cyberheaven will be determined by choice, not by divine fiat. Although one's postmortem mind could remain a program in a hard drive, such a condition would defeat the purpose of achieving immortality. Of course, the hard drive on which the mind ran could be programmed with a rich virtual-reality environment, and the mind program could live, as if in some version of the Terasem Heaven, as a purely virtual being moving through delightfully varied worlds in the Cloud. The future world could be banks of self-maintaining servers endlessly running programs that ran billions of human personalities in billions of virtual-reality universes.

But Itskov does not seem interested in this iteration of the afterlife. He wants his avatars to live in our existing three-dimensional world or in some variant of that world. At the same time, however, he understands that it sometimes might be more convenient, more entertaining, more creative to inhabit a different prosthesis/body for at least some parts of one's immortality. This ability to be mobile is what Itskov means when he talks about everyone becoming multi-bodied. As we move more deeply, both psychologically and temporally, into the avatar experience, the attachment to the original body will tend to lessen. There will be less memory of how it was to be embodied. Although the initial experience of moving from the body will be very disorienting, as suggested above, in time the opposite likely will happen. The very people who wanted to go back to the old body, and who cherished the avatar for its likeness to that body, might well show themselves as willing to adopt a new shape to accomplish things that their enhanced intelligence could imagine but that their old avatar body never could do.

Being multi-bodied will be especially useful for those who port to distant planets and into alternate universes. Different topographies require different bodily forms and capabilities, and good technology can design such bodies. There is no reason, for example, why future people could not be their own vehicles, whatever world they live on. On Earth, such body/vehicles might first look like Segways with faces and arms, with wheels projecting from their legs. As time passed and people reflected on this design, they would surely come up with models with removable wheels or with smaller ones that could morph into feet as needed. And if some sort of rolling underpinning proved more useful, feet might disappear altogether.

The idea of interchangeable bodies would have symbolic social implications as well. We could decide, for example, that traditional avatar bodies—ones that looked just like the flesh individual they originally represented—should be the norm for more formal occasions. Other body forms could be "worn" for less-formal occasions or in situations where one needed to get specific tasks done. In a more distant future, nanobot minds might be able to enter the motherboards of copiers or computers and become the relevant CPUs for the time it takes to complete a specific task. There might be specially designed student bodies with built-in keyboards, recorders, and cameras, as well as foldable desk extensions. Of course, going to class might happen purely for the sake of tradition because no one would have to go to school at all. All relevant knowledge could be uploaded to one's silicon mind, and universities, like so many other institutions, would disappear as physical sites.

We could go on with such playful speculations, but the point is clear. We soon and then progressively would come to understand that biological bodies or their robotic copies were not strictly necessary, although they could be important for sentimental or ritual reasons. Inevitably the robotic copy of such a body, as well as its need to look exactly like the biological original, would become more and more the exception. In time there would be people who had little to no memory of what they once looked like. Even if they did remember it would not matter much, because there might be dozens or even hundreds of other things that they had looked like over the course of a very long deathless life; some of the non-biological forms might even be remembered more vividly and fondly as being truer representations of an individual's inner self. Therefore, in the cultures of the future, there would be no theoretical or emotional connection between being *this* mind and having *that* body. The flesh body gradually would lose its privileged place in both memory and metaphysics, and the creedal phrase "the resurrection of the body" would cease to compute.

We also have to wonder what would happen to Earth when avatar bodies left for distant planets or other dimensions. One can be sure that there still would be conservatives who would not give up their remotely controlled avatars. There also, inevitably, still would be flesh people—perhaps many of them—who refused to morph into minded machines. Some of these people might take advantage of medical enhancements to extend lifespan, but they still would be defined by living in their biological bodies. These people would be left behind by the "cosmic expansion," so that flesh bodies would persist for at least a few generations; and if flesh bodies persist, so will biological reproduction. As avatars on distant planets are developing alternate bodies, conservative holdouts on Earth might be producing children.

This question is part of a larger issue: What happens to childhood in a world in which the ideal is that people now in existence should never die? How, in fact, will the entire understanding of human life span, purpose, and relations be affected? What happens, for example, to children and young people in this near-future world in which their parents and grandparents never die? What happens to young bodies when older bodies remain young or become young again? This is an especially pointed and poignant question if we realize that deceased grandparents would come back to the world as fit young beings who might look younger—and better—than their natural grandchildren. More radically, the older people might have disconnected from their biological bodies and show up as cars, birds, or colored clouds, far more interesting and elusive than their laggard grandchildren.

Here is a disturbing thought. In a near-future world in which the older people are prettier and fitter than the young, and are indeed immortal, there could arise a suicide culture among the young so that they could ironically attain youth and beauty by killing themselves and coming back as an idealized artificial avatar. If the whole point is to defeat death, mightn't one defeat it by embracing it early, before aging could impose its ravages? Wouldn't premature death be more attractive than aging in a non-aging society?

Will having a flesh body become a sign of inferiority? Will there be a business in used avatar robots left behind by people who have become holograms or swarms? Will these used avatars be sold cheaply to people who cannot afford a new robot of their own? Will there be cut-rate practitioners who promise to turn minds into code, or will the government create programs to subsidize the move to avatar platforms for the less advantaged? Will there be cheap generic robots offered by lower-end retailers like Walmart? In the film *Surrogates*, Bruce Willis buys just this sort of inexpensive replacement when his custom-made avatar is destroyed.

Most importantly—and disturbingly—will the government also institute programs for voluntary and even perhaps compulsory sterilization so no more flesh people will be born? Providing postmortem avatars for a fixed, diminishing population would be infinitely easier and more economical than trying to provide such entities for a population that keeps renewing itself. Even if robotic avatars do not need food or shelter, they do need recharging, and they do take up space, so birth rates might be brought down to zero to make digital immortality feasible for as many people as possible.

The next issue that bears examination before moving on is the question of intellectual and emotional changes that having new bodies will bring. Physical disease would be a thing of the past for the multi-bodied. However, would emotional balance also be programmed into the new bodies, obliterating the scars of childhood and the emotional and behavioral limitations imposed by genetic defects? This certainly would be both a possibility and a temptation. If we could, wouldn't we want to jettison all the crippling emotional baggage associated with our flesh bodies? Modifying or suppressing a few lines of code could make us sane, prudent, and with non-addictive personalities. We no longer would suffer depression or anxiety attacks, or harbor dark paranoid fears and resentments. Thus, as we moved from one body to another, we would be saner, more peaceful people. And when we dealt with flesh people, we would have the advantage of seeing things more clearly, in an emotional sense, than they did.

But this raises a question. If we program out our devils, will this also deprive us of our angels? Do we need a less "smooth" psyche to be creative and inventive? Could such "leveling out" of our dark places diminish the possibilities of the production of those who would write great novels, make brilliant scientific discoveries, and produce biting satire? Is there a real connection between a certain degree of madness and creativity? But if everyone is relentlessly sane, will such productions even interest us? Conversely, if we eliminate imbalance, will we make it impossible for tortured souls to create the technologies that will make the rest of us happier? Although such questions are fueled by conjecture—and unanswerable—they suggest a way that a "perfected" world might not necessarily be one that is fulfilling.

Another significant indicator of a radical change to who we may become as humans and the world in which we reside rests on one of the premises on which Ray Kurzweil and other transhumanists base their ideas: At the Singularity, superintelligent machines will appear. They will begin to replicate themselves and their intellectual growth will be exponential rather than linear. One of the more intriguing and at the same time unsettling aspects of Itskov's program, and of any transhumanist program, is that once such machines appear, they will keep autonomously making smarter and smarter versions of themselves. Once we begin to become machines ourselves, no longer constrained by our throwback bodies but moving freely from one inorganic body to the next, we will also grow more intelligent at an exponential rate. If Ray Kurzweil's Law of Accelerated Returns (LOAR) holds true, then this must be the case.[20,21]

Within a short time, the minds in full-on avatars will be much smarter than the minds in people running brain-computer interface robots or hybrids with organic brains, and will be much, much smarter than the minds of in-the-flesh people. Machine intelligence does not have to waste time adjusting to a complicated collection of vulnerable organic components, nor does it have to do much to adapt to an environment. Its whole meaning as a machine is to optimize the conditions under which it operates; for a machine that is rationally conceived and executed, being ever more reasonable and growing ever smarter is built into the very fabric of machine existence. Machines on this level exist to be smart, that is, to keep operating at peak efficiency for as long as they can.

Thus, to return to our reflections about generational relationships, the deceased grandparent who returns to his still-living spouse, and to his children and grandchildren, is not only fitter and saner than they are, but much, much smarter, and dedicated to getting even more so as a hedge against breaking down or wearing out. Reintegrating the deceased, re-bodied, and re-brained elder into the still living family might be more challenging than one would suppose. Old Granddad will no longer be the doddering shadow of his former self. He will be fast-moving, brilliant, and, yes, prone to getting impatient with his hopelessly slow flesh descendants. Until everyone in the family has died and been reborn there might very well be asymmetry between revamped avatar people and "meat" or hybrid people.

This asymmetry in intelligence could be yet another reason for the development of suicide cults. Not only would postmortem people have better bodies, they also would be smarter and saner than their children and grandchildren, and there would be inevitable pressures on the young to join their elders (and betters) in death, so that they too could reap the benefits of digital immortality.

But even in a world with no new flesh people, would there still be babies? What about reproducing in a virtual way? Will there be physicians and geneticists and programmers who will know exactly how to splice together different "double helices," or more precisely their digital equivalents, to create new program patterns on secure servers? In principle, there is no reason why two intelligent avatars who are in love cannot enlist the experts to make them a "mind" child, whom they can then download into an infant avatar body or a baby swarm, mimicking human birth and childrearing. Even though there probably would not be any sort of learning curve for this superintelligent child, one can imagine timed programs that would begin to operate in the child's brain at predetermined intervals, thereby making him appear to grow up and learn, even though the maturation process was really just the triggering of new digital programs.

"Children," in this new world would be artificially crafted programs, as multi-bodied as adults—but would this make them any less human? This brings us right up to the deepest issue that the re-creation of flesh humans as intelligent machines raises. Will Itskov's avatars—carefree, unaffected by loss or fear, scrubbed clean of anxiety, and superintelligent—still be human? Are humans, as Itskov's project suggests, even *meant* to be citizens of a neo-humanity?

To sum up, what being multi-bodied could mean is that we would soon, and then progressively, come to understand that biological bodies or robotic copies of such are not necessary, although they could be important for sentimental reasons. Inevitably the robotic copy of such a body, as well as its need to look exactly like the biological original, would become more and more the exception. In time there would be some people who had little or no memory of what they once looked like. Even if they did remember, it would not matter much because (1) there might be dozens of things that they had looked like, and some of the nonbiological ones might get the nod as being truer representations of this or that individual's inner self, the mind; and (2) there would be no theoretical or felt connection between being *this* mind and having *that* body. The new minds in the new bodies would be smarter every minute. Being multi-bodied is only one aspect of development in a world in which exponentially more intelligent minds would devise forms of embodiment that neither we, nor Itskov, can possibly imagine.

Goal 4. Extending into Multi-Realities

The fourth goal, "To extend our environment to multi-reality," follows from the third. Becoming multi-bodied and creating an environment that can be described as "multi-reality" seem to fit together. But what might Itskov mean? He could mean two quite different things. If he believes in current cosmology, then he would believe that we inhabit a multiverse in which many parallel universes coexist. If this were true, then we might develop as yet unknown ways to port from one universe, or reality, to another, and we might devise ways to remake ourselves so that we will retain the same minds but become the type of being who can enter, for example, an alternate universe with a different number of dimensions and a different physics. Our plasticity could become such that we could move not only from one place to another, but from one *kind* of place to another.

Or, probably, Itskov means something different. There is no reason that we cannot build an advanced version of an Oculus Rift headset into the robot "*du jour*."[22] Once we do this, it will be simple to project a mind into any number of alternate realities while the body remains in one place. Consider this thought experiment: I adopt a virtual reality–generated body that fits perfectly into an undersea virtual-reality world, so that my fish-form slides wakelessly through virtual waves. Of course I need not adopt a literal fish body, but I can flip easily from one virtual reality to another, living in one body after another in virtual space. Alternatively, I can enter the now retro world of cyberspace, using my headgear to jack into an Internet virtual reality that could be a game world or a more sophisticated version of Second Life. Some of these games could be retro contests in which I can be "killed"; there might even be games in which I can experience virtual "death." In any event, the liberation of mind from body not only leads to multi-bodies but also to multi-realities in which those bodies can live.

Virtual-reality environments could take a literary or cinematic form. We could hunt down the white whale with Ahab, resist Calypso with Odysseus, plot trysts with Emma Bovary, and discuss the "Royale" hamburger with John Travolta. Any and all fictional experiences could be ours for the price of a new virtual-reality program. Of course, new bodily forms also would produce new literature and film, or their future cognates, and these certainly would be interactive.

A final, and very interesting, meaning of the fourth goal could be that as we adopt a wider variety of bodies we will also re-engineer the external world and our relationships in that world to suit that variety. If there are no more chairs or cars, there could be other things that would suit body shapes and sizes that we can now merely imagine. For example, what passes for furniture in the near future will be as multi-form as the bodies that use it.

Relationships, too, will tend to be as polymorphous as the furniture. If I can adopt a multitude of shapes, then I also can adopt a multitude of sexualities, family relationships, and friendships. Gender, age, ethnicity, and cultural background all always will be under constant revision, to the point that none of these traditional markers will really exist as markers unless I choose to have them do so. I might spend Monday—if there are such things as Mondays—as a Korean American family man living in Los Angeles. Tuesday, I might morph into a transgender Serbian. Wednesday I might be a kestrel soaring over the cliffs of Dover.

Who I am, as well as where I am, will be purely a matter of choice as I move freely from one body and one reality into another. Think of a near-future world in which we have opened wormholes to alternate realities, built virtual-reality headsets into our faces, and retooled the public world to accommodate very different kinds of bodies. All of these things are possible and each easily could become a feature of cybernetic immortality. In fact, the great variety of ways "to be" could be a mundane characteristic of the world 50 years from now. This could do a good deal to alleviate the potential boredom of minds that are immortal in a mortal world in which there is no depthless God into which one can lose oneself.

Goal 5. Controlling Reality Through Thought

The fifth goal, to "Control reality by thought," as we have seen with the other goals, might have more than one meaning. On one level, Itskov might mean roughly the same thing as we mean when we say that a brain-computer interface can control a prosthetic device by thinking about controlling it. Extended to reality in general, this goal could be describing a world in which many objects are "wired," imbedded with the necessary uptakes to be moved through thinking about them. The technology could be similar to that used to control prostheses, or it could represent an extension and elaboration of the software and hardware used to remotely control avatars. In any event, we can conceive of a future world in which the very objects that surround us, retooled to suit our new post-human bodies, are not only parts of multi-realities but are also *responsive* parts. As technology develops, it will digitize not only our brains and our bodies but also the whole physical world.

A second meaning simply could be that if we produce virtual-reality worlds in which we live and move, then these worlds would be entirely created and controlled by thought. But what is genuinely interesting about this idea is the notion that, as time passes, the difference between virtual realities and "real" realities will diminish. The trajectory is toward a world or worlds in which technological reason controls more and more of what we now see as "other," as the resistant "real." As with Rothblatt but in less radically developed form, Itskov's transhumanist/posthumanist vision tends more and more toward full-on metaphysical digitalism in which all of reality eventually becomes embodied code, and in which nothing, ultimately, is other than, or different from, the mind.

Goal 6. The Creation of Personal Universes

The sixth goal is remarkable and richly evocative: "To allow each human being to create a personal universe."[23] In this new world, we are multi-bodied, and we live in multi-realities. Our thoughts control the world, either the virtual one, the real one, or both. Now, with the mind's power having transformed our bodies and the world around them, we have achieved the power for each of us to make his or her very own universe—perhaps as a virtual landscape within which we can choose to live for as much of our lives as we decide; as a reality over which we have complete control and that no one else can enter without our permission; or as a planet or moon that we alone inhabit, inviting and disinviting whomever we choose.

Let's assume that the boundaries between realities, virtual and "real," have been compromised and perhaps obliterated because thought now controls every world in which we live. Every world is an artifact. Nature has disappeared as a freestanding reality. Trees, shrubs, grass, ocelots—all are digital representations, or robotic copies, or virtual, or something else created by untrammeled reason. There is no "out there" out there in our ordinary sense because everything that exists is not only matter reworked, but is also matter rendered as a programmed artifact just as our robot bodies are matter reworked to appear as "natural" as flesh. There is no need for the vagaries and inefficiencies of "real" nature when its robotized or virtualized copy—in Jean Baudrillard's word, a "simulacrum"—can form or surround.[24] And there will be plenty to go around. With space colonization and possible wormholes to other universes, the powers of virtualization, and the extension of robotics nanotechnology to the material world, it will not be difficult to give every individual mind its own universe as a playground in which it can be a god.

That this vision is surprisingly libertarian, in the sense of deifying individualism in splendid isolation, should not surprise us. Rothblatt is unusual in emphasizing collective consciousness. Much of the transhumanist and posthumanist mainstream is committed to Itskov's level of Ayn Randian individualism.[25]

The ideal existence for the Itskovian avatar is to be alone with himself or herself in a universe created and maintained by his or her own mind, not as a delusion but as a real set of objects created by digital programs and projected into a space that the mind creates, sustains, and endlessly changes at will. In Itskov's "Heaven," every individual ends up as the god in his or her universe. We can invite visitors if we choose. But if each of us becomes smart enough to create a complete universe, our own version of the "real," we also will be smart enough to determine how to create unique patterns of information—minds—who will become our company forever in a world of our own making.

Goal 7. Managing History

Itskov's final, more communal goal is "To manage the course of history."[26] One can infer that such "management" might mean that the fully realized avatars will now obliterate history. If minds control all events and everyone has his or her own universe, if there is perfect freedom to adopt any shape or form of life one wishes, and if everyone lives forever, then every possible source of human conflict will have been eliminated. Consequently, there no longer will be the events that create history: class conflict, national rivalries, clashes over scarce resources, or feelings of inferiority or of having been wronged. Once these motives for conflict disappear, history, as Francis Fukuyama predicted a bit prematurely at the turn of the millennium, also will disappear.[4] Itskov's new world order will be completed when events have come under the complete control of reason and when nothing untoward disrupts the digitization and full rationalization of the "real." Thus, Itskov joins Karl Marx, Hegel, and Plato in conceiving a perfectly rational world from which all chance and all history have been banished.[27]

Nothing confirms the fundamental rationalism of the transhumanist vision more than this, Itskov's final vision, and nothing more vividly captures his deepest longing: to create a perfectly safe world in which nothing disturbing can happen and in which every individual rules as a timeless, benign god in his or her own designer universe. As visions of Heaven go, things could be worse.

This is the new world order—a world created in totality by a new species—the neo-human, the next stage in evolution, one envisioned, propelled, and controlled by ourselves, and with only ourselves, each one all alone, as the divine inhabitants. Rothblatt's collective consciousness and shared Godness have been replaced by a fragmented multiverse in which each mind is the sole aim of its own development and in which boundaries that can be crossed, from mind to mind, have been replaced by impenetrable borders between forever incompatible private universes.

Chapter 10

The (Post)Human Future?

This long, circuitous journey that I began at Hollywood Forever cemetery has traced a technical and conceptual revolution that promises to bring the dead online in the very near future, culminating in the transhumanist project of actualizing immortality for the dead on the Internet. This revolution challenges fundamental notions about what it means to be human and even what it means simply to be alive, because it argues that we have to abandon our biological bodies to become who we truly are. This idea disrupts traditional religious ideas at their core, challenging the fundamental idea that divine beings control what happens to us after we die. In the new paradigm, human reason controls the postmortem future. We become immortal because we will soon devise the technological means to live forever as digital patterns of information in the Cloud. We begin a final consideration of this extraordinary move of putting the dead online by examining a series of objections to this potential change in how we understand our life and death. These objections come from several perspectives that see this project as not simply problematic but downright dangerous—what historian Francis Fukuyama has identified as one of "the world's most dangerous ideas."[1]

Although there have been no substantial objections to online memorials, archival sites, or most social media legacy pages, there is a growing cultural resistance to the fact that we spend too much of our time on screens and, hence, are altering for the worse how we relate to one another.[2] If we cannot make it out to the cemetery to visit our dead, but have turned even them into characters on a smartphone app, what have we come to? Are even the dead no longer sacred?

There also are more particular objections to mistaking the virtual presence of the dead on Facebook pages for their real presence. If everyone we have ever known shows up online, including the dead, won't we lose a vital distinction between the virtual and the real? Hasn't that boundary already been compromised too much?

Lastly, don't we compromise the respect due to the dead by posting garish homemade memorials on YouTube, however heartfelt those might be? And what about the level of sheer disrespect for the dead that one finds on MyDeathSpace, as well as in the endless YouTube videos of car, train, and airplane crashes, and in the horror of the beheading videos posted by terrorist groups?

But most memorial and social media sites are viewed as benign. Such sites even seem to have a positive social value, as anyone who visits the 9/11, Hurricane Katrina, and online cemetery sites can learn. It seems a good thing to use the Internet to keep the dead close to our hearts. It is when we take up the more troubling question of creating online avatars of the dead that distress and anxiety increase exponentially.

There seem to be many reasons for this unease. One is the concern that when avatars have developed further, they will have the power to create the illusion of "presence," leading people to suspend disbelief and to invest emotions and loyalty into what essentially are philosophical zombies. Or, as was shown in "Be Right Back," such replicas of the dead will disappoint us precisely because they are *not* good enough copies. In both instances, however, we see living humans inviting mindless machines into their lives, dangerously blurring the boundaries between the human and the nonhuman. Donna Haraway predicted this in her 1991 essay, "A Cyborg Manifesto,"[3] but she was referring to entities that would combine elements of the human and the machine. Avatars of the dead have nothing human about them but their programming, so letting them into our lives as if they were people seems at the outer limits of the unsettling.

Transhumanism, however, which embraces the idea that we actually can insert our first-person identities into such onscreen avatars, opens up a very different world with much higher emotional and metaphysical stakes, and we encounter vigorous and sustained objections from several important quarters. For some time, popular culture has been in the forefront of sounding a kind of alarm.

POPULAR CULTURE'S DYSTOPIC VISIONS

The products of popular culture, as was shown with "Be Right Back," have both foreseen and tested these ideas before they have been enacted. Popular culture—film, print and graphic novels, computer games—has vividly represented these possible futures in people's everyday imaginings for many decades. It took websites, online games, and social media, as well as the concept of cyberspace, to create new places for the dead in the worlds that computers opened up. In a similar vein, as much as the final transit of the dead from mindless avatar to first-person subject needs the theories of mind that we have sketched out, that move also needed representation in popular media to make people more familiar—and more comfortable—with the new world they might soon be asked to enter. Four films serve as illustrations of both the visionary appeal and dystopic alarm that the prospect of moving minds from "meat" bodies to digital "ghosts" can arouse. We have already discussed *Avatar* and *Surrogates* in chapter nine, but here we meet them in a different context.

Each film presents the reality of mind portability, but each offers a different scenario about how this can happen and what it might mean. Central to the plot of *Avatar* (2009) is the idea that a human mind, an identity, can be transferred from a human brain and body to the brain and body of a synthesized biological avatar. In the film, Jake Sully, a paraplegic human whose mind inhabits an avatar of the native people whose culture Jake's company is destroying, joins the natives and, when he is fatally injured fighting the humans, has his identity permanently ported from his body to that of his avatar.

Surrogates (2011), by contrast, presents a near-future society in which flesh-and-blood humans stay at home and use brain-computer-interface to remotely control android robots called "Surries"—all of which are young, attractive, slender, and well dressed—to go about the world and do their business, even as their hidden controllers age.

Transcendence (2014) tells the story of a fatally injured scientist who uploads his consciousness to a quantum computer and expands his mind from there to control the entire Internet.

Chappie (2015) relates how a police robot in South Africa gets reprogrammed to have human feelings and ends up helping a fatally wounded human upload his consciousness to a robot.

Three of these four films feature scenarios in which dying people transfer their identities to other platforms—robots, genetically engineered clones, hard drives—to continue their lives. In *Surrogates*, minds are not literally transferred out of bodies, but they are projected into computer-driven substitute bodies. In *Chappie*, *Transcendence*, and *Avatar*, a human mind travels from a dying or aging body into a form that is less vulnerable.

All of these films postulate that transferring a mind, intact, from a dying or aging human to a computerized "Other," is possible and morally complex. Two of the films suggest that it is a bad thing to do. In *Chappie*, a put-upon robot that has become human saves his human creator by capturing the human's mind as a computer program, then porting that mind to a robot. Both of them then have to go into hiding from authorities who will stop at nothing to destroy such machine-human hybrids. In *Transcendence* the authorities do everything they can to destroy a scientist whose wife had uploaded his mind to a quantum computer, even at the cost of depriving the world of digital connections forever. In *Avatar*, by contrast, Jake Sully's mind is ported from his dying body into his avatar through a combination of technologies and mystical practices—an affirmation of the moral superiority of the pre-technological indigenous people, the "Na'vi," whose plight Jake has embraced. But even in this case, mind transfer is not designed to provide personal immortality, but rather to allow the character to escape from a world that is evil to one that is purer and more innocent. Only in *Transcendence* is the issue of mind transfer to achieve immortality an issue, but the transfer is made only because the character whose mind is transferred, Will Caster, would die otherwise. In this case the uploaded scientist at first becomes amorally power-mad, as well as oddly benevolent, controlling humans with nanobot invaders even as he uses his vast new intelligence to create an ecologically sustainable paradise. In that film, the government destroys Will and shuts down the Internet because Will had *become* the Internet, and the government fears that he will become too powerful. Thus, he must be destroyed. Here, mind transfer to achieve immortality is a morally ambiguous event, producing both evil and good that the powers-that-be cannot tolerate.

Chappie and *Avatar* both suggest that human ways are too corrupt to tolerate good people, and so these people are forced to flee for their lives into alternate forms of existence. In these two films, mind transfer is a mixed form of both transcendence and escape. We do not transfer our minds to achieve immortality, but to protect ourselves from evil authorities.

In *Surrogates* humans lose their agency and sense of purpose as they grow too dependent on their robot avatars. Even though this film does not include full-blown mind transfer, it represents a stage on the way to such transfer, as Dmitry Itskov saw when he referenced both it and

Avatar in his discussions of his Avatar Project. And *Surrogates*, like the other films, ends badly in the sense that at the climax the character played by Bruce Willis deactivates all the robot surrogates and returns humanity to itself.

These four films represent a strong theme in twenty-first-century popular culture narratives: Artificial intelligence and evolving digital technologies will make it possible to transfer human minds to other formats, but such endeavors will either not turn out well or will be squelched by a hostile authority. Either people cannot handle digital immortality, or they won't be allowed to have it even if it benefits them. Thus, although these films affirm that digital immortality can be achieved, at best its benefits are limited. Only in *Avatar,* a film in which the protagonist moves his mind from one sort of biological body to another, is there any suggestion that the transfer will open up new spiritual and emotional vistas—but, interestingly, these new vistas are found in the indigenous world and not the technological one, a not-so-subtle condemnation of a vision of a technological world both ruthless and morally empty. And the world of technology has its own concerns and doubts about the prospects of mind transfer and digital immortality.

Mind uploading thus is on our cultural radar, but computer-driven versions of human identity remain deeply suspect. Even films that present artificial intelligence "personalities," such as Samantha in *Her* and Ava in *Ex Machina*, suggest that minds housed in digital machines— whether those minds are copies of the minds of the dead or minds created by AI programs—should be objects of suspicion, the nature of which is examined next.

TECHNOLOGICAL CONCERNS

Several objections to what I am calling this new revolution have arisen from the technological world that spawned it. One objection is the "We're too stupid, or the problem is just too complex, or we cannot write the software" objection. At the heart of this objection is the idea that although we can dream about mind uploading and unlimited human enhancement, we never will do more than approach this dream asymptotically, never quite achieving what we hope and need to achieve to make the transhumanist program into a reality.[4]

The only plausible response to these objections, which we need not rehearse here in detail, is that we will have to wait and see. My limited technical knowledge and understanding of such matters constrains me from making any sort of definitive pronouncements on these issues. On the one hand, I fully appreciate how daunting it will be to scan every one of the brain's neurons and its many connections to other neurons into a database, and then to translate that information into digital code. On the other hand, I am aware of Moore's Law about the exponential growth of computing speed and power and memory capacity, as well as Ray Kurzweil's LOAR (Law of Accelerated Returns),[5] and think that there is a good chance that we soon will have the hardware we need to copy the human brain.

This essentially is how Dmitry Itskov addresses such objections, as was shown in chapter nine. Itskov argues that, in science, everything that people claim is impossible eventually becomes possible. Thus, what we regard as technically beyond our reach today needs only the next brilliant invention to make into a reality.

I am not convinced, however, that such a radical move will be needed. I am deeply sympathetic to Kurzweil's "patternism" and Rothblatt's pragmatic functionalism concerning mind replication. On balance, therefore, I take the "We're too stupid" arguments seriously, but I do not find them to be completely convincing, because I believe that we will be able to create plausible copies of individual minds using information culled from data, rather than by slavishly reproducing every neuron in the brain.

The second set of objections is more philosophical and formal. These objections assert that no matter how sophisticated we make our digital devices and their programs, the best a computing device can do is to sort things into their proper categories; but a device never can achieve the self-awareness necessary to create genuine subjective identity. Computers, according to thinkers like John Searle, are brilliant sorters, but they cannot know what they are sorting and, more importantly, that they are doing so. Searle rejects as incoherent the idea that any digital device running a program can be self-aware, that it is reflexive, so that it knows what it is and that it is. Searle's final judgment is that computers just can't think.

Searle makes his case using the now-famous Chinese Room argument.[6] He asks us to imagine an individual in a closed room. The room is filled with Chinese symbols that the individual can move around and arrange in sequences. The premise is that Chinese writers write strings of symbols that ask questions in Chinese. They pass these questions, or symbol-strings, through a slot in the closed door of the room, as the questions are passed in the original version of the Turing Test. The individual inside the room does not speak a word of Chinese, but he has books and books of instructions written in English that tell him which symbols to string together if one sees this or that sequence of symbols. So, he knows that if he sees "%^&," he can send back either "*()" or "@#$," depending on whether the original string does or does not have a "~" attached after a gap.

Let's say our individual is very attentive and very fast and that he gets the symbol-strings right almost every time. Searle's first claim is that if he does this, the people writing the notes will judge that he speaks Chinese, just as the interrogator in the Imitation Game judges that the computing machine is thinking if it answers his questions as a human would answer them.

Searle's second claim is that the note writers will be wrong to think this, because all the man in the room is doing is arranging shapes in sequences in accordance with the rules laid out in his guidebooks. He has no idea what the sequences mean, no sense of what Searle calls the semantics of the strings, although he has an excellent grasp of the syntax, that is, the rules of arrangement.

We should add that the guides the person in the room is using provide only correspondences with no explanation of why this string "deserves" that string as a response. Thus, the person in the room never can learn more about Chinese because there is no meaning involved in the correspondence rules.

Therefore, Searle concludes computers sort brilliantly, but think not at all: they know the rules for arranging symbols correctly, but have no idea of the meaning behind the symbols that dictates how they get arranged. Thus, according to Searle, we can program a processing unit to respond differentially to inputs in such a way that it appears to be self-aware—it will pass a Turing Test, but it will be one of David Chalmers's "philosophical zombies," a being that does everything that a person would be expected to do, but which has nothing going on inside, no subjective experience. This is Searle's man in the room. His behavior indicates that he knows Chinese, but all he is doing is matching symbols. In the same way our philosophical zombie is programmed with sorting rules: input X, output Y, with no subjective experience in between.

Thomas Nagel captured the heart of this objection in his famous essay titled "What Is It Like to Be a Bat?"[7] There, Nagel objects to the inadequacy of physicalist accounts of human consciousness. His point is that when we try to reduce descriptions of first-order subject awareness to descriptions of brain states, we miss what might be most important about the phenomenon we are trying to describe.

Nagel gets at this by yet another thought experiment. Consider the bat. Bats use something called echo-location to fly in the dark without dashing themselves against obstacles that they cannot see. They emit high-pitched squeaks that bounce off hidden obstacles and let the bat know when to turn or duck or fly higher. Nagel says that it is a futile exercise for you or me to try to imagine what having echo-location would be like. His point is that whatever this is like, there is something it is like, some irreducibly subjective way it feels, and is, to be echo-locating. Not only that, but bat A's echo-location experience is not the same as bat B's echo-location experience. So, there is irreducibly something it is like, as a type, to be *a* bat, and there is something it is uniquely like to be *this* bat.

If computers are unreflecting sorting devices, then there is subjectively nothing it is like to be whatever it is they are. The way this works out as an objection to the transhumanist desire to upload minds is that critics warn that it is possible to create a plausible replica that will *appear* to have subjective experience. The critics warn that transhumanists who mistakenly believe that they are transferring their identities as digital programs to online avatars, for example, will simply die. The avatars will be exactly like the Eternime replicas or the Pinchas Gutter hologram—well-spoken, carefully crafted lookalike chatbots with no subjective inwardness. Mind transfer then is nothing more than an expensive, and finally a stupid, form of suicide. What appears to be a step into a brave new world is no step at all. What we will end up with is a universe filled with *apparent* people, simulacra of subjects, talking with each other, and not one of them understanding what is going on, or even that *anything* is going on. It will be an entire world in which there is *no* "there" there, anywhere. Rothblatt's collective consciousness will *say* it is self-aware, should anyone ever be there to ask, but the response will be exactly like that of the man in the Chinese Room—lacking any essential meaning. Or Itskov's god in his or her own universe will be a god without a scintilla of awareness, a god that doesn't know it is a god and that, moreover, has no idea what a god is.

And another objection, based on Derek Parfit's teletransportation thought experiment,[8] argues that if we are destructively uploaded from our body to another, we will disappear as "us." Parfit hypothesizes what would happen if there were a machine that could destroy my body and with it, of course, my mind, atom by atom, and send the patterns for each atom to Mars via radio waves. There, the radio signals would assemble a perfectly cognate new set of atoms and reassemble a perfect replica of me. What we will have is a superb perfect copy, but not the original entity.

Parfit "proves" that this new being will not really be me (shades of the transporter in *Star Trek*!) by offering an alternate scenario in which the machine sends the pattern for a perfect copy of me to Mars but leaves me intact on Earth. Would there then be two of me, or would there be an original and a replica? We know from Rothblatt's remarks on the mind-clones that she would have no problem with this because her notion of identity is much looser, more pragmatic, and, dare I say it, more post-modern and performative than essentialist.

I think Nagel, Parfit, and Searle have crafted brilliant thought experiments about personal identity, and I think every one of them needs to be taken into account by anyone contemplating mind uploading in the near future, along with Chalmers's own thought experiment, the philosophical zombie, which we have used throughout the book.

Recall that Chalmers's idea is that it is possible to think of an entity that is indistinguishable in any way from a biological human, but that differs in the important respect that there is nothing it is like to be that thing. In our case, we are saying that there could be something that looks, walks, talks, and smells like a human being, even like a human being we know intimately, and that entity is not really a human at all but a very well-made, mindless robot.

The common riposte to all these brilliant thought experiments is: If I meet this entity, outside the Chinese Room, and ask it if it is my late Uncle Albert, and it says yes, and, moreover, it knows things that Albert never put online or in a public form anywhere, and which only Albert and I know, I am willing to say that this is for all practical purposes my Uncle Albert whose mind was uploaded to a machine body, to an online avatar, to a hologram. I might or might not opt for the mind-uploading procedure for myself, but I am convinced that there is no way for me, as an outside interrogator, to know whether the being who purports to be Uncle Albert is or is not Uncle Albert, absent some egregious error on the entity's part that suggests it is not Albert but a nefarious copy. Thus, however brilliant the thought experiments might be, they ultimately are moot, because if we can produce an online entity that passes Turing Tests, that is, convinces us that it is who it says it is, then there is no way for the interrogator to de-termine whether he or she is interacting with a mindless program.

This is the essence of Rothblatt's response to the thought experiments, as was examined in chapter six. As long as the online intelligence con-vinces a panel of experts that it is the subject it claims to be, this is good enough for Rothblatt.

There are two other significant worlds that also have strong concerns which might be the most telling: the philosophical world of phenomenologists and existentialists, and that of the ethicists, and the religious world, populated by a variety of theologians from various faith traditions.

OTHER PHILOSOPHICAL OBJECTIONS: THE PROBLEM OF EMBODIMENT AND THE ISSUE OF MORALITY

The further philosophical concerns arrange themselves into two categories: (1) embodiment questions generated by existentialism and phenomenology, supplemented by the concerns of gender and race theorists; and (2) questions that deal with issues of morality and ethics.

The "We belong in a biological body" objection, which is rooted in both gender-identity theories on the one hand and post-Heideggerian phenomenologies of the body on the other, argues that being human *means* being embodied. If we extract minds, as information patterns, from their existential situatedness, what we end up with will not be human. I will, for purposes of narrative economy, restrict my remarks to a consideration of the phenomenological/existential camp, as represented by Maurice Merleau-Ponty's work on perception and embodiment or George Lakoff and Mark Johnson's on symbols and language.[9] Merleau-Ponty's idea is that human consciousness and the biological body are necessary conditions one for the other. Human awareness and self-awareness are simply inconceivable absent the experienced connections between thinking and bodying. We might succeed in creating some weird distortion of a human being by transferring the patterns of our mind to a different nonbiological substrate, but what we get we would not want to get. Such a being could not help but be one sort of monster or another; we can be sure that it could not be human.

The reason that is offered is that the human brain is so deeply wired into the body's different systems, and especially the central nervous system, that if we abstract the algorithms in the mind that refer in complex ways to a biological body, the collection of algorithms implanted in a nonbiological medium will be wildly maladaptive because so many of the mind's responses have to do with a body that no longer is there. If the mind works at all outside its body, it will work in different, unpredictable ways. Whatever it becomes, it cannot by definition be us; and it is problematic whether such a transplanted mind even will qualify as being human. We might not end up with improved copies of ourselves at all, but rather with a new, independent entity that we not only will not be able to control but which we will not even be able to understand.

Thus, making new versions of ourselves could lead to the creation of a race of aliens who might turn out to be demons that bring about the deaths of their creators. Philosophical concern here meets popular culture's obsession with dystopic narratives of technology's potential evil.

This fear is nicely concretized in the work that the American philosophers Lakoff and Johnson have done on the connections between language and embodiment. They make a strong case that many of our most important concepts, especially in the realm of ethics, are couched in metaphors that are based in the particulars of the human body. Once we remove this point of reference by taking the body from its mind, these concepts could gradually lose their significance. Additionally, when we lack the body needed to generate emotion, we will change.

Let me be clear. Neither Merleau-Ponty nor Lakoff and Johnson would say that a mind abstracted from its body and implanted in another kind of body would have no emotions or moral concepts, but that all of these would undergo radical, mostly negative, transformations. The deepest insight here is that, existentially, being fully human simply is unthinkable if we do not include the body as a necessary reference. We might be able to reproduce something in purely digital form, but we would almost certainly not want to know what it is that we have produced.

Consider this thought experiment. Your biological body has died and you have been imported to an online avatar. You are programmed to see a rich virtual world around you. You feel the ground under your feet, you smell the air, you move through the scene. But this is *not* your old body. If this body falls from a cliff or pitches forward off a roof, or drives his car into a wall doing 80 miles an hour, nothing happens that would have happened were you in your "meat" body. You have experiences but they have to be qualitatively different. What philosophers call the "*qualia*," the immediate felt perceptions, hold no undertones of possible hurt or danger. Under these circumstances, you could and probably would become almost entirely self-referential. Digital immortality could usher in an era of unprecedented self-absorption. As noted when assessing Itskov's initiative, he would have each individual play the god in his or her universe.

If one favors such a life, then digital immortality is the direction in which we should be headed. But if one values social interaction, mutual support, and interdependence, then the prospect of a world filled with self-centered dead souls living each in his or her own universe is not edifying and challenges most understandings of what it means to be human.

This vision could be the scenario if those who are digitally immortal retain some analog of their bodily shapes and remain at roughly our present level of intelligence. But the transhumanists, as shown herein, predict other things that the philosophers do not address. If we add Ray Kurzweil's idea that intelligent machines—and a human now would be one of those—will, by their very nature as rational organizations built to sustain themselves, constantly work to improve themselves, another layer is included in the experiment.

What does Kurzweil's idea mean, in practice? I offer another thought experiment. One of the features of the flesh is it opacity. Another is its resistance. We often do not understand what moves us to act, and we as often grow frustrated because our bodies will not allow us to do what we want to do. Both of these features shape our identity. If I am an on-line avatar or a hologram, there is no literal flesh to offer its opaque motives, no flesh to resist my wishes. I can think my way completely into my avatar body and know everything about it, changing it to fit what I want to do, and reprogramming it so that it is not moved by obscure forces beyond my knowledge and control.

I become, then, a being that constantly revises his body to make it entirely his own. The body then becomes more and more *ideal*; that is, more a pure projection of mind, a notion rather than a thing. I have no clear idea at all what this would mean for my personal identity. But it would almost certainly mean that I would only occupy an idealized vir-tual or robotic body for as long as I remained psychologically tied to the idea that I needed to live in a human body. I would soon cease to look anything like a biological human being.

Whatever form the rationalized "body" of the future might take, I do know that making my body entirely reasonable would free me from worrying about it. This would give me more time to think for thinking's pure sake and make me correspondingly less driven by feelings and dreams. In my superintelligent condition, with a body that needed nei-ther dreams nor feelings, I might soon become as psychologically unrec-ognizable as I was physically unrecognizable.

Whether this trajectory toward a new, disembodied identity is a nega-tive move or not depends on how one conceives of the relationship be-tween minds and bodies. If minds are self-contained systems that can move without loss from one setting to another—a deeply Platonic no-tion—then the disembodiment sketched out above might be a good thing. If, however, we believe that minds belong in biological bodies to remain human minds, then the trajectory could not be more unwelcome. The uncanny disembodied something that this thought experiment sug-gests that we would become fundamentally abrogates the Heideggerian insight that human beings are "*Dasein*"—"being-there." If we can keep changing our "there," or even create it digitally, then Heidegger's characterization becomes a bad joke. To be human requires a stable location, and that is all there is to it.

A new category of objections is a variation on the last one, but this time inflected by a commitment to the idea that human beings have an internal moral compass. There has been a good deal of discussion about whether we can program moral principles into artificial intelligence. Such figures as Francis Fukuyama and Stephen Hawking, among others, have expressed serious reservations about—and have even warned against—the wisdom of creating superintelligent robots because such entities might not understand, or take seriously, the moral rules that bind our societies together.[10] Even committed transhumanists such as Nick Bostrom have issued warnings on the topic, noting that an artificial intelligence designed to make paper clips might come up with the idea to turn the entire world into paper clips, including all humans!

But human beings who achieve digital immortality are not AI machines; they are people whose minds have been translated into digital code. We have to assume that this coding includes their moral principles and intuitions along with everything else, especially if we think of moral principles as rational rules, in the manner of the Kantian categorical imperative. Thus, we can expect uploaded people to have very different moral sensibilities than AI creations such as Ava in *Ex Machina* or Samantha in *Her*.

But how (or if) these moral sensibilities will actuate is, of course, an unknown. As noted above when discussing the effects of biological disembodiment on personal identity, who can say what will happen to moral rules once the intelligence of uploaded people begins to increase exponentially, once they are freed from their bodies? And what effect will the removal of feelings of loss and pain have on moral judgment? Even if we think of moral decision making as a purely rational enterprise, such decision making needs to incorporate judgments about the pain certain decisions might cause in those affected by our moral decisions. But can a being who no longer feels pain be trusted to make decisions that take pain into account?

One can conjecture, then, that even though uploaded people are not pure AI creations, their altered "life" conditions might cause them to suffer lapses in moral sensitivity attendant on the loss of the capacity to experience pain.

Thus, disembodiment or re-embodiment might change identity beyond recognition, and moral judgment might be altered for the worse in erstwhile biological humans who live in bodies that have no pain qualia.

But, conversely, we also cannot know for certain how these changes in identity will manifest themselves. In fact, these changes might be a good thing, because there is nothing that dictates that beings who once felt pain, and now do not, should be morally insensitive. But there is no uncertainty, no lack of clarity in how the religious world evaluates these possibilities. As one might guess, the concerns are momentous and severe.

RELIGIOUS DOUBTS

The final set of objections I want to take up are religious, which fall into three areas of concern.[11] First, the proposals for digital immortality that we have examined thus far are either purely secular (Itskov) or pantheist (Rothblatt). Neither acknowledges the creative and sustaining presence of a transcendent divinity, and this levels the hierarchy of being in an unacceptable way for traditional religious conceptions of human experience. If there is no transcendent God to impose rules, for example, how can we trust the collective efforts of humanity—whose history in this regard is anything but edifying—to create and enforce universal compassion and respect? Further, in the absence of such a God and the salvation He offers, what gives life purpose?

The nub of this objection is that if we eliminate God altogether or, as in the Terasem case, have collective human intelligence create God, then there will be no reassuring and judging Other to let us know that the fate of the cosmos rests in His (or Her) metaphoric hands and to offer us guidance and hope. Although the transhumanist universe is not one of Camusian or Sartrean existential *malaise*, empty of meaning and purpose, there still is the sense in both the 2045 Initiative and Terasem that humans are ultimately on their own, dependent entirely on their own resources to make the human project work.

This position rejects the idea that we humans depend on any context, whether that be Darwinian natural selection or Divine providence and judgment. Itskov, Rothblatt, and the other transhumanists in general are supremely confident that human beings are able to shape their own fates and, in fact, that the entire enterprise amounts to controlling human fate by controlling evolution. As shown, there even is a strong undercurrent of belief in a shared human destiny, the idea that we are *fated* to achieve collective apotheosis—an idea that becomes a kind of "faith," but one divorced completely from any traditional conception.

This world of digital immortality is, as we have come to understand, ultimately a world with no metaphysical up or down. It is a world without transcendence, despite what Terasem says about transcending space and time. Ultimately, there is no mystery here, no Other in whom one can lose oneself, no depthless Being outside oneself into whose care one can commit oneself. The world of digital immortality is relentlessly adult and relentlessly one-dimensional.

A second objection, raised by Robert M. Geraci in his *Apocalyptic AI*,[12] is that transhumanist views of Internet afterlife are essentially religious, but in a dualist Gnostic sense that hinges on a complete rejection of the body, as if the body were inherently evil, what Plato described as a "prison" for the soul. Thus, transhumanism as a religion takes up a severely anti-body, dualist theme, setting it apart from most, but not all, of mainstream Christian, Jewish, and Muslim belief. The tendency in both Itskov and Rothblatt to favor a future in which the material universe is replaced by a virtual emulation lends credibility to such claims. At the same time, we must not forget that transhumanists are for the most part materialists who always imbed minds in some material substrate or other. Minds for most transhumanists always will be patterns of information, data bits, rather than immaterial Gnostic souls. But this belief gestures back, in its turn, to the phenomenologist's objection that transhumanists reject the biological mortal body and would prefer that minds be housed in machines.

The third religious objection asks: Don't these proposals commit us to an incredible act of hubris? If we try to take charge of immortality, which has been the gods' prerogative since Gilgamesh tried to resurrect his lost friend Inkidu, aren't we assuming that human beings can take control of their own destinies, and successfully usurp the place of the gods? Self-absorption, as noted earlier, is a central piece of Itskov's initiative in that he envisions each individual playing god in his or her universe. Is this not exactly how Scripture, in the Book of Genesis, defines sin: "*Eritis sicut dii*,"[13] or "They would be as gods"? Isn't the transhumanist proposal to create digital immortality a direct challenge to the First Commandment, "I am the Lord thy God. Thou shalt put no other gods before Me"? And doesn't it, in the last analysis, establish a parallel Heaven to compete with the one offered by the Judeo-Christian-Islamic God?

If, in the near future, believing Christians or Muslims were offered the chance at digital immortality, would they be right to take that chance? Would this be tantamount to choosing a humanly produced Heaven over one created by God? Or would this, as the Terasem proposals suggest, be entirely compatible with traditional Heavens? First one goes to earthly Heaven, as an avatar, then to religious Heaven, as a spirit or resurrected body. We might imagine that such a proposal would inevitably create a kind of war of the Heavens between proponents of digital Heaven and those who prefer a traditional Godly Heaven.

Because it is a foundational tenet of traditional Western theologies that humans have no business usurping God's prerogatives, transhumanists would have to be considered sinners; and good Christians, Jews, and Muslims would have to steer clear of their blandishments. But if the transhumanists could offer what appeared to be a real digital immortality immediately available, would some believers defect and choose this visible immortality over one that they could not see?

Could the triumph of transhumanist immortality spell the death of traditional religious belief, or its replacement by Terasem's trans-religion or Itskov's libertarian self-absorption? Or, might the mainstream Western religions eventually join with transhumanism, as Martine Rothblatt suggests they will, and as certain strains in contemporary Christian theology, especially, suggest that they will? Is there a genuine spiritual convergence between Teilhard de Chardin's Omega Point and Martine Rothblatt's "Godness"? And is this why the Terasem Foundation sponsored a virtual 2015 conference on Terasem and Teilhard, appropriately held at Terasem's virtual island in Second Life?[14]

FINAL THOUGHTS: THE EVOLVING AMERICAN DEATH NARRATIVE

We have been on a long and circuitous journey and now we approach its end. At the heart of the questions we have been asking is whether we are seeing a true, new salvation that will lead us to a better world—a new Heaven as "neo-humans"—or whether this is a foray to a nightmare world as adumbrated by popular culture's dystopic visions of a future in which humans disappear as humans, to be replaced by mindless or heartless humanoid machines.

The new American death narratives that we are collectively creating as I write this book offer four themes that are, interestingly, reflective of the history of American death narratives: optimism about the fate of the dead; a belief that the boundary between life and death is permeable and easily crossed, going both ways; a do-it-yourself sense of entitlement in describing/designing the afterlife; and a willingness to enlist technologies, old and new, to represent and enable the new death narrative and to furnish the afterlife.

These themes have emerged from what can be understood as a historical struggle to wrest control of the dead, and of the stories we tell about them, from a corporatized funeral industry and a powerful medical-hospital establishment. Prior to the Civil War, in what I have called the Axial Age of American death narratives, ordinary citizens had control of the dead, including the stories about where personal identity went after death and what it did when it got there.

The cultural upheavals of the 1960s and the social crisis that the AIDS epidemic provoked began to loosen the grip of morticians, doctors, and cemetery managers over the dead and the stories we tell about them. Medicine was initially helpless in the face of the AIDS epidemic in the 1980s, so sufferers more often returned home or to hospices to die—beyond the control of morticians and doctors. The era saw the appearance of non-traditional funeral services. Events conspired to produce a situation in which ordinary people began to reassert control over stories about what dying and the afterlife mean.

This return of death narratives to the control of ordinary people showed up in the least controllable of all social forms, the realm of popular culture. New Heaven narratives started to make their appearance in films and novels. Near-death experience became hugely popular, as did a renascent spiritualism. Movies about benign ghosts proliferated. Evangelical Christians produced compelling narratives about the End Times and the Rapture. After 9/11 this new Heaven literature proliferated even more, as death again came to the forefront of the public's consciousness.

During the same period all this was going on, however, other things were afoot that would push death narratives in wildly unexpected new directions. Personal computers and the Internet were becoming part of the cultural landscape at the height of the AIDS crisis, and the importance of digital devices had been adumbrated by leaders of the 1960s mind-expansion movement, such as Timothy Leary. Intelligent machines appeared on the far horizon of our awareness, and things would never be the same again.

Intelligence had been liberated from the biological body. Once this happened, a new meaning for dying and the afterlife could not help but emerge. Machines can last forever. We build machines. Our identities can be turned into programs. They can then be moved to machines. If all of this happens, then I have achieved immortality. Thus, as professional grief counselors took over mainstream death narratives, the outlines of a new death narrative were emerging. Transhumanism is the home of this new death narrative. Those who are making that narrative also propose that they control not only the story about death and the afterlife, but also the actual process of getting there and staying there.

Its major claim, as has been shown, is that it is time to begin producing the technologies that will free us from biological evolution and from our bodies. The more radical transhumanists embrace the idea that this liberation from organic evolution, and thus from the biological body, should take the form of finding ways for people to retain their identities while jettisoning the biological body and the death that goes with it. The transhumanist image of death and the afterlife today is that of a mind uploaded to an online avatar, a humanoid robot, or a hologram, there to reside in digital immortality. If the transhumanists are correct, however, then it won't be long before that mind begins to develop new forms of existence that we can neither predict nor comprehend. Computing machines will provide a new virtual place in which individual personalities can appear online, there to develop as their own internal logic will dictate.

What has been of particular interest and, hence, a focus of this study is the work of the two *practical* transhumanists who promise a literal Internet afterlife either now or in the very near future. Martine Rothblatt and Dmitry Itskov are trying to put the trans–posthumanist project in play and thereby create a new death narrative and a new death experience. Their work displays the optimism, permeability, do-it-yourself confidence, and faith in the uses of technology that characterized the death narratives and practices throughout our history. Additionally, they share that earlier period's unwillingness to lose the dead to another—and an alien—world. Where earlier generations of Americans have rejected the idea of young people dying and being lost to death, the transhumanists, moved by an analogous impatience, reject the idea of privileged *old* people, or any people, dying.

Whatever objections one might have to transhumanism, it does present itself as an implacable opponent of all forms of human suffering, even if it proposes to solve the problem of suffering by turning human beings into undying machines.

Finally, we should note that despite the powerful objections and profound and understandable concerns of traditional religious perspectives, there are religious people who see no tension between religious faith and transhumanist projects. In the spirit of the visionary Jesuit paleontologist Teilhard de Chardin, many current religious thinkers envision a future in which the new death narratives and the old cross-fertilize each other rather than cancel each other out. They argue that if we can meet or become God as minds in machines as well as we can in the vestments of the flesh, then there ultimately is no difference between traditional salvation and cyberresurrection.

But this is a huge "if." My long journey has taken us to a world beyond physical death in which flesh people have all but disappeared, and are replaced by online avatars living in virtual worlds or by evanescent holograms flitting in and out of space-time. These are worlds where minds live forever, but where Earth is derelict, peopled by a few "meat" humans kept as living museum exhibits. There are robots, biologically enhanced clones, people made of swarms of computers as tiny as cells. They live all over the multiverse, slipping through wormholes from one kind of space-time to another, assuming innumerable different forms, none of which defines them. This world, or these worlds, bear little resemblance to traditional religious images of Heaven.

If we were to look for a loved one in this afterlife, we would find "him or her" distributed over scores of provisional identities, living different lives in different worlds, ultimately at home everywhere, but with no fixed residence except in his or her thoughts. He or she would be dauntingly intelligent, immediately jacked into the single Great Mind that all the dead share. We almost certainly would have little or no idea of what he or she was "talking" about—the thoughts would appear in our awareness without him or her having to speak—and, as to emotions, I have no idea what they would be, or even *if* they would be.

This would be a world without God, if by "God" we mean a transcendent separate Being who creates and judges. The Great Mind to which everyone belonged always would be creating and re-creating all of Being to make it better, which would mean to make it more perfectly virtual. Being itself, now also a part of the Great Mind, would constantly be making new and more rational versions of itself, in which more and more, and better and better versions of our beloved dead person would be replicating themselves. One also can surmise that we would not belong in such a world. It would be changing all the time, getting away from us, developing beyond any hope of our understanding it. I have no idea whether it would be visible or tangible, or whether it would be *anywhere* that we could locate it.

This afterlife would definitely *not* be a static Heaven of golden streets and mansions, or the tame light shows and sweet Jesuses of the afterlives we find in popular fiction. It would be the realm of pure Mind unleashed. If you choose to join this ride—and it really *is* a ride—then you and I have a future that I am incapable of writing about and you are incapable of understanding even if I could write about it.

Welcome to Internet afterlife, and to virtual salvation in the twenty-first century!

"Et introibo ad altare Dei.
Ad Deum, qui laetificat juventutem meam."
("I will go up into the altar of God. To God, who gives joy to my youth.")
—Opening of traditional Roman Catholic mass

Notes

CHAPTER 1: INTRODUCTION: JOURNEYING INTO NEW WORLDS OF THE DEAD

1. Stephen Mitchell. *Gilgamesh: A New English Version*. New York: The Free Press, 2004.

2. Martin Heidegger. *Being and Time*. New York: Harper, 1962, 279–304.

3. Hannah Arendt. *The Human Condition*. Chicago: University of Chicago Press, 1958, 17.

4. "Summerland: An Introduction." Wicca Chat. http://www.wicca-chat .com/gardnarianbos.htm. Accessed February 5, 2016.

5. Emanuel Swedenborg and George F. Dole. *Heaven and Hell*. New York: Swedenborg Foundation, 1984.

6. Jacques Derrida. *Aporias: Dying—Awaiting (One Another at) the "Limits of Truth" (mourir—s'attendre Aux "limites De La Vérité.")* Stanford, CA: Stanford University Press, 1993, 6–11.

7. Kevin D. O'Neill. "Death, Lives, and Video Streams." *Mortality* 13, no. 2 (2008).

8. By "death narratives" I mean the stories we generate to explain where the dead go, who they become, and what their relationship to the living means. *See God in the Machine* by Anne Foerst. On pages 13–22 of the book she defines humans as "*homo narrans*." Foerst writes (page 13), "I believe that humans are, before anything else, story-tellers." She writes further, on page 17, that "[h]umans have a need to tell stories, to make sense of the world."

On the importance of creating stories about the dead and our relationship to them, *see also* Joseph Roach, *Cities of the Dead*, and Richard Pogue Harrison, *Dominion of the Dead*. The magisterial study of the stories we tell about the dead is Philippe Aries, *Now and at the Hour*. *See also, Over Her Dead Body*, by

Elisabeth Bronfen, and *Death and Representation*, by Sarah Webster Goodwin and Elizabeth Bronfen.

    9. Stanley B. Burns. *Sleeping Beauty: Memorial Photography in America*. Altadena, CA: Twelvetrees Press, 1990.

    10. Nathaniel Hawthorne. *The House of the Seven Gables*. New York: Dodd and Mead, 1950.

    11. Elizabeth Stuart Phelps. *Beyond the Gates*. Boston: Houghton, Mifflin, 1883. *The Gates Ajar*. Cambridge: Belknap Press of Harvard University Press, 1964. *The Gates Between*. Boston: Houghton, Mifflin and Company, 1887.

    12. "Elizabeth Stuart Phelps Ward (1844–1911). Critical and Biographical Introduction." Warner et al., comp. 1917. *The Library of the World's Best Literature*. http://www.bartleby.com/library/prose/5551.html. Accessed February 5, 2016.

CHAPTER 2: BEGINNINGS: ONLINE MEMORIALIZATION AND HAUNTED SOCIAL MEDIA

    1. The world of online memorials lives *online*, therefore I invite my readers to make reading this book an interactive experience by going from the pages to a screen as they read. This is, after all, a book about Internet afterlife, and it is meant to be read with one eye on a screen. This suggestion holds good for every chapter of the book with the possible exception of Chapter Four.

The Digital Beyond offers an almost bewildering array of services to help people manage death online. Its list of online services includes nearly 60 sites that offer memorials, smartphone apps, archival sites, and email messaging sites. http://www.thedigitalbeyond.com/online-services-list/ (accessed April 26, 2016).

Some of the sites are no longer functioning—the online world is volatile—but there are many others that Digital Beyond does not list, including the Facebook-based Sanctri and imorial.com. Additionally, a site such as Legacy .com offers roughly 100 memorial sites that Legacy sets up and maintains. Some of these are memorials of public tragedies, but many are dedicated to universities, professions, military installations, and even awards such as the Oscars and Emmys. http://www.legacy.com/ns/memorial-sites/ (accessed April 26, 2016).

    2. You will see just how extensive the online world of group memorials is as you read, and even more as you explore the Internet. Google virtually any public tragedy—shootings, terrorist attacks, tornadoes, hurricanes, floods, school shootings—and you will find online memorials.

    3. The Digital Beyond has a nearly exhaustive list of memorial sites of every kind. EverPlans has almost as many links, and Legacy.com offers a plethora of online memorials that it sets up and maintains for an almost startling range of groups. Legacy also offers links to associated services, such as estate planning, funeral arrangements, and grief counseling. It offers special celebrity memorials—a service also provided by other sites. Hollywood Forever's "Library of Lives" has a stable of online celebrity memorials dedicated to the many Hollywood figures who are interred there, such as Peter Lorre, Jayne Mansfield, and Errol Flynn.

4. I again invite the reader to visit Facebook and to think of any public tragedy—even "smaller" ones such as police shootings of African American citizens—and check for memorial sites. Because Facebook groups are far easier to set up and maintain than are free-standing websites, Facebook has become home to many memorials that would not otherwise be established or maintained.

5. Rather than reproduce these messages and tributes as part of the text of this book, I invite the reader to make this a more interactive experience. Visit some of these sites and be touched, saddened, and even heartbroken by what you will find there.

6. More scholarly information about traditional American funeral customs and practices is available from the following sources.

Habenstein, Robert Wesley, and William M Lamers. *The History of American Funeral Directing*. Eighth ed. Brookfield, WI: National Funeral Directors Association, 2014.

Hoy, William G. *Do Funerals Matter? The Purposes and Practices of Death Rituals in Global Perspective*. New York: Routledge, 2013.

Laderman, Gary. *Rest in Peace: A Cultural History of Death and the Funeral Home in Twentieth-Century America*. New York: Oxford University Press, 2003.

Sloane, David Charles. *The Last Great Necessity: Cemeteries in American History*. Baltimore: Johns Hopkins University Press, 1991.

Yalom, Marilyn. *The America Resting Place: Four Hundred Years of History Through Our Cemeteries and Burial Grounds*. Boston: Houghton Mifflin, 2008.

7. *See* Margaret Wertheim, *The Pearly Gates of Cyberspace: A History of Space from Dante to the Internet*, 2000, and C. J. Sofka (1997), "Social Support 'Internetworks,' Caskets for Sale, and More: Thanatology and the Information Superhighway." *Death Studies* 21(6): 553–74.

8. For a riveting account of the intensely divisive political struggles over who would control how 9/11 is remembered, I highly recommend William Langewiesche's *American Ground: Unbuilding the World Trade Center*. New York: North Point Press, 2002.

9. Again, rather than burdening readers with the endlessly long URLs for YouTube videos, I tentatively suggest that spending a little time with this book in one hand and the other hand on a keyboard, and search YouTube for its special brand of heartbreaking memorials. There is something alternately touching and disruptive about experiencing amateur video tributes to children who have died tragically. Strictly speaking, I cannot recommend such a search, but know that it will alter the way you see the world.

10. "What Is a Facebook Memorial?" Digital Memorials. November 29, 2009. https://mediamemoryandhistory.wordpress.com/what-is-a-facebook-memorial/. Accessed January 7, 2016.

11. *See* "Ghosts in the Machine: Do the Dead Live on In Facebook?" Patrick Stokes, University of Hertfordshire, *Philosophy and Technology* (forthcoming). https://www.academia.edu/953807/Ghosts_in_the_Machine_Do_the_Dead _Live_On_in_Facebook. Accessed July 2, 2015.

12. John Dobler. "Ghosts in the Machine: Mourning the MySpace Dead." In Trevor J. Blank ed. *Folklore and the Internet: Vernacular Expression in a Digital World*. Logan, UT: Utah State University Press, 2009.

13. Carol Zaleski. *Otherworld Journeys: Accounts of Near-Death Experience in Medieval and Modern Times*. New York: Oxford University Press, 1987. This book is the most nuanced and perceptive study conducted by a scholar who is not a routine skeptic.

14. Reflecting the volatility of online sites, one well-known website of this type, DeathSwitch, recently ceased operating.

15. LivesOn has attracted a good deal of online media attention. An example can be found on the Mashable site. http://mashable.com/2013/02/26/liveson /#kCh.WZ3XUqq3. Accessed April 14, 2016.

CHAPTER 3: THE RISE OF THE AVATAR

1. Sherry Turkle. *Alone Together: Why We Expect More from Technology and Less from Each Other*. New York, NY: Basic Books, 2012.

2. Zach Waggoner. *My Avatar, My Self: Identity in Video Role-playing Games*. Jefferson, NC: McFarland, 2009.

3. *See*, for example, the websites listed below.

http://lslwiki.net/lslwiki/wakka.php?wakka=AgentAndAvatar (accessed April 14, 2015)

https://en.wikipedia.org/wiki/Automated_online_assistantCHATBOT (accessed April 13, 2015)

https://www.chatbots.org (accessed April 14, 2015)

http://mashable.com/2015/11/16/dbot-chatbot/#X509_vTkE8qa (accessed April 14, 2015)

http://www.computerworld.com/article/3018162/emerging-technology/the-dark-side-of-the -coming-chatbot-revolution.html (accessed April 14, 2015)

These sites define "chatbot," and the chatbot.org site provides information about how a person can create his or her own chatbot. The *Mashable* and *Computer World* pieces warn against possible future problems with these AI interactive "personal assistants." On what these are, consult the Wikipedia reference concerning "Automated online assistant."

To learn about the Apple chatbot, Siri, and the Windows version, Cortana, the reader can also consult the following sites.

http://www.imore.com/siri (accessed April 26, 2016)

http://www.apple.com/ios/siri/ (accessed April 14, 2015)

http://windows.microsoft.com/en-us/windows-10/getstarted-what-is-cortana   (accessed April 14, 2015)

Google is developing an automated online assistant, *see* http://www .businessinsider.com/google-tests-new-artificial-intelligence-chatbot-2015-6 (accessed April 14, 2015); and the IKEA furniture store chain has had its chatbot, Anna, for some time, *see* https://www.chatbots.org/virtual_assistant/anna _sweden/ (accessed April 14, 2015).

4. The concept of cyberspace as a virtual world created by computer networks, which has its own continuous landscapes and into which one literally and figuratively can disappear, first appeared in memorable ways in the work of Vernor Vinge (*True Names*) and in that of the cyberpunk cultural icon William Gibson, whose *Neuromancer*, originally published in 1984, made both the concept of cyberspace and that of the "matrix" as a parallel virtual world, part of our shared culture. Gibson's famous description of "cyberspace" is worth citing.

Cyberspace. A consensual hallucination experienced daily by billions of legitimate operators, in every nation, by children being taught mathematical concepts. . . . A graphic representation of data abstracted from banks of every computer in the human system. Unthinkable complexity. Lines of light ranged in the nonspace of the mind, clusters and constellations of data. Like city lights, receding. (*Neuromancer*, p. 49).

Gibson defines the matrix in virtually the same way. *Neuromancer,* p. 3. The protagonist, Case, spent his youth "jacked into a custom cyberspace deck that projected his disembodied consciousness into the consensual hallucination that was the matrix."

5. William Gibson. *Neuromancer*. London: Harper Voyager, 2013.

6. Neal Stephenson. *Snow Crash*. New York: Bantam Books, 2000.

7. It is a tribute to the creative vitality and multiplicity of the cyberworld that there does not seem to be any direct causal influence between *Neuromancer* and *The Matrix*, even though both use the term "matrix" and both tell dark stories about "consensual hallucination."

8. The Dixie Flatliner (a.k.a. McCoy Pauley) is the first example of Internet afterlife. This friend of Case's is kept alive as a ROM by Sense/Net, for his specialized hacker knowledge. Dixie hates his condition, because he is about nothing but the past and even though he seems human, he really is not. He is a digital being without genuine sentience. *See*, e.g., *Neuromancer*, at p. 129. Dixie's plight is poignantly captured on page 103.

"I'm dead, Case."
"How's it feel?"
"It doesn't."
"Bother you?"
"What bothers me is, nothin' does."

9. Online computer games have been a part of our lives since the 1970s. As they developed better graphics, players could see themselves represented by progressively more lifelike avatars, which, depending on the game, could be adapted more closely to what one wished the avatar to be.

There are now avatars in console games—such as Wii, Xbox, and Sony PlayStation—as well as avatars in online MMORPGs (Massively multi-player online role playing game), and in MMOs in general (Massively multi-player online game), including first-person shooter and quest games.

Academics have studied online games for years. Classic studies such as Sherry Turkle's *Life on the Screen* (1997) and Janet Murray's *Hamlet and the*

Holodeck (1997) are supplemented today, for example, by the important contributions of Pat Harrigan and Noah Wardrup-Fruin (*First Person: New Media As Story, Performance, and Game* (2006), *Second Person: Role-Playing and Story in Games and Playable Media* (2010), and *Third Person: Authoring and Exploring Vast Narratives* (2009)), among many others.

Technoself studies, an interesting sub-field, has developed around the question of what happens to our identities when we replicate ourselves in virtual online worlds. *See,* e.g., Rocci Luppicini, *Handbook of Research on Technoself: Identity in a Technological Society* (2 vols.). Ottawa: University of Ottawa, 2013.

10. Second Life is the most well-known, but certainly not the only, alternative non-gaming online world. For information about joining Second Life, visit http://secondlife.com/?utm_source=Bing&utm_medium=texteng&utm_term=Branded&utm_content=2ndLifeGeneral&utm_campaign=SecondLifeVirtualWorldBuy (accessed January 15, 2016). Other, less-developed "worlds" include Kitely, Cloud Party, and There, Inc.—none of which use the open source software developed by Linden Labs, the company that created Second Life. Sites that share the Linden software include, among others, OSGrid and Virtual Highway. All of these links are available at http://www.answers.com/Q/What_are_websites_like_second_life (accessed January 15, 2016).

Avatars are absolutely essential to alternate-world sites because on such sites everyone that a user meets takes the form of an agent avatar—that is, of an avatar directly representing an autonomous subject.

11. Chalmers's initial discussion of this famous and controversial concept can be found in Chalmers's 1996 work, *The Conscious Mind*, p. 104.

We make use of one version of his idea, namely that of a "behavioral zombie." The idea here is that the virtual being acts like a human but is not a biological entity. Chalmers's zombie generally is seen as a biological being. For the idea of a behavioral zombie, see, for example, http://www.funnelbrain.com/c-1034884-behavioral-zombie.html (accessed October 15, 2015).

12. To see what the transhumanists believe, see Chapter Five of this book, which includes an outline of transhumanist beliefs as well as many references to useful sources on transhumanism.

As a quick reference, one can do worse than consult "The Transhumanist FAQ 3.0," available online in its entirety at http://humanityplus.org/philosophy/transhumanist-faq/ (accessed August 8, 2015). This is a collective document written and rewritten over the past two decades by successive generations of transhumanist thinkers. The FAQ originally was associated with Max More's Extropy Institute in the early 1990s. It migrated to the WTA (World Transhumanist Association) in 1998. That organization later changed its name to humanity+, under whose aegis the Transhumanist FAQ, 3.0, is published and maintained.

One could also look at "A History of Transhumanist Thought," published in its entirety online at http://www.nickbostrom.com/papers/history.pdf (accessed August 11, 2015).

13. *See,* e.g., Christopher Hugh Partridge, *Introduction to World Religions*, p. 148, at Books.Google.com. *See also* Stephen Prothero, *God Is Not One: The Eight Rival Religions That Run the World*, p. 174.

For a use of the word "avatar" by someone who believes in such entities, *see* Nicholas Russell, *A Crash Course in Spirituality—Book 1: Welcome to the Spiritual Path* (2012).

14. Garriott originally used the word "avatar" to describe his game agent to remind players that the avatars represented real-life individuals who should follow moral codes. Incidentally, Garriott was the person who in 1997 coined the MMORPG to replace the less appealing MMO designation.

15. The best study of this identification between game players and their avatars is Zach Waggoner, *My Avatar, My Self: Identity in Video Role-Playing Games* (2009). *See also* Jesper Juul, *Half-Real: Video Games Between Real Rules and Fictional Worlds* (2011).

16. There is no settled nomenclature for the different kinds of game, instant message, and virtual world avatars. I use "first-person avatars" to mean virtual entities that are directly moved by autonomous subjects. I use "native avatars" or "agent" avatars to mean virtual entities whose moves are controlled by the software that runs the game or the virtual world or the instant messaging environment.

There are two levels of such embodied agents. The entities that players encounter and must contend with in video games—police and enemy soldiers—are embodied agents who are only minimally interactive. Intelligent embodied agents, or conversational/autonomous embodied agents, are computer-generated entities that appear to be human in that they adapt to circumstances, learn, and change.

For a discussion of the difference between first-person avatars and computer-created agents, *see*, for example, Celso M. De Melo, Peter J. Carnevale, and Jonathan Gratch, "Agent or Avatar? Using Virtual Confederates in Conflict Management Research." University of Southern California–Marshall School of Business, Institute for Creative Technologies (USC). Available at ict.usc.edu /pubs/Agent%20or%20Avatar%20Using%20Virtual%20Confederates%20 in%20Conflict%20Management%20Research.pdf (accessed April 14, 2016).

See also https://www.chatbots.org/avatar/ for a rough-and ready definition and http://intelligent.software.informer.com/download-intelligent-avatar/ (accessed January 11, 2016), where you can download intelligent avatar programs.

The USC site makes clear how murky avatar nomenclature remains.

17. To see what this service offers, go to http://eterni.me, and to sign up if you are moved to do so. *See also* http://www.cnet.com/news/eterni-me-lets-you -skype-with-the-dead/#! and http://www.nbcnews.com/technology/unlively-chat -skype-dead-eterni-me-2D12024238 (accessed February 1, 2016), *inter alia*, for discussion of the site and its services.

18. The original Intellitar site is dormant, as is the virtualeternty.com site. For skeptical reviews from 2010, *see* http://www.cnet.com/news/intellitar-ava tars-a-poor-substitute-for-afterlife/#! and http://www.popsci.com/technology /article/2010-10/intellitar-provides-digital-clone-creep-out-future-generations (accessed November 27, 2015). *See also* the 2007 report, available at http:// abcnews.go.com/icaught/Story?id=3421980&page=1&nfo=/desktop_newsfeed _ab_refer_homepage (accessed November 27, 2015).

19. For a description of what this software intends, *see* http://research
.microsoft.com/apps/pubs/default.aspx?id=64157 (accessed December 5, 2015).
See also Total Recall, especially the prescient Chapter Seven, "Everyday Life and
Afterlife," pp. 137–56, in which Gemmell and Bell reject the possibility of genuine Internet afterlife. They do however argue that replicas of the dead are a
plausible option and a likelihood in the near future.

20. The avatar prototypes that ICT is developing as well as its research projects can be found at http://ict.usc.edu (accessed December 12, 2015).

21. For a detailed discussion of this program, *see* http://ict.usc.edu/proto
types/pts/ (accessed December 12, 2015).

22. Please see http://ict.usc.edu/news/new-dimensions-in-testimony-project
-and-ict-research-featured-in-australias-saturday-paper/ (accessed   December
18, 2015).

See, e.g., http://www.huffingtonpost.com/2013/02/02/holocaust-holograms-
survivors-usc_n_2606718.html (accessed December 18, 2015); http://www
.today.com/series/are-we-there-yet/holograms-add-new-dimension-holocaust
-survivors-story-t20511 (accessed December 19, 2015), https://video.search.ya
hoo.com/search/video;_ylt=AwrTHQ_g.dBWT2gAAQ1XNyoA;_ylu=X3oD
MTEydmluZGpyBGNvbG8DZ3ExBHBvcwMxBHZ0aWQDQjExNzhfMQRz
ZWMDc2M-?p=Pinchas+Gutter+Hologram+Youtube&fr=aaplw#id=1&vid=1
8381b1eb66d3dee5f2bc5191407fa21&action=view (accessed   December   20,
2015). For more information visit the Shoah Foundation site at USC.

23. I use extended hypothetical thought experiments here because there is
very little written about what the experience of interacting with replicas of the
dead would entail. This is, as far as I know, the first and only book to think
through the implications of such meetings on a practical level.

24. An excellent overview and history of the concept of the Uncanny Valley
can be found at http://tvtropes.org/pmwiki/pmwiki.php/Main/UncannyValley
(accessed August 29, 2015).

For the "Yuck Factor," *see* https://www.newscientist.com/article/mg21528731
-800-the-yuck-factor-the-surprising-power-of-disgust/ (accessed August 29, 2015).

25. As of this writing, the entire "Be Right Back" episode is available on
YouTube at https://search.yahoo.com/search?ei=utf-8&fr=aaplw&p=%22Be+
Right+Back%22+youtube (accessed July 11, 2015). Comments and reviews for
the show can be found at http://www.avclub.com/tvclub/berighback106152 (ac-
cessed July 11, 2015). *See also* http://www.imdb.com/title/tt2290780/ (accessed
July 11, 2015) for cast, plot summary, and user reviews.

CHAPTER 4: CAN THE MIND BE PORTABLE? THEORIES
OF MIND FROM PLATO TO TURING

1. Homer and Richmond Lattimore. *The Odyssey of Homer.* New York:
Harper & Row, 1967, Book 11. E. R. Dodds. *The Greeks and the Irrational.*
Berkeley, CA: University of California Press, 2004.

2. Peter Kingsley. *In the Dark Places of Wisdom.* Inverness, CA: Golden Sufi
Center, 1999.

3. Plato, Benjamin Jowett, and Justin Kaplan. *Dialogues of Plato.* New York: Pocket Books, 1951.

4. Plato. *Phaedo*, 73c–75c.

5. John Cottingham. *Rene Descartes: Meditations on First Philosophy.* Meditation Two. Cambridge, UK: Cambridge University Press, 2015.

6. John Locke. *An Essay Concerning Human Understanding.* Part II, Chapter 27, Of Identity and Diversity. Section 9, Personal Identity. New York: Dover Publications, 1959, 286–87.

7. Homer. *The Odyssey of Homer*, translated by Richmond Lattimore. New York: Harper and Row, 1967, Book 18, line 416 ff.

8. Jewish Virtual Library. "Golem." https://www.jewishvirtuallibrary.org /jsource/Judaism/Golem.html. Accessed February 7, 2016. Leonora Cohen Rosenfield. *From Beast-Machine to Man-Machine; Animal Soul in French Letters from Descartes to La Mettrie.* New York: Octagon Books, 1968.

9. Radiolab Podcast Articles. "A Clockwork Miracle." http://www.radiolab .org/story/140632-clockwork-miracle/. Accessed February 7, 2016. Gaby Wood. *Living Dolls: A Magical History of the Quest for Mechanical Life.* London: Faber and Faber, 2002.

10. *History of Computers and Computing.* "Jacques de Vaucanson." http:// history-computer.com/Dreamers/Vaucanson.html. Accessed February 7, 2016.

11. Computer History Museum. "The Babbage Engine." http://www.com puterhistory.org/babbage/. Accessed February 7, 2016.

12. Alan M. Turing. "Computing Machinery and Intelligence." *Parsing the Turing Test*, 2009. doi: 10.1007/978-1-4020-6710-5_3.

13. Home Page of the Loebner Prize. http://www.loebner.net/Prizef/loebner -prize.html. Accessed February 7, 2016.

CHAPTER 5: MOVING MINDS: TRANSHUMANISM AND THE PATH TO INTERNET AFTERLIFE

1. Max More. "On Becoming Posthuman." *Free Inquiry*, Fall 1994.

2. Yuval Noah Harari. *Sapiens: A Brief History of Humankind.* New York: Harper, 2015.

3. David Christian. *Big History. The Big Bang, Life on Earth, and the Rise of Humanity.* Chantilly, VA: Teaching, 2008.

4. Richard Dawkins. *The Selfish Gene.* Oxford: Oxford University Press, 1989.

5. Galen Strawson. "*Sapiens: A Brief History of Humankind* by Yuval Noah Harari—Review." *The Guardian.* September 11, 2014. http://www.theguardian .com/books/2014/sep/11/sapiens-brief-history-humankind-yuval-noah-harari- review. Accessed February 17, 2016.

6. The modern use of the terms "transhumanism" usually is traced to a passage in Julian Huxley's remarks in *New Bottles for New Wine*, published in 1957. In that book, Huxley writes:

I believe in transhumanism: once there are enough people who can truly say that, the human species will be on the threshold of a new kind of existence, as different from ours as ours is from that of Peking man. It will at last be consciously fulfilling its real destiny.

He discusses transhumanism from page 13 to page 17. *See* http://www.hux ley.net/transhumanism/ (accessed March 7, 2015).

F. M. Esfendiary, who changed his name to FM-2030, was one of the earliest intellectuals who built his public career around the themes of transhumanism. He identified himself as a futurist in the 1970s, and in 1989 published *Are You a Transhuman?*

7. Aubrey de Grey and Michael Rae. *Ending Aging: The Rejuvenation Breakthroughs that Could Reverse Human Aging in Our Lifetime.* New York: St. Martin's Press, 2007. *See also* https://www.ted.com/talks/aubrey_de_grey _says_we_can_avoid_aging?language=en (accessed February 23, 2015).

8. http://www.cryonics.org (accessed February 23, 2015).

9. If the reader would like a rough-and-ready introduction to the major transhumanist writers, please refer to the following sources.

Books

Bostrom, Nick. *Superintelligence: Paths, Dangers, Strategies.* Oxford: Oxford University Press, 2014.

Clark, Andy. *Natural-Born Cyborgs: Minds, Technologies, and the Future of Human Intelligence.* Oxford: Oxford University Press, 2003.

Hansell, Gregory R., and William Grassie, eds. *H+/-: Transhumanism and Its Critics.* Xlibris Corporation, 2011.

Hayles, N. Katherine. *How We Became Posthuman: Virtual Bodies in Cybernetics, Literature, and Informatics.* Chicago: University of Chicago Press, 1999.

Kurzweil, Ray. *The Age of Spiritual Machines.* New York: Viking, 1999.

More, Max, and Natasha Vita-More, eds. *The Transhumanist Reader.* Malden, MA: Wiley-Blackwell, 2013.

YouTube Videos

Bostrom, Nick: https://www.youtube.com/watch?v=P0Nf3TcMiHo (accessed December 19, 2014)

Case, Amber: https://www.youtube.com/watch?v=z1KJAXM3xYA (accessed September 1, 2015)

Kurzweil, Ray: https://www.youtube.com/watch?v=RIkxVci-R4k (accessed December 15, 2014)

Sosa, Jason: https://www.youtube.com/watch?v=1Ugo2KEV2XQ (accessed February 8, 2016)

Vita-More, Natasha: https://www.youtube.com/watch?v=8LucitzhNQ8 February 28, 2016

Readers also can refer to the Metanexus Institute (http://www.metanexus .net/about-metanexus-institute [accessed January 2, 2016]) and the H+ online journal site (http://hplusmagazine.com [accessed January 2, 2016]).

10. David Chalmers. "Mind Uploading: A Philosophical Analysis." In Russell Blackford and Damien Broderick, eds. *Intelligence Unbound: The Future of Uploaded and Machine Minds*. Malden, MA: Wiley, 2014, 102–18.

11. Randal Koene is the most vocal proponent of Whole Brain Emulation (WBE). His website, "Carboncopies," at http://www.carboncopies.org (accessed January 10, 2016), collects essays and other materials dealing with WBE.

CHAPTER 6: MARTINE ROTHBLATT AND THE VIRTUALLY HUMAN

1. Martine Rothblatt. *Virtually Human: The Promise—and the Peril—of Digital Afterlife*. New York: St. Martin's Press, 2014, 3, 307 (hereinafter referred to as "*VH*").

2. *VH*, 3, 306.

3. Sebastian Seung. *Connectome: How the Brain's Wiring Makes Us Who We Are*. Boston: Houghton Mifflin Harcourt, 2012.

4. *VH*, 13.

5. *VH*, 15.

6. *VH*, 14.

7. *VH*, 15.

8. *VH*, 69–72.

9. *VH*, 88–89.

10. *VH*, 285.

11. *VH*, 89.

12. *VH*, 83–84.

13. *VH*, 84–85.

14. *VH*, 84–85.

15. *VH*, 84.

16. *VH*, 33.

17. *VH*, 264ff.

18. *VH*, 265.

19. *VH*, 265.

20. *VH*, 276.

CHAPTER 7: THE TRUTHS OF TERASEM

1. Martine Rothblatt. *Virtually Human: The Promise—and the Peril—of Digital Afterlife*. New York: St. Martin's Press, 2014, 305 (hereinafter referred to as "*VH*").

2. Max More. "The Extropian Principles (Version 3.0): A Transhumanist Declaration." Extropy Institute, 1998. Max More first coined the term in the mid-1980s. His Extropy Institute closed in 2006, declaring that its work was done. The Extropy Institute was been followed by the World Transhumanist Association, which recently renamed itself as Humanity+. The "Extropist Manifesto" was written by Breki Tomasson and Hank Pellissier and published online in January 2010.

3. The Danish transhumanist philosopher Nick Bostrom published this piece in 2001. A complete copy can be found at: http://www.humanscience.org/docs /Bostrom%20(2001)%20Are%20You%20Living%20in%20a%20 Computer%20Simulation.pdf (accessed March 7, 2015).

4. The term "the Singularity" first was used in this manner in 1993 by the futurist and cyberpunk author Vernor Vinge. Kurzweil appropriated the term in his 2006 book, *The Singularity Is Near*, attributing the idea to John von Neuman and I. J. Good. Kurzweil predicts that by the year 2045 human life will change forever when we have created the technology able to produce levels of intelligence that will make the biological body both unnecessary and a burden.

5. *VH*, 265.

6. *VH*, 265.

7. *VH*, 275.

8. *VH*, 276.

9. This Czech opera was written by Janacek, based on a play by Karl Capek. It was first produced in 1926. As an interesting and ironic side note, Karl Capek was the person who in 1920 first introduced the word and the concept of "robot," in his play *R.U.R.*

10. Rudolph Otto wrote about the religious phenomenon of the "*numen*"— "the holy"—emphasizing God's complete *otherness*, and Karl Barth's "*totaliter aliter*," which means "wholly other." The phrasing is from St. Augustine's *Confessions*.

CHAPTER 8: DMITRY ITSKOV AND THE IMMORTALITY BUTTON

1. David Segal. "This Man Is Not a Cyborg. Yet." *The New York Times*, June 1, 2013. *See also* "About Us." on 2045.com (accessed October 16, 2015).

2. David Segal. "This Man Is Not a Cyborg. Yet." *The New York Times*, June 1, 2013. George Dvorsky. "The Russian Eccentric Who Wants to Make Surrogates a Reality." *GIZMODO*, June 3, 2013. Bianca Bosker. "Dmitry Itskov Knows that He'll Live Forever: Here's How He's Living Now." *Huffington Tech*, June 18, 2013.

3. *See* Teihard de Chardin. *The Phenomenon of Man*. New York: Harper Perennial, 1959. *See also* Dmitry Itskov's talk, "The Path to Neo-humanity as the Foundation of the Ideology of the 'Evolution 2045' Party" (http://2045.com /articles /30869/html), where Itskov does state that "the ability to unite in a collective gigantic mind, the noosphere," will be a defining characteristic of what he calls "neo-humanity." How this plays out is discussed in chapter nine.

4. Itskov had several religious figures speak at the GF 2045 Conference in New York City, including Swami Vishnudevananda Giri Ji Maharaj, Mahayogi "Pilot" Baba, Rabbi Alan Brill, and retired Orthodox Archbishop Lazar Puholo. Itskov posted on the 2045.com website a discussion of his meeting with the Dalai Lama, but it is unclear how much support the Dalai Lama offered to Itskov's movement. What he says about the steps of neo-humanity is presented in chapter nine.

5. Itskov mentions this problem in more than one place. The analysis figures into his "Russian Experience" talk (http://2045.com/articles /2910.html [accessed December 9, 2015]), from which this quote was taken, and also in the "Path" talk mentioned above, as well as in his call to arms, "Fellow Immortalists!" (http://2045.com/news/33999.html [accessed December 11, 2015]).

6. Itskov. "Russian Experience," p. 7.

7. Itskov's near-Gnostic suspicion of the body is noted by those who write about him and interview him. Bosker and Segal note his personal asceticism. Michelle Ealey, in her 2013 "Exclusive Interview with Dmitry Itskov, Founder of Global Future 2045" for *SF*, as well as Andrew Couts in his article, "How One Russian Millionaire Wants to Save the World with Immortal Cyborgs," published by *DigitalTrends* in March 2013, however, cite Itskov's passion to rid people of their biological bodies.

8. In the "Ideology" essay, Itskov writes that who we really are—conscious minds—"will inevitably begin to come into conflict with the limited protein-based carrier—the biological body."

9. The term "ideological paradigm" crops up in virtually everything Itskov writes. He means that we need to redirect our collective energies away from short-sighted self-satisfaction and toward larger goals, which seem focused on defeating death by devising ways to replace the "meat" body.

10. Immortality Button, Slide 2, "The 2045 Initiative Solution."

11. *See* Andre Breton, *Nadja*; and Jean-Paul Sartre, *No Exit* and *Nausea*. Also worth examining is Albert Camus, *The Stranger* and *The Myth of Sisyphus*.

12. Sigmund Freud. *Beyond the Pleasure Principle*. London, Vienna: International Psycho-Analytical, 1922. Freud argues that there is something in human awareness deeper than Eros, which is the drive for pleasure. This is the desire for rest, for cessation, that haunts every living being, if only because the business of living is so taxing.

13. The text of this letter is available at http://2045.com/articles/30158.html (accessed December 23, 2015).

14. The text of this letter is available at http://gf2045.com/read/209/ (accessed December 23, 2015).

15. *See* http://motherboard.vice.com/blog/russian-billionaire-dmitry-itskov -plans-on-becoming-immortal-by-2045 (accessed December 24, 2015).

16. *See* http://www.prnewswire.com/news-releases/steven-seagal-asks-for -russian-pm-vladimir-putins-support-in-immortality-research-121948323.html (accessed April 23, 2015).

17. These films are discussed at length in the analysis of Itskov's vision, and in chapter ten when we take up objections to transhumanist proposals. Itskov understands that James Cameron's movie *Avatar* uses the idea of an avatar in a somewhat different sense than Itskov uses it, and he also appreciates that *Surrogates* takes a distinctly dim view of what Itskov calls Avatar A, but neither the differences nor the skepticism with regard to avatars discourages Itskov in the least. As David Segal wrote in his *New York Times* piece, "This Man Is Not a Cyborg. Yet." *The New York Times*, June 1, 2013. Itskov perhaps is the world's "most ambitious utopian."

18. The Defense Advanced Research Projects Agency (DARPA), the U.S. Department of Defense's robotic research arm, calls its program to develop surrogate soldiers the "Avatar Project."

19. Immortality Button, Slide 5. Most versions of this stage of the Avatar Project postulate that we will transplant the *brain*, rather than the entire head, but in this version of the project Itskov calls for complete head transplantation.

20. The video "Two Headed Dogs Demikhov Shocking Experiment Footage," is available at https://www.bing.com/videos/search?q=demikhov's+dog&view=detail&mid=EC3C12763419E8FA9527EC3C12763419E8FA9527&FORM=VIRE2. *See* Demikhov's obituary at nytimes.com/1998/11/25/world/vladimir-p-demikhov-82-pioneer-in-transplants-dies.html (accessed January 1, 2016). For information about Dr. Robert White, an American who experimented with transplanting monkey heads, *see* http://motherboard.vice.com/blog/dr-robert-white-transplanted-first-monkey-head (accessed January 1, 2016).

21. *See* the Avatar Project diagram on the main 2045.com website. There are two different versions of the diagram but they agree in listing four Avatars.

22. For details on this concept, *see* http://usatoday30.usatoday.com/tech/news/robotics/2005-04-07-ants-nasa_x.htm (accessed April 26, 2016) and http://motherboard.vice.com/read/why-the-us-military-is-funding-tiny-autonomous-flying-robots (accessed January 7, 2016).

23. Immortality Button, Slide 8, "Select Your Avatar Requirements."

24. For further reading on Itskov and related issues, some suggested resources are listed below.

Baele, Yannick. "Archives Mensuelles: Mai 2013." *Mai.* n.p. May 20, 2013.

Bennetts, Marc. "Seuls Les Riches Seront Immortels." *Vid.me.* n.p. October 24, 2014.

Borghino, Dario. " 'Avatar' Project Aims for Human Immortality by 2045." *Gizmag*, July 25, 2012.

Bosker, Bianca. "Dmitry Itskov Knows He'll Live Forever; Here's How He's Living Now." *The Huffington Post.* n.p. July 22, 2013.

Corbyn, Zoe. "Live Forever: Scientists Say They'll Soon Extend Life Well Beyond 120." *The Guardian.* n.p. January 11, 2015.

Couts, Andrew. "How One Russian Millionaire Wants to Save the World . . . with Immortal Cyborgs." *Digital Trends.* n.p. March 28, 2013.

Couts, Andrew. "Land of the God-Men: Inside the Wild Movement to Turn Us into Immortal Cyborgs." *Digital Trends.* n.p. June 20, 2013.

Dambrot, Stuart Mason. "The World According to Itskov: Futurists Convene at GF2045 (Part 2)." Phys.org. August 1, 2013.

"Dmitry Itskov on the Philosophy of Immortality." *YouTube.* n.p. June 19, 2013.

"Dmitry Itskov Wants to Live Forever." *Forbes Magazine.* June 19, 2013.

Drummond, Katie. "Russian Mogul's Plan: Plant Our Brains in Robots, Keep Them Alive Forever." *Wired.com.* Conde Nast Digital. February 29, 2012.

Dvorsky, George. "The Russian Eccentric Who Wants to Make Surrogates a Reality." *Io9.* Gizmodo, June 3, 2013.

Ealey, Michelle. "Exclusive Interview with Dmitry Itskov, Founder of Global Future 2045." ScienceFiction.com RSS (n.d.): n.p.

Isaacson, Betsy. "The Men Who Would Cure Death." *Newsweek*. n.p. March 13, 2015.

Kavoussi, Bonnie. "Dmitry Itskov, Russian Billionaire, Plans Immortality Research Center." *Huffington Post*. August 28, 2012.

Koene, Randal A. "A Review of the 2013 Congress in New York City." 2045 Initiative. October 1, 2013.

Kumar, Niraj. "Hologram Avatar and Rainbow Bodies." *Society for Asian Integration* (n.d.): n.p.

Lewis, Tanya. "The Singularity Is Near: Mind Uploading by 2045?" *Yahoo! News*. Yahoo! June 17, 2013.

"The Madness of Dmitry Itskov." *Cryptogoncom* RSS. n.p. February 29, 2012.

Pachal, Pete. "Russian Billionaire Wants to Create Cyborgs for Real." *Mashable*. n.p. Apr. 1, 2013.

Paquette, Emmanuel. "*Ces Milliardaires Qui Rêvent D'acheter L'immortalité.*" *Sciences*. n.p. January 13, 2014.

Pisani, Bob. "Immortality by 2035?" *CNBC*. n.p. June 14, 2013.

Regalado, Antonio. "So, You Wanna Be an Android?" *MIT Technology Review*. n.p., June 18, 2013.

CHAPTER 9: ITSKOV AND NEO-HUMANITY

1. This can be viewed on the 2045 website, Slide 10. http://2045.com/articles/29105.html. Accessed April 14, 2016.

2. Dmitry Itskov. "Russian Experience," p. 7.

3. Ibid.

4. I researched this information from a variety of online sites, including those listed below.

http://data.worldbank.org/indicator/IS.VEH.NVEH.P3 (accessed December 11, 2015)

http://www.autoblog.com/2014/03/12/who-can-afford-the-average-car-price-only-folks-in-washington/ (accessed December 11, 2015)

http://www.carwale.com/tata-cars/ (accessed December 11, 2015)

http://www.vtpi.org/tca/tca0501.pdf (accessed December 11, 2015)

https://www.truecar.com/car-cost (accessed December 11, 2015)

http://www.zigwheels.com/newcars/Tata (accessed December 11, 2015)

5. Itskov. "The Russian Experience," p. 7. Itskov does not specify which non-fossil fuel sources he means. For some speculation on near-future new energy sources, and also on possible new battery technologies, which will be important for powering avatars, please visit the following websites.

http://cleantechnica.com/2015/05/15/new-battery-technology-will-fundamentally-change-the-way-the-grid-operates/ (accessed December 16, 2015)

http://www.alternative-energy-news.info/technology/future-energy/ (accessed December 16, 2015)

http://www.scientificamerican.com/report/alt-energy/ (accessed December 16, 2015)

6. Itskov. "The Russian Experience," p. 7.

7. Ibid. Itskov does not name the studies that find that only 2 percent of people accept death, and his single anecdote is a thin scaffolding on which to hang a large claim—that death is not natural—on which the plausibility of much of his vision depends. But as I wrote earlier, Itskov is not a moderate thinker.

8. *See* Sigmund Freud. 1915. "Thoughts for the Times on War and Death." http://panarchy.org/freudl/war.1915.htm (accessed July 1, 2014).

9. Martin Heidegger. *Being and Time.* "Division Two, Dasein and Temporality," nos. 46–53, p. 279–311. For more on this topic, *see also* Ernest Becker's book, *The Denial of Death* (1997), and Geoffrey Gorer's famous article, "The Pornography of Death" (1955). https://www.unz.org/Pub/Encounter -1955oct-00049 (accessed November 22, 2014).

10. *See* Eric Steinhart, *Your Digital Afterlives*; and Martine Rothblatt, *Truths of Terasem.* Steinhart is an invigorating—if unnerving—philosopher who, as far as I can tell, is the individual who has extended Rothblatt's ideas about transforming the real into the virtual into a complete, detailed metaphysics that he calls "digitalism." Steinhart seems to work at the conceptual edge of transhumanism. He is not often mentioned, but I predict that his comprehensive vision of an endlessly self-perfecting machine/virtual universe will receive more recognition and will flesh out Itskov's and Rothblatt's practical but relatively underdeveloped theories. Steinhart is a challenging read but is very much worth the effort.

11. Itskov. "Russian Experience," p. 7.

12. The pros and cons of mind uploading, which apply in Itskov's case, have been touched on in the discussion of transhumanism in chapter five and are revisited in chapter ten. For further clarification, however, readers might wish to consult the following sources.

The pro-mind uploading thinkers include Marvin Minsky (*The Emotion Machine,* 2006), Hans Moravec (*Mind Children,* 1988), Michio Kaku (*The Future of the Mind,* 2014), and of course Randal A. Koene. Koene is affiliated with Itskov's 2045 Initiative, published a review of the GF2045 Conference, and maintains the most active mind-uploading website, that of his nonprofit foundation, carboncopies.org, which is an ongoing source of information about developments in the field.

The con side of the mind-uploading argument, which is sketched out in Chapter Ten, is nicely represented by the thinking of Kenneth D. Miller, whose short but precise piece in the *New York Times* summarizes the case well. *See* "Will You Ever Be Able to Upload Your Mind?" http://www.nytimes .com/2015/10/11/opinion/sunday/will-you-ever-be-able-to-upload-your-brain .html?_r=0 (accessed January 23, 2016). Of course, Itskov's response to this objection has nothing to do with either side of the argument, even though Randal A. Koene—one of the world's most outspoken proponents of Whole Brain Emulation, and the person who wrote the most detailed proposal for mind uploading—is Itskov's chief science officer for the 2045 Initiative. But, as Itskov himself says, he is neither philosopher nor scientist.

13. For an overview of this issue, see the *Stanford Encyclopedia of Philosophy* http://plato.stanford.edu/entries/induction-problem/ (accessed January 22, 2016);

https://www.princeton.edu/~grosen/puc/phi203/induction.html (accessed January 22, 2016); and https://www.youtube.com/watch?v=sd8cxXfPJU4 (accessed January 22, 2016).

14. The original version of the Chinese Room idea is sometimes traced back to Gottfried Leibniz' mill analogy in his *Monadology*, Section 17 (GP VI, 609/AG 215). John Searle's modern iteration appeared in a 1980 issue of *Behavioral and Brain Sciences* under the title, "Minds, Brains, and Programs." For summaries and commentary on the original argument, *see*, *inter alia*, http://plato.stanford.edu/entries/chinese-room (accessed February 10, 2016); and http://www.mind.ilstu.edu/curriculum/searle_chinese_room_chinese_room.php (accessed February 10, 2016).

15. This issue is referenced elsewhere, especially in chapter six, but the issue is first broached in Chalmers's 1996 publication, *The Conscious Mind: In Search of a Fundamental Theory*, and in his 1995 paper "Facing Up to the Problem of Consciousness."

16. Itskov. "Russian Experience," at p. 8.

17. Leading transhumanists such as Anders Sandberg and Nick Bostrom write extensively about the importance of building a moral compass into our future, superintelligent machine-bodied selves. *See*, e.g., http://www.nickbostrom.com/ethics/transhumanist.pdf (accessed January 3, 2016), in which Bostrom discusses transhumanist ethics, and http://www.tandfonline.com/doi/full/10.1080/0952813X.2014.895113#.VtTklcfS4dU (accessed January 3, 2016), in which Sandberg writes about "The Ethics of Brain Emulation."

18. Itskov. "Russian Experience," at p. 8.

19. "The path to neo-Humanity as the foundation of the ideology of the 'Evolution 2045' party." http://2045.com/articles/30869.html (accessed March 17, 2016). Slide 12 is titled, "The Goals of Neohumanity in the Third Millennium."

20. *See* http://www.kurzweilai.net/the-law-of-accelerating-returns (accessed April 26, 2016).

21. The possibilities and the perils of exponentially developing superintelligence are a central issue in the whole transhumanist project, but one which, again, Itskov is aware of but seems to think will work itself out. For discussions of what superintelligence might mean, for good or ill, see, for example, the list provided below.

Barrat, James. *Our Final Invention: Artificial Intelligence and the End of the Human Era.* New York: Thomas Dunne Books, 2013.

Blackford, Russell, and Damien Broderick. *Intelligence Unbound: The Future of Uploaded and Machine Minds.* Chichester, UK: John Wiley and Sons, 2014.

Bostrom, Nick. *Superintelligence: The Coming Machine Intelligence Revolution.* Oxford: Oxford University Press, 2013.

Brain, Marshall. *The Second Intelligent Species: How Humans Will Become as Irrelevant as Cockroaches.* Cary, NC: BYG Publishing, 2015.

Grossman, Lev. "2045: The Year Man Becomes Immortal." *Time.* February 10, 2011. http://content.time.com/time/magazine/article/0,9171,2048299,00.html. Accessed March 7, 2015.

Kurzweil, Raymond. *The Age of Spiritual Machines: When Computers Exceed Human Intelligence.* New York: Penguin Books, 2000.

22. See the website for Oculus equipment at https://www.oculus.com/en-us/ (accessed August 25, 2015). For a more detailed story and assessment, *see* http://www.wired.com/2014/05/oculus-rift-4/ (accessed August 25, 2015).

23. Itskov. "Russian Experience," Slide 12.

24. For a substantive discussion of Baudrillard's idea, which deserves more attention than it has been afforded in discussions of transhumanism to this point, *see* http://web.stanford.edu/class/history34q/readings/Baudrillard/Baudrillard _Simulacra.html (accessed December 1, 2013). *See also* Baudrillard's two classics, "*Simulacra and Simulation,*" and "*Symbolic Exchange and Death.*"

25. For discussions of Rand's individualism and objectivism, see http://ayn randlexicon.com/lexicon/individualism.html (accessed August 23, 2015); and http://atlassociety.org/objectivism/atlas-university/new-to-ayn-rand (accessed August 23, 2015).

26. Itskov. "Russian Experience," Slide 12.

27. *See* Francis Fukuyama's 1992 *The End of History and the Last Man* (New York: The Free Press, 1992), in which he discusses all three thinkers with reference to the end of history. *See also* Sheldon Wolin's *Politics and Vision* (Boston: Little, Brown, 1960), for an interesting variation on some of the same themes. For briefer discussions consult http://internationalpoliticaltheory .blogspot.com/2011/11/hegel-on-end-of-history.html (accessed August 7, 2015); and https://www.marxists.org/reference/subject/philosophy/works/us/fukuyama .htm (accessed August 11, 2015).

CHAPTER 10: THE (POST)HUMAN FUTURE?

1. Francis Fukuyama. "Transhumanism." *Foreign Policy*, No. 144 (Sept.-Oct. 2004), 42–43. In an article written as a response to identifying "the world's most dangerous ideas," Fukuyama rejects the idea that we can ally ourselves with intelligent machines and still remain human.

2. Sherry Turkle was one of the earliest such critics, a role she plays to this day. Please see her earlier work, *Life on the Screen*, written in the 1990s, as well as her more recent work, *Alone Together*, in which she speculates on how new technologies (such as smartphones), and new social media sites have led to fragmented lives and identities in which face-to-face contact becomes less frequent and less important.

3. A PDF of "The Cyborg Manifesto" is available online at http://www.fac ulty.umb.edu/gary_zabel/Courses/Art%20and%20Philosophy%20in%20 SL%20and%20Other%20Virtual%20Worlds/Texts/cyborg_manifesto.pdf (accessed January 7, 2016).

4. There are many places to find summaries of technical objections to mind uploading and digital immortality. I confine myself to references anyone can access online. Maciamo Hay, for example, raises objections in his brief essay in H+ magazine (http://hplusmagazine.com/2014/04/24/mind-uploading-wont-lead-to

-immortality/ [accessed January 23, 2016]). *See also* George Dvorsky's eight objections to the feasibility of mind uploading at http://io9.gizmodo.com/you-ll -probably-never-upload-your-mind-into-a-computer-474941498 (accessed January 23, 2016). *See also* Kenneth D. Miller's objections at http://www.nytimes .com/2015/10/11/opinion/sunday/will-you-ever-be-able-to-upload-your-brain .html?_r=3 (accessed January 23, 2016). Dominic Fairfax presents both sides of the discussion at http://thinkalongtheselines.blogspot.com (accessed January 23, 2016).

This review of Satel and Lilienfeld's book about neuroscience, *Brainwashed*, also captures some of the current scientific skepticism about whether we can port human identity to the Internet. http://metanexus.net/product/brainwashed -seductive-appeal-mindless-neuroscience (accessed January 23, 2016).

5. Kurzweil discusses how LOAR works at his very active website http:// www.kurzweilai.net/the-law-of-accelerating-returns (accessed February 1, 2016). Discussions of the principle also are found in his writing, *The Singularity Is Near*.

6. Searle introduced the Chinese Room thought experiment in "Minds, Brains, and Programs," published in *Behavioral and Brain Sciences* in 1980. Since then it has become a staple in discussions about whether computers can think, even though Searle himself later wrote that there is nothing in principle that would prevent a more advanced computer from thinking. A PDF of the original article can be found at http://cogprints.org/7150/1/10.1.1.83.5248.pdf (accessed April 9, 2015).

7. Thomas Nagel, "What Is It Like to Be a Bat?" *Philosophical Review* LXXXIII 4 (October 1974). A PDF of the article can be found online at http:// organizations.utep.edu/Portals/1475/nagel_bat.pdf (accessed April 22, 2015).

8. Derek Parfit introduced the teletransportation experiment in his book, *Reasons and Persons*, published in 1986. Thus, over a span of roughly 30 years, philosophers published four pivotal thought experiments on the subjects of artificial intelligence, mind transfer, and personal identity: Teletransportation, in 1962; The Bat, in 1974; The Chinese Room, in 1980, and Philosophical Zombies, in 1996. All of these can be read as glosses on different aspects of Turing's Imitation Game thought experiment of 1950, which itself can be read as a comment on Leibnitz' Mill argument found in Section Seventeen of the *Monadology* (which I do not discuss herein for reasons of narrative economy).

9. *See* George Lakoff and Mark Johnson, *Metaphors We Live By* and *Philosophy in the Flesh*, as well as Maurice Merleau-Ponty, *Phenomenology and Perception* and *Visible and Invisible*. Good discussions of Lakoff and Johnson on embodiment can be found at https://www.nytimes.com/books/first/l/lakoff -philosophy.html (accessed June 6, 2015); and at http://digitalcommons.macal es-ter.edu/cgi/viewcontent.cgi?article=1143&context=philo (accessed June 7, 2015).

Discussions of Merleau-Ponty's ideas on embodiment can be found at http:// ejap.louisiana.edu/EJAP/1996.spring/dreyfus.1996.spring.html;   http://ndpr .nd.edu/news/24867-merleau-ponty-and-derrida-intertwining-embodiment -and-alterity/ (accessed June 19, 2015); https://embodimentblog.wordpress .com/tag/merleau-ponty/ (accessed June 19, 2015); and in many other sources.

On feminism and embodiment, one can look at Iris Marion Young's canonical "Throwing Like a Girl: A Phenomenology of Feminine Body Comportment, Motility and Spatiality," as well as at Judith Butler's "The Body in Its Sexual Being," and "Sexual Ideology and Phenomenological Description," all cited in "Feminism, Phenomenology and Embodiment," by Steven Connor. http://www.stevenconnor.com/cp/femphen.htm (accessed July 1, 2015).

The rise and influence of postgenderism, which is much more in line with transhumanist aspirations and fits Rothblatt's perspective about identity in that it argues that in the future gender can be transcended, can be traced through the groundbreaking essay, "The Cyborg Manifesto," by Donna Haraway, which embraces a postgender position but ultimately stops short of endorsing the morphing of people into machines. A PDF of the text can be found online at http://www.faculty.umb.edu/gary_zabel/Courses/Art%20and%20Philosophy%20in%20SL%20and%20Other%20Virtual%20Worlds/Texts/cyborg_manifesto.pdf (accessed January 19, 2016).

Shulamith Firestone suggests an early version of postgenderism in her 1970 *Dialectic of Sex.*

10. The fear that the future development of superintelligent machines/people could mean the end of humanity, or its enslavement, is embraced by such scientific and technological luminaries as Elon Musk and Stephen Hawkings.

For dire predictions about the future of digital intelligence, *see* George Dvorsky's writings at http://io9.gizmodo.com/10-horrifying-technologies-that-should-never-be-allowed-1635238363 (accessed January 19, 2016). For a more balanced but wary approach to the topic, *see* Patrick Lin's *Robot Ethics*, and http://www.economist.com/node/21556234 (accessed June 5, 2015), an *Economist* piece on "Robot Ethics."

Even convinced transhumanists such as Nick Bostrom worry about the ethics of superintelligent beings (http://www.nickbostrom.com/ethics/ai.pdf [accessed August 8, 2015]), and both Martine Rothblatt and Dmitry Itskov worry extensively about building a moral compass into immortal online minds and robots.

11. There is an extensive literature on the connections between transhumanism and religion. Some of it is neutral or intermittently positive, such as Craig Detweiler's *iGods* and Anne Foerst's *God in the Machine,* as well as Margaret Wertheim's classic, *The Pearly Gates of Cyberspace.*

Other works, such as Mercer and Trostle's collection, *Religion and Transhumanism*, present a range of opinions about the possibility of religion coming to terms with transhumanism and technoimmortality. Ronald Cole-Turner's *Transhumanism and Transcendence* presents a similar range of theological opinion from Brent Water's severe skepticism to Michael Burdett's and David Grumett's optimisms, based on the theology of the Jesuit visionary Teilhard de Chardin.

Jeannine Thweatt-Bates presents an interestingly nuanced position, using Haraway's notion of the human-machine hybrid as a counter to the fully digitized immortal mind in her *Cyborg Selves.*

Martine Rothblatt argues extensively, in *Truths*, that world religions ultimately will have no problem with technoimmortality, seeing it as a waystation on the road to Heaven. Dmitry Itskov enlists religious figures at his conferences, although his connections to formal religion, if any, are unclear.

I am aware that there was a Transhumanism and Religion conference in 2014 (http://brighterbrains.org/articles/entry/religion-and-transhumanism-the-future-of-faith-ethics-and-philosophy-may-10 [accessed January 22, 2016]), at which representatives of mainstream religions as well as Wicca and Terasem representatives spoke. The conference was hosted by IEET—the Institute for Ethics and Emerging Technology—which is headed by Nick Bostrom and James Hughes, both leading advocates of transhumanism.

As a final note, I cannot help but mention that there is an active Mormon Transhumanist Association (http://news.transfigurism.org/2015/11/2016-con ference-of-mormon-transhumanist.html [accessed January 22, 2016]) which holds annual conferences. On the other hand, various Catholic sites and jour-nals reject transhumanism out of hand, or raise serious questions about it, for example the Catholic News Agency and the Jesuit magazine *America* (http:// www.catholicnewsagency.com/news/can-we-delete-death-transhumanisms -lofty-goal-meets-a-catholic-response-11222/ [accessed January 21, 2016]; http://americamagazine.org/issue/501/article/transhumanism [accessed January 21, 2016]).

For an interesting perspective on how traditional religious believers might react to transhumanist proposals about digital immortality, *see* https://www .singularityweblog.com/transhumanism-goes-to-campus/ (accessed January 24, 2016).

These references are by no means exhaustive. The connections between reli-gious belief and proposals for digital afterlife are complex and ongoing, and my references only scratch the surface.

12. Robert M. Geraci, *Apocalyptic AI: Visions of Heaven in Robotics, Artificial Intelligence, and Virtual Reality*. Geraci also writes about visions of the sacred in online video games, in his *Virtually Sacred: Myth and Meaning in World of Warcraft and Second Life*.

The idea that transhumanism is a crypto-religion has been in the air for some time. Marcie Gainer invokes this theme in her 2015 post "Transhumanism— The Final Religion?" which can be found on the Disinformation website at http://disinfo.com/2015/07/transhumanism-the-final-religion/ (accessed January 29, 2016). Of course, Martine Rothblatt's Terasem overtly calls itself a "transreligion."

13. Genesis, Book 3, Chapter 5: "You will be like God," the serpent speaking to Eve.

14. *See,* e.g., the Disinformation post on Cole-Turner's *Transhumanism and Transcendence*. *See also* Micah Redding's post on the Motherboard website in 2015 (http://motherboard.vice.com/read/why-i-became-a-christian-transhu manist [accessed July 21, 2015]). For the Terasem conference, *see* http://terase mcentral. org/events.html (accessed August 1, 2015). The virtual conference was titled, "10th Annual Workshop on Geoethical Nanotechnology, Terasem Island Conference Center, Second Life, Monday, July 20, 2015."

Bibliography

"2012 Truths of Terasem [Kindle Edition]."*2012 Truths of Terasem EBook: Terasem Movement.*" Amazon.com.au, Kindle Store. http://www.amazon .com.au/2012-Truths-Terasem-Movement-ebook/dp/B007PSYDQC. Accessed February 9, 2016.

"2045 Initiative." 2045 Strategic Social Initiative. http://2045.com/articles/30158 .h. Accessed February 11, 2016.

"2045 Initiative." 2045 Strategic Social Initiative. http://2045.com/. Accessed January 6, 2016.

"2045 Initiative." Twitter. https://twitter.com/2045Initiative. Accessed February 16, 2016.

"2045 Initiative Will Sponsor Research in Cybernetic Immortality." Science World Report. March 25, 2013. http://www.scienceworldreport.com/articles /5783/20130325/cybernetic-immortality-2045-strategic-social-initiative .htm. Accessed January 7, 2016.

"The 5 Point Online Memorial Code of Ethics." The Online Memorial Code of Ethics. http://thememorialcode.org/. Accessed January 7, 2016.

"9/11 Pentagon Visitor Education Center Project Information." National 9/11 Pentagon Memorial. http://pentagonmemorial.org/. Accessed January 7, 2016.

Ackerman, Diane. *The Human Age: The World Shaped by Us.* 2014 ed. New York, NY: W.W. Norton, 2014.

"Advanced Social Robots." http://www.robotindroboto.com/. Accessed January 7, 2016.

Albom, Mitch. *The Five People You Meet in Heaven.* New York: Hyperion, 2003.

Albom, Mitch. *For One More Day.* New York: Hyperion, 2006.

Albom, Mitch. *Tuesdays with Morrie: An Old Man, a Young Man, and Life's Greatest Lesson.* New York: Doubleday, 1997.

Alexander, Eben. *Proof of Heaven: A Neurosurgeon's Journey into the Afterlife.* New York, NY: Simon and Schuster, 2012.

Allenby, Braden R., and Daniel R. Sarewitz. *The Techno-Human Condition.* Cambridge, MA: MIT Press, 2011.

Ancestry.com. http://www.1000memories.com/. Accessed February 5, 2016.

Anthony, Del Monte Louis. *The Artificial Intelligence Revolution: Will Artificial Intelligence Serve Us or Replace Us.* Louis A. Del Monte, 2013.

Antonio. "So, You Wanna Be an Android?" *MIT Technology Review.* http://www.technologyreview.com/view/516226/so-you-wanna-be-an-android/. Accessed February 26, 2016.

Appleyard, Bryan. *How to Live Forever or Die Trying: On the New Immortality.* London: Simon & Schuster, 2007.

Arendt, Hannah. *The Human Condition.* Chicago: University of Chicago Press, 1958.

Ariès, Philippe. *The Hour of Our Death.* New York: Knopf, 1981.

Armstrong, Stuart. *Smarter than Us: The Rise of Machine Intelligence.* Berkeley: MIRI, 2014.

"Avatar A / 2045 Initiative." http://2045.com/project/avatar. Accessed February 14, 2016.

" 'Avatar' Project Aims for Human Immortality by 2045." http://www.gizmag.com/avatar-project-2045/23454/. Accessed January 7, 2016.

"The Babbage Engine." http://www.computerhistory.org/babbage/. Accessed February 7, 2016.

Bachrach, Judy. *Glimpsing Heaven: The Stories and Science of Dying and Returning.* Washington, DC: National Geographic Books, 2014.

Baele, Yannick. "Articles Tagués: Dimitri Itskov." May 20, 2013. https://yannickbaele.wordpress.com/tag/dimitri-itskov/. Accessed February 26, 2016.

Barrat, James. *Our Final Invention: Artificial Intelligence and the End of the Human Era.* London: St. Martin's Griffin, 2015.

Baym, Nancy K. *Personal Connections in the Digital Age.* Cambridge, UK: Polity, 2010.

"Be Right Back." IMDb. http://www.imdb.com/title/tt2290780/. Accessed January 7, 2016.

Bell, C. Gordon, and Jim Gemmell. *Total Recall: How the E-Memory Revolution Will Change Everything.* New York: Dutton, 2009.

Bell, C. Gordon, and Jim Gemmell. *Your Life, Uploaded: The Digital Way to Better Memory, Health, and Productivity.* New York: Plume, 2010.

Benedikt, Michael. *Cyberspace: First Steps.* Cambridge, MA: MIT Press, 1992.

Benford, Gregory, and Elisabeth Malartre. *Beyond Human: Living with Robots and Cyborgs.* New York: Forge, 2007.

Bennetts, Marc. "*Dossier Seuls Les Riches Seront Immortels.*" *Les Gros Titres Du SCELVA.* October 24, 2014. https://lesgrostitresduscelva.wordpress.com/2014/10/24/dossier-seuls-les-riches-seront-immortels/. Accessed February 26, 2016.

Bennetts, Marc. "How Dmitry Itskov Plans to Live for Ever | The Times." *The Times.* June 26, 2014. http://www.thetimes.co.uk/tto/life/article4130109.ece. Accessed February 26, 2016.

"Be+Right+Back+Black+Mirror+Youtube—Yahoo Video Search Results." https://video.search.yahoo.com/search/video;_ylt=AwrSbDZwf79W wD0AZeVXNyoA;_ylu=X3oDMTEydmluZGpyBGNvbG8DZ3ExBHBv cwMxBHZ0aWQDQjExNzhfMQRzZWMDc2M-?p=Be%2BRight%2B Back%2BBlack%2BMirror%2BYoutube&fr=aaplw#id=1&vid=f66b83c 1d1cc87ce35ac102040b83d6e&action=view. Accessed February 13, 2016.

Bisceglio, Paul. "How Social Media Is Changing the Way We Approach Death." *The Atlantic*. August 20, 2013. http://www.theatlantic.com/health /archive/2013/08/how-social-media-is-changing-the-way-we-approach -death/278836/. Accessed January 7, 2016.

Blackford, Russell, and Damien Broderick. *Intelligence Unbound: The Future of Uploaded and Machine Minds*. Malden, MA: John Wiley & Sons, 2014.

Blank, Trevor J. *Folklore and the Internet: Vernacular Expression in a Digital World*. Logan, UT: Utah State University Press, 2009.

Blascovich, Jim, and Jeremy Bailenson. *Infinite Reality: Avatars, Eternal Life, New Worlds, and the Dawn of the Virtual Revolution*. New York: William Morrow, 2011.

Blum, Edwin A., and Jeremy Royal Howard. *Holman KJV Study Bible: King James Version of the Holy Bible*. Nashville, TN: Holman Bible Publishers, 2012.

Borghino, Dario. " 'Avatar' Project Aims for Human Immortality by 2045." July 25, 2012. http://www.gizmag.com/avatar-project-2045/23454/. Accessed February 29, 2016.

Borgman, Erik, Stephan Erp, and Hille Haker. *Cyberspace-Cyberethics-Cybertheology*. London: SCM, 2005.

Bosker, Bianca. "Dmitry Itskov Knows He'll Live Forever; Here's How He's Living Now." *The Huffington Post*. http://www.huffingtonpost.com/2013/06/17 /dmitry-itskov_n_3455807.html. Accessed January 7, 2016.

Bostrom, Nick. "Introduction to Transhumanist Thought." *Journal of Evolution and Technology* 14(1) (April 2005). Accessed January 17, 2016. doi:10.1057/9781137342768.0004.

Bostrom, Nick. "Introduction: The Transhumanist FAQ." *Transhumanism and the Body*. Accessed February 13, 2016. doi:10.1057/9781137342768.0004.

Bostrom, Nick. *Superintelligence: The Coming Machine Intelligence Revolution*. Oxford: Oxford University Press, 2013.

Bostrom, Nick. "Transhumanist FAQ." Humanity+. http://humanityplus.org/ philosophy/transhumanist-faq/. Accessed January 17, 2016.

Bowman, Emma. "From Facebook to a Virtual You: Planning Your Digital Afterlife." NPR. February 12, 2015. http://www.npr.org/sections/alltech considered/2015/02/12/385753136/from-facebook-to-a-virtual-you-plan ning-your-digital-afterlife. Accessed January 17, 2016.

Braidotti, Rosi. *The Posthuman*. 2013 ed. Malden MA: Polity, 2013.

Brain, Marshall. *The Second Intelligent Species*. Cary, NC: BYG Publishing, 2015.

Braude, Ann. *Radical Spirits: Spiritualism and Women's Rights in Nineteenth-Century America*. Boston, MA: Beacon Press, 1989.

Bronfen, Elisabeth. *Over Her Dead Body: Death, Femininity, and the Aesthetic.* New York: Routledge, 1992.

Bukatman, Scott. *Terminal Identity: The Virtual Subject in Postmodern Science Fiction.* Durham: Duke University Press, 1993.

Burns, Stanley B. *Sleeping Beauty: Memorial Photography in America.* Altadena, CA: Twelvetrees Press, 1990.

Burpo, Todd, and Lynn Vincent. *Heaven Is for Real: A Little Boy's Astounding Story of His Trip to Heaven and Back.* Nashville, TN: Thomas Nelson, 2010.

Cantor, Norman L. *After We Die: The Life and Times of the Human Cadaver.* Washington, DC: Georgetown University Press, 2010.

Caputi, Jane. *Goddesses and Monsters: Women, Myth, Power, and Popular Culture.* Madison: University of Wisconsin Press/Popular Press, 2004.

Carboncopies.org Foundation. http://www.carboncopies.org/. Accessed January 7, 2016.

Carroll, Evan, and John Romano. *Your Digital Afterlife: When Facebook, Flickr and Twitter Are Your Estate, What's Your Legacy?* Berkeley, CA: New Riders, 2011.

Case, Amber. "We Are Already Cyborgs." YouTube. http://www.youtube.com/watch?v=cUzFtWNOOOU. Accessed February 9, 2016.

Casey, John. *After Lives: A Guide to Heaven, Hell, and Purgatory.* Oxford: Oxford University Press, 2009.

Castricano, Carla Jodey. *Cryptomimesis: The Gothic and Jacques Derrida's Ghost Writing.* Montréal: McGill-Queen's University Press, 2001.

Cave, Stephen. *Immortality: The Quest to Live Forever and How It Drives Civilization.* New York: Crown Publishers, 2012.

Chalmers, David John. *The Conscious Mind: In Search of a Fundamental Theory.* New York: Oxford University Press, 1996.

Chardin, Pierre Teilhard De, Julian Huxley, and Bernard Wall. *The Phenomenon of Man.* New York: Harper, 1959.

Christian, David. *Big History. The Big Bang, Life on Earth, and the Rise of Humanity.* Chantilly, VA: Teaching, 2008.

"Christian Memorials." Christian Memorials. http://www.christianmemorials.com/memorials/list.asp?char=G. Accessed January 7, 2016.

Clark, Andy. *Natural-Born Cyborgs: Minds, Technologies, and the Future of Human Intelligence.* Oxford: Oxford University Press, 2003.

"A Clockwork Miracle." Radiolab Podcast Articles. http://www.radiolab.org/story/140632-clockwork-miracle/. Accessed February 7, 2016.

Cole-Turner, Ronald. *Transhumanism and Transcendence: Christian Hope in an Age of Technological Enhancement.* Washington, DC: Georgetown University Press, 2011.

"Company Overview of Intellitar, Inc." *Businessweek.com.* http://investingbusinessweek.com/research/stocks/private/snapshot.asp?privcapId=99203572. Accessed August 4, 2014.

Cottingham, John. *Rene Descartes: Meditations on First Philosophy.* New York: Cambridge University Press, 2015.

Couts, Andrew. "Land of the God-Men: Inside the Wild Movement to Turn Us into Immortal Cyborgs." *Digital Trends*. June 20, 2013. http://www.digi taltrends.com/cool-tech/inside-dmitry-itskovs-global-future-2045-confer ence/. Accessed February 26, 2016.

"Create a Beautiful & Informative Online Obituary in Just a Few Minutes with Memorial." Memorial. http://creatememorial.com/c/25-off. Accessed January 7, 2016.

"Create a Free Memorial Website for Your Loved Ones." MemoryIsLife. http:// en.memoryislife.com/. Accessed January 7, 2016.

"Create a Simple Memorial Website for a Loved One Who Has Passed Away." Memorial Website. http://www.ilasting.com/. Accessed January 7, 2016.

"Create Online Memorial Website to Honor Friends & Family." http://memory-of.com/public/. Accessed January 7, 2016.

"Create Online Memorial Websites in Memory of Your Loved Ones at Remembered.com." https://remembered.com/. Accessed January 7, 2016.

"Create Your FREE FOREVER Memorial Now!" Free Online Memorial Websites, Honor Your Lost Loved One. http://never-gone.com/. Accessed January 7, 2016.

"Create Your Free Talking Avatar with a Photo of You!" http://www.2bmovie .com/index.html. Accessed January 7, 2016.

Cronin, Melissa. " 'Mind Uploading' & Digital Immortality May Be Reality By 2045, Futurists Say." *The Huffington Post*. http://www.huffingtonpost .com/2013/06/18/mind-uploading-2045-futurists_n_3458961.html. Accessed January 17, 2016.

Cross, John of the, and Lloyd Hildebrand. *Dark Night of the Soul: And Other Great Works*. Orlando, FL: Bridge-Logos, 2007.

"Cyberspace Is Dead. Gone." Thistlwood. August 4, 2014. http://www .thistlwood.com/cyberspace-is-dead-gone/. Accessed January 17, 2016.

Davenport, John J. *Narrative Identity, Autonomy and Morality*. New York, NY: Rutledge, 2012.

Dawkins, Richard. *The Selfish Gene*. Oxford: Oxford University Press, 1989.

De Grey, Aubrey D. N. J, and Michael Rae. *Ending Aging: The Rejuvenation Breakthroughs that Could Reverse Human Aging in Our Lifetime*. New York: St. Martin's Press, 2007.

"Dead Man's Switch." https://www.deadmansswitch.net/. Accessed January 7, 2016.

Dennett, Daniel Clement. *Consciousness Explained*. London UK: Lane, the Penguin Press, 1992.

Derrida, Jacques. *Aporias: Dying—Awaiting (One Another at) the "Limits of Truth" (mourir—s'attendre Aux "limites De La Vérité")*. Stanford, CA: Stanford University Press, 1993.

Descartes, René, and David Weissman. *Discourse on the Method and Meditations on First Philosophy*. New Haven: Yale University Press, 1996.

Detweiler, Craig. *IGods: How Technology Shapes Our Spiritual and Social Lives*. Grand Rapids, MI: Brazos Press, 2013.

"The Digital Beyond." http://www.thedigitalbeyond.com/. Accessed January 7, 2016.

"Digital Memorials." http://www.digital-memorial.com/. Accessed January 7, 2016.

"Dmitry Itskov on "Project 'Immortality 2045'—Russian Experience, at Singularity Summit 2011." YouTube. https://www.youtube.com/watch?v=zEi3ZAYheT0. Accessed February 11, 2016.

DocuBank—Immediate Access to Healthcare Directives & Emergency Medical Information—Anywhere, Anytime, 24/7/365. http://www.docubank.com/. Accessed January 7, 2016.

Dodds, E. R. *The Greeks and the Irrational.* Berkeley, CA: University of California Press, 2004.

Dollimore, Jonathan. *Death, Desire, and Loss in Western Culture.* New York: Routledge, 1998.

Drexler, K. Eric. *Engines of Creation.* Garden City, NY: Anchor Press/Doubleday, 1986.

Drummond, Katie. "Russian Mogul's Plan: Plant Our Brains in Robots, Keep Them Alive Forever." Wired.com. February 29, 2012. http://www.wired.com/2012/02/dmitry-itskov/. Accessed February 27, 2016.

Dupuy, Jean-Pierre. "H-: Cybernetics Is an Antihumanism: Advanced Technologies and the Rebellion Against the Human Condition." http://www.metanexus.net/essay/h-cybernetics-antihumanism-advanced-technologies-and-rebellion-against-human-condition. Accessed February 13, 2016.

Dupuy, Jean-Pierre. "Rationally Speaking | Official Podcast of New York City Skeptics—Current Episodes—RS17—Transhumanism." http://rationallyspeakingpodcast.org/show/rs17-transhumanism.html. Accessed February 13, 2016.

Eadie, Betty J., and Curtis Taylor. *Embraced by the Light.* Placerville, CA: Gold Leaf Press, 1992.

Ealey, Michelle. "Exclusive Interview with Dmitry Itskov, Founder of Global Future 2045." ScienceFiction.com RSS. http://sciencefiction.com/2012/03/19/exclusive-interview-with-dmitry-itskov-founder-of-global-future-2045/. Accessed February 26, 2016.

Easton, Thomas A. *Silicon Karma.* Clarkston, GA: White Wolf Publishing, 1997.

Eden, Amnon H., and Eric Steinhart. *Singularity Hypotheses: A Scientific and Philosophical Assessment.* Heidelberg: Springer, 2012.

Edward, John, and Natasha Stoynoff. *Final Beginnings.* New York: Princess Books, 2004.

"Elizabeth Stuart Phelps Ward (1844–1911). Critical and Biographical Introduction." Warner et al., comp. 1917. *The Library of the World's Best Literature.* http://www.bartleby.com/library/prose/5551.html. Accessed February 5, 2016.

Esfandiary, F. M. *Optimism One.* New York: Popular Library, 1978.

Eterni.me. http://eterni.me/. Accessed February 14, 2016.

"Eterni.Me Company Offering Immortality & Skype Chats with the Dead."
YouTube. http://www.youtube.com/watch?v=_zwFfPJdyPo. Accessed
February 14, 2016.

"Eterni.me Lets You Skype with the Dead." CNET. http://www.cnet.com/news
/eterni-me-lets-you-skype-with-the-dead/#! Accessed February 14, 2016.

"Eterni.me Will Create a Computer Version of You for When You Die." http://
www.gizmag.com/eterni-me-death-avatar/31053/. Accessed February 14,
2016.

"Everplans." https://www.everplans.com/. Accessed January 7, 2016.

"Facebook Logo." National September 11 Memorial & Museum. https://www
.facebook.com/911memorial. Accessed January 7, 2016.

Faust, Drew Gilpin. *This Republic of Suffering: Death and the American Civil
War*. New York: Alfred A. Knopf, 2008.

Feenberg, Andrew. "Active and Passive Bodies." *Techné: Research in Philosophy
and Technology* 7(2) (Winter 2003): 125–30. Accessed January 17, 2016.
doi: 10.5840/techne2003725.

FM-2030. *Are You a Transhuman? Monitoring and Stimulating Your Personal
Rate of Growth in a Rapidly Changing World*. New York, NY: Warner
Books, 1989.

"FM-2030: Are You Transhuman?" YouTube. http://www.youtube.com
/watch?v=eaS9QBdVHMs. Accessed February 9, 2016.

Foerst, Anne. *God in the Machine: What Robots Teach Us about Humanity and
God*. New York: Dutton, 2004.

Forever Remembered® Obituary Service, Funeral Home Web Sites. http://www
.forever-remembered.com/. Accessed January 7, 2016.

"ForeverMissed Online Memorials." ForeverMissed.com. http://www.forever
missed.com/. Accessed January 7, 2016.

Frankish, Keith, and William M. Ramsey eds. *The Cambridge Handbook of
Artificial Intelligence*. Cambridge: Cambridge University Press, 2014.

"Free Online Memorial Website." For Loved One with Memorial Book
and Family Tree. http://www.last-memories.com/. Accessed January 7,
2016.

"FREE Online Memorial Websites for Loved Ones, Tributes, Funeral and Death
Notices—Skymorials." http://www.skymorials.com/. Accessed January 7,
2016.

Frenkel, James, and Vernor Vinge. *True Names by Vernor Vinge and the Opening
of the Cyberspace Frontier*. New York: Tor, 2001.

Friedberg, Anne. *The Virtual Window: From Alberti to Microsoft*. Cambridge,
MA: MIT Press, 2006.

"Future." Yuval Harari. http://www.ynharari.com/future/articles/humans-have-
passed-their-expiry-date/. Accessed January 17, 2016.

Gainer, Marcie. "Transhumanism - The Final Religion? - Disinformation."
Disinformation. July 21, 2015. Accessed February 13, 2016. http://disinfo
.com/2015/07/transhumanism-the-final-religion/.

Gallacher, Patrick J. *The Cloud of Unknowing*. Kalamazoo, MI: Medieval
Institute Publications Western Michigan University, 1997.

Garreau, Joel. *Radical Evolution: The Promise and Peril of Enhancing Our Minds, Our Bodies—and What It Means to Be Human*. New York: Doubleday, 2005.

Geraci, Robert M. *Apocalyptic AI: Visions of Heaven in Robotics, Artificial Intelligence, and Virtual Reality*. New York: Oxford University Press, 2010.

Geraci, Robert M. *Virtually Sacred: Myth and Meaning in World of Warcraft and Second Life*. New York: Oxford University Press, 2014.

"GF2045: Global Future 2045—International Congress." GF2045. http://gf2045.com/read/209/. Accessed February 11, 2016.

Gibson, William. *Neuromancer*. London: Harper Voyager, 2013.

Gilbert, Sandra M. *Death's Door: Modern Dying and the Ways We Grieve*. New York: W.W. Norton, 2006.

Goodwin, Sarah McKim Webster, and Elisabeth Bronfen. *Death and Representation*. Baltimore: Johns Hopkins University Press, 1993.

Grassie, William. "Introduction." Metanexus. http://www.metanexus.net/essay/introduction. Accessed September 4, 2015.

Grau, Oliver. *Virtual Art: From Illusion to Immersion*. Cambridge, MA: MIT Press, 2003.

Gray, John. *The Immortalization Commission: Science and the Strange Quest to Cheat Death*. New York: Farrar, Straus and Giroux, 2011.

Green, James W. *Beyond the Good Death: The Anthropology of Modern Dying*. Philadelphia: University of Pennsylvania Press, 2008.

Greene, Richard, and K. Silem Mohammad. *Zombies, Vampires, and Philosophy: New Life for the Undead*. Chicago, IL: Open Court, 2010.

Gucciardi, Anthony. "Russian Scientist Says Immortality Possible for Wealthy Elite by 2045." *Natural Society*. August 1, 2012. http://naturalsociety.com/russian-scientist-says-immortality-possible-for-wealthy-elite-by-2045/. Accessed February 29, 2016.

"H-: Transhumanism and the Posthuman Future: Will Technological Progress Get Us There?" http://www.metanexus.net/essay/h-transhumanism-and-posthuman-future-will-technological-progress-get-us-there. Accessed February 13, 2016.

Habenstein, Robert Wesley, and William M. Lamers. *The History of American Funeral Directing*. Milwaukee, WI: Bulfin Printers, 1962.

Hall, J. Storrs. *Beyond AI: Creating the Conscience of the Machine*. Amherst, NY: Prometheus Books, 2007.

Hansell, Gregory R., William Grassie, Russell Blackford, Nick Bostrom, and Jean Pierre Dupuy. *H±: Transhumanism and Its Critics*. Philadelphia, PA: Metanexus Institute, 2011.

Harari, Yuval Noah. *Sapiens*. 2015 ed. New York, NY: Harper, 2015.

Haraway, Donna Jeanne. *Simians, Cyborgs, and Women: The Reinvention of Nature*. New York: Routledge, 1991.

"The Hard Problem of Consciousness." *Internet Encyclopedia of Philosophy*. http://www.iep.utm.edu/hard-con/. Accessed January 7, 2016.

Harrison, Robert Pogue. *The Dominion of the Dead*. Chicago: University of Chicago Press, 2003.

Hawthorne, Nathaniel, and Basil Davenport. *The House of the Seven Gables*. New York: Dodd, Mead & Co., 1950.

Hayles, Katherine. *How We Became Posthuman: Virtual Bodies in Cybernetics, Literature, and Informatics*. Chicago, IL: University of Chicago Press, 1999.

Hayles, Katherine. *My Mother Was a Computer: Digital Subjects and Literary Texts*. Chicago: University of Chicago Press, 2005.

Hayworth, Kenneth. "Killed By Bad Philosophy." Fight Aging! https://www.fightaging.org/archives/2014/03/killed-by-bad-philosophy.php. Accessed January 17, 2016.

Heidegger, Martin. *Being and Time*. New York: Harper, 1962.

"Here's How to Hide Your Private PC Files Instantly—Just By Dragging Them Into Your Own "Virtual Vault"! Plus: Shred the Original Files From Your Disk, Permanently!" Virtual Vault Pro. http://www.virtualvaultpro.com/vault/. Accessed January 7, 2016.

Hertzfeld, Don. "World of Tomorrow." IMDb. http://www.imdb.com/title/tt4171032/. Accessed February 19, 2016.

Holeton, Richard. *Composing Cyberspace: Identity, Community, and Knowledge in the Electronic Age*. Boston: McGraw-Hill, 1998.

Holland, Sharon Patricia. *Raising the Dead: Readings of Death and (Black) Subjectivity*. Durham, NC: Duke University Press, 2000.

"Home—Hanson Robotics Ltd." Hanson Robotics Ltd RSS. http://www.hansonrobotics.com/. Accessed January 7, 2016.

"Home Page of The Loebner Prize in Artificial Intelligence." http://www.loebner.net/Prizef/loebner-prize.html. Accessed February 7, 2016.

"Home." Terasem. http://terasemfaith.net/. Accessed January 7, 2016.

Homer, and Richmond Lattimore. *The Odyssey of Homer*. New York: Harper & Row, 1967.

"How One Russian Millionaire Wants to Save the World . . . with Immortal Cyborgs." *Digital Trends*. March 28, 2013. http://www.digitaltrends.com/cool-tech/dmitry-itskov-2045-initiative/. Accessed January 7, 2016.

Howarth, Glennys, and Oliver Leaman. *Encyclopedia of Death and Dying*. London: Routledge, 2002.

"Human Destiny Is to Eliminate Death—Essays & Debates on Immortality." Goodreads. http://www.goodreads.com/book/show/19409198-human-destiny-is-to-eliminate-death-essays-debates-on-immortality. Accessed February 15, 2016.

"Humanity+. Transhumanist FAQ." http://humanityplus.org/philosophy/transhumanist-faq/. Accessed February 9, 2016.

Hurricane Katrina Memorial Site: Notable Deaths & Obituaries. http://www.legacy.com/memorial-sites/hurricane-katrina/. Accessed January 7, 2016.

"Hurricane Katrina Memorials." http://katrinamemorials.com/. Accessed January 7, 2016.

"I Remember You—Free Online Memorials." http://www.irememberyou.com/. Accessed January 7, 2016.

"If I Die—the Digital Afterlife Facebook Application." If I Die Facebook App. http://ifidie.net/. Accessed January 7, 2016.

"If You Plug Twitter Into a Digital Avatar, Can You Live Forever?" Wired.com. http://www.wired.com/2013/09/lifenaut/. Accessed January 7, 2016.

Ihde, Don. "Of Which Human Are We Post?" September 1, 2011. http://www.metanexus.net/essay/h-which-human-are-we-post. Accessed January 17, 2016.

Immortality. Amherst, NY: Prometheus Books, 1997.

"Intellitar Avatars a Poor Substitute for Afterlife—CNET." *CNET*. http://www.cnet.com/news/intellitar-avatars-a-poor-substitute-for-afterlife/#!. Accessed January 7, 2016.

"Intellitar Launches Live Beta of Virtual Eternity Cloning Technology." *Marketwire*. http://www.marketwired.com/press-release/Intellitar-Launches-Live-Beta-of-Virtual-Eternity-Cloning-Technology-1338945.htm. Accessed February 14, 2016.

"Intellitar's 'Digital Clones' Creepily Preserve Your Legacy for Future Generations." *Popular Science*. http://www.popsci.com/technology/article/2010-10/intellitar-provides-digital-clone-creep-out-future-generations. Accessed January 7, 2016.

"Interview with a Robot | The New York Times." YouTube. http://www.youtube.com/watch?v=uvcQCJpZJH8. Accessed January 7, 2016.

Isaacson, Betsy. "Next Up for Silicon Valley: Solving Death." *Newsweek*. March 5, 2015. http://www.newsweek.com/2015/03/13/silicon-valley-trying-make-humans-immortal-and-finding-some-success-311402.html?piano_t=1. Accessed February 26, 2016.

Istvan, Zoltan. *The Transhumanist Wager*. Futurity Imagine Media LLC, 2013.

Itskov, Dmitry. "Dmitry Itskov on 'Project Immortality 2045'—Russian Experience" at Singularity Summit 2011. YouTube. October 16, 2011. http://www.youtube.com/watch?v=zEi3ZAYheT0. Accessed February 29, 2016.

Itskov, Dmitry. " 'Evolution 2045'—The Party of Intellectual, Technological and Spiritual Breakthrough. Manifesto." 2045.com. August 22, 2012. http://evolution.2045.com. Accessed February 29, 2016.

Itskov, Dmitry. "The Path to Neo-Humanity as the Foundation of the Ideology of the 'Evolution 2045' Party." 2045 Initiative. http://2045.com/articles/30869.html. Accessed December 7, 2015.

"Jacques De Vaucanson." *History of Computers and Computing, Automata*. http://history-computer.com/Dreamers/Vaucanson.html. Accessed February 7, 2016.

Jewish Virtual Library. https://www.jewishvirtuallibrary.org/jsource/Judaism/Golem.html. Accessed February 7, 2016.

"Journal of Life—Living Memories." http://www.journal-of-life.com/. Accessed January 7, 2016.

Kaku, Michio. *The Future of the Mind: The Scientific Quest to Understand, Enhance, and Empower the Mind*. New York: Doubleday, 2014.

Kant, Immanuel, Theodore Meyer Greene, Hoyt H. Hudson, and John Silber. *Religion Within the Limits of Reason Alone*. New York: Harper & Row, 1960.

Keister, Douglas. *Stories in Stone: A Field Guide to Cemetery Symbolism and Iconography*. Salt Lake City: Gibbs Smith Publisher, 2004.

Kelly, James P., and John Kessel. *Digital Rapture: The Singularity Anthology*. San Francisco, CA: Tachyon Publications, 2012.

Kingsley, Peter. *In the Dark Places of Wisdom*. Inverness, CA: Golden Sufi Center, 1999.

Klaver, Elizabeth. *Images of the Corpse: From the Renaissance to Cyberspace*. Madison, WI: University of Wisconsin Press, 2004.

Koene, Randal A. Carboncopies.org Foundation. http://www.carboncopies.org/. Accessed February 29, 2016.

Koene, Randal A. "GF2045(2013) Proceedings: Dr. Randal A. Koene—Carboncopies.org Foundation." http://www.carboncopies.org/gf2045 -2013-proceedings/gf2045-2013-proceedings-koene. Accessed February 29, 2016.

Koene, Randal A. "Review of GF2045-2013 in New York—Carboncopies.org Foundation." http://www.carboncopies.org/review-of-gf2045-2013-in -new-york. Accessed February 29, 2016.

Kroehling, Richard. "2B—The Era of Flesh Is Over." http://www.2bmovie.com/. Accessed February 19, 2016.

Kurzweil, Ray. *How to Create a Mind: The Secret of Human Thought Revealed*. New York: Viking, 2012.

Kurzweil, Ray. *The Singularity Is Near*. London: Duckworth, 2006.

Kurzweil, Raymond. *The Age of Spiritual Machines: When Computers Exceed Human Intelligence*. New York: Penguin Books, 2000.

"Kurzweil AI | Accelerating Intelligence." Kurzweil AI 2045 The Year Man Becomes Immortal; Comments. http://kurzweilAI.net/2045-the-year-man -becomes-immortal. Accessed January 7, 2016.

Laderman, Gary. *Rest in Peace: A Cultural History of Death and the Funeral Home in Twentieth-Century America*. New York: Oxford University Press, 2003.

Laderman, Gary. *The Sacred Remains: American Attitudes Toward Death, 1799–1883*. New Haven: Yale University Press, 1996.

Lakoff, George, and Mark Johnson. *Metaphors We Live By*. Chicago: University of Chicago Press, 1980.

Lakoff, George, and Mark Johnson. *Philosophy in the Flesh: The Embodied Mind and Its Challenge to Western Thought*. New York: Basic Books, 1999.

"Last Will and Testament Forms." Create My. http://www.createmywill.com/. Accessed January 7, 2016.

"Legacy.com | Where Life Stories Live On." Legacy.com. http://www.legacy .com/. Accessed January 7, 2016.

Leibniz, Gottfried Wilhelm, and George R. Montgomery. *Discourse on Metaphysics; Correspondence with Arnauld; Monadology*. La Salle, IL: Open Court, 1980.

Lepore, Jill. *The Mansion of Happiness: A History of Life and Death*. New York: Alfred A. Knopf, 2012.

"Lewis Lapham Ponders His Mortality." Salon.com. http://www.salon
.com/2013/09/24/lewis_lapham_ponders_his_mortality_partner/easxy
bib. Accessed February 24, 2016.

Lewis, Tanya. "Dossier Seuls Les Riches Seront Immortels." Les Gros Titres Du
SCELVA. October 24, 2014. https://lesgrostitresduscelva.wordpress
.com/2014/10/24/dossier-seuls-les-riches-seront-immortels/. Accessed
February 26, 2016.

Lewis, Tanya. "The Singularity Is Near: Mind Uploading by 2045?" LiveScience.
June 17, 2013. http://www.livescience.com/. Accessed January 7, 2016.

"Library of Lives." https://www.facebook.com/libraryoflives. Accessed January
7, 2016.

"LifeNaut." YouTube. http://www.youtube.com/user/LifeNaut. Accessed
February 14, 2016.

"LifeNaut—Mind File—Bio File." https://www.lifenaut.com/index.html.
Accessed January 7, 2016.

"LifeNaut." LifeNaut Home 30 Comments. https://www.lifenaut.com/. Accessed
January 6, 2016.

"LifeNaut Project. Eternalizing Consciousness Using a Virtual Avatar." Machine
Consciousness. http://www.conscious-robots.com/en/conscious-machines
/machine-consciousness-projects/eternalizing-consciousness-using-an
-artificial-intelligenc.html. Accessed January 7, 2016.

"LivesOn." http://liveson.org/. Accessed January 7, 2016.

"LivesOn: New Service to Let You Tweet When You're Dead." ABC News.
February 22, 2013. http://abcnews.go.com/blogs/technology/2013/02
/_liveson-new-service-to-let-you-tweet-when-youre-dead/. Accessed January 7, 2016.

"LivesOn Will Let You Tweet from Beyond the Grave." Mashable. http://mash
able.com/2013/02/26/liveson/. Accessed January 7, 2016.

Lizza, John P. Persons, Humanity, and the Definition of Death. Baltimore, MD:
Johns Hopkins University Press, 2006.

Locke, John. An Essay Concerning Human Understanding. New York: Dover
Publications, 1959.

"Locke on Personal Identity." http://www.academia.edu/743927/Locke_on
_Personal_Identity. Accessed January 7, 2016.

Luciano, Dana. Arranging Grief: Sacred Time and the Body in Nineteenth-
Century America. New York: New York University Press, 2007.

"The Madness of Dmitry Itskov." Cryptogon.com RSS. February 29, 2012.
http://www.cryptogon.com/?p=27819. Accessed February 26, 2016.

Magerstädt, Sylvie. Body, Soul and Cyberspace in Contemporary Science Fiction
Cinema: Virtual Worlds and Ethical Problems. Basingstoke, U.K.: Palgrave
Macmillan, 2014.

Martin, Douglas. "Futurist Known as FM-2030 Is Dead at 69." The New York
Times. July 10, 2000. http://www.nytimes.com/2000/07/11/us/futurist
-known-as-fm-2030-is-dead-at-69.html. Accessed February 13, 2016.

McAvan, Emily. The Postmodern Sacred: Popular Culture Spirituality in the
Science Fiction, Fantasy and Urban Fantasy Genres. Jefferson, NC:
McFarland & Company, 2012.

McDannell, Colleen, and Bernhard Lang. *Heaven: A History*. New Haven: Yale University Press, 1988.

Mcdonald, Brent. "Interview with a Robot." *The New York Times*. June 24, 2010. http://www.nytimes.com/video/science/1247468035233/interview-with-a-robot.html. Accessed January 7, 2016.

McLaughlin, Budd. "Huntsville-Based Intellitar Can Make that Electronic Message Personal." *The Huntsville Times*. Intellitar. http://blog.al.com/huntsville-times-business/2011/02/huntsville-based_intellitar_ca.html. Accessed January 7, 2016.

"Memorialization Request | Facebook." https://www.facebook.com/help/contact/651319028315841. Accessed January 7, 2016.

Mercer, Calvin R. *Religion and Transhumanism: The Unknown Future of Human Enhancement*. Santa Barbara: Prayer, 2014.

Mercer, Calvin R. *Transhumanism and the Body: The World Religions Speak*. Palsgrave Studies in the Future of Humanity and Its Successors. New York, NY: Palgrave Macmillan, 2014.

Merleau-Ponty, Maurice. *Phenomenology of Perception*. London: Routledge, 2012.

Meyer, Richard E. *Cemeteries and Gravemarkers: Voices of American Culture*. Ann Arbor, MI: UMI Research Press, 1989.

Miller, Kenneth. "Will You Ever Be Able to Upload Your Brain?" *The New York Times*. October 10, 2015. http://www.nytimes.com/2015/10/11/opinion/sunday/will-you-ever-be-able-to-upload-your-brain.html. Accessed February 29, 2016.

Miller, Lisa. *Heaven: Our Enduring Fascination with the Afterlife*. New York: Harper, 2010.

"Mind Uploading Home Page." http://www.ibiblio.org/jstrout/uploading/. Accessed January 7, 2016.

"Mind Uploading." Mind Uploading Home Comments. http://www.minduploading.org/. Accessed January 17, 2016.

Minsky, Marvin Lee. *The Emotion Machine: Commonsense Thinking, Artificial Intelligence, and the Future of the Human Mind*. New York: Simon & Schuster, 2006.

Mitchell, Stephen. *Gilgamesh: A New English Version*. New York: Free Press, 2004.

MobileReference. *Two Treatises of Government by John Locke*. Boston: MobileReference.com, 2008.

Moravec, Hans P. *Mind Children: The Future of Robot and Human Intelligence*. Cambridge, MA: Harvard University Press, 1988.

"Morbid Momento [sic] or Apt Memorial?" Post-Mortem Photography. http://www.post-mortem-photography.com/index.html. Accessed January 7, 2016.

More, Max. "H+: True Transhumanism." February 9, 2009. http://www.metanexus.net/essay/h-true-transhumanism. Accessed January 17, 2016.

More, Max, and Natasha Vita-More. *The Transhumanist Reader: Classical and Contemporary Essays on the Science, Technology, and Philosophy of the Human Future*. London: Wiley-Blackwell, 2013.

Moreman, Christopher M., and A. David Lewis. *Digital Death: Mortality and Beyond in the Online Age*. Santa Barbara, CA: Praeger, 2014.

Mosco, Vincent. *The Digital Sublime: Myth, Power, and Cyberspace*. Cambridge, MA: MIT Press, 2004.

Muehlhauser, Luke, and Stuart Armstrong. "Can We Really Upload Johnny Depp's Brain?" http://www.slate.com/articles/technology/future_tense /2014/04/transcendence_science_can_we_really_upload_johnny_depp_s _brain.html. Accessed January 7, 2016.

My Last Will | MyLastWill.com. http://mylastwill.com/. Accessed January 7, 2016.

MyDeath Space. http://www.facebook.com/MyDeathSpace. Accessed January 7, 2016.

"National September 11 Memorial & Museum | World Trade Center Memorial." http://www.911memorial.org/. Accessed January 7, 2016.

"A New Kind of Eternal Life: The Growing Christian Transhumanism Movement—Disinformation." Disinformation. August 18, 2015. http:// disinfo.com/2015/08/new-kind-eternal-life-growing-christian-transhu manism-movement/. Accessed February 13, 2016.

The New Science of Religion. http://newscienceofreligion.com/. Accessed September 4, 2015.

O'Neill, Kevin D. "Death, Lives, and Video Streams." *Mortality* 13, no. 2 (2008): 174–86. Accessed January 7, 2016. doi: 10.1080/1357627080195 4435.

Online Memorial. http://www.valleyoflife.com/. Accessed January 7, 2016.

"Online Memorial." Imorial. http://imorial.com/. Accessed January 7, 2016.

"Online Memorial of Jeanne Simpson." Create a Free Memorial Website for Your Loved Ones. http://demo1en.memoryislife.com/. Accessed January 7, 2016.

"Online Memorial Websites—Free, Special Memorials—MuchLoved." MuchLoved. http://www.muchloved.com/. Accessed January 7, 2016.

"Online Memorials | Free Online Memorials | Virtual Memorials." http://www .memoryrain.com/. Accessed January 7, 2016.

Online Memorials, Online Memorial Tributes, and Unique Memorial Gifts. http://www.preciousmemoriesandmore.com/. Accessed January 7, 2016.

"Online Pet Memorials." Onlinepetmemorials.com. http://www.onlinepetme morials.com/about.php. Accessed January 7, 2016.

"Online Service to Record Your Life Story, Funeral and Legacy." Afternote. https://www.afternote.com/. Accessed February 5, 2016.

Oppy, Graham. "The Turing Test." Stanford University. April 9, 2003. http:// plato.stanford.edu/entries/turing-test/. Accessed January 7, 2016.

Pagden, Anthony. *The Enlightenment and Why It Still Matters*. Oxford: Oxford University Press, 2013.

Pet Memorial Website. Free Online Memorial for Your Loved Pets. http://www .pets-memories.com/. Accessed January 7, 2016.

Pet Memorials Online - Critters.com. Accessed January 7, 2016. http://www .critters.com/.

Peters, Ted. "Transhumanism as a New Religious Movement." *Ted's Timely Take.* http://tedstimelytake.com/transhumanism-new-religious-movement-4/. Accessed February 13, 2016.

Phelps, Elizabeth Stuart. *Beyond the Gates.* Boston: Houghton, Mifflin, 1883.

Phelps, Elizabeth Stuart. *The Gates Ajar.* Cambridge: Belknap Press of Harvard University Press, 1964.

Phelps, Elizabeth Stuart. *The Gates Between.* Boston: Houghton, Mifflin and Company, 1887.

Philosophical Zombie. http://philosophicalzombie.net/. Accessed January 7, 2016.

Pigliucci, Massimo. "Rationally Speaking: The Zombification of Philosophy (of Mind)." Rationally Speaking. July 2008. http://rationallyspeaking.blogspot.com/2008/07/zombification-of-philosophy-of-mind.html. Accessed January 17, 2016.

Piore, Adam. "The Neuroscientist Who Wants to Upload Humanity to a Computer." *Popular Science.* May 18, 2014. http://www.popsci.com/article/science/neuroscientist-who-wants-upload-humanity-computer. Accessed January 17, 2016.

Piper, Don, and Cecil Murphey. *90 Minutes in Heaven: My True Story.* Grand Rapids, MI: Revell, 2009.

Pisani, Bob. "Whoa, Immortality by 2035? Mind-Blowing Investing." CNBC. June 14, 2013. http://www.cnbc.com/id/100817288. Accessed February 26, 2016.

Plato, Benjamin Jowett, and Justin Kaplan. *Dialogues of Plato.* New York: Pocket Books, 1951.

Prentiss, E. *Stepping Heavenward.* Uhrichsville, OH: Barbour Publishing, 1998.

Rabaté, Jean-Michel. *The Ghosts of Modernity.* Gainesville: University Press of Florida, 1996.

Rainie, Harrison, and Barry Wellman. *Networked: The New Social Operating System.* Cambridge, MA: MIT Press, 2012.

"The Rapture of the Nerds." *Time.* http://time.com/66536/terasem-trascendence-religion-technology/. Accessed February 13, 2016.

Redding, Micah. "Why I Became a Christian Transhumanist." *Motherboard.* http://motherboard.vice.com/read/why-i-became-a-christian-transhumanist. Accessed February 13, 2016.

Regalado, Antonio. "So, You Wanna Be an Android?" *MIT Technology Review.* June 18, 2013. http://www.technologyreview.com/view/516226/so-you-wanna-be-an-android/. Accessed February 26, 2016.

Ricciardi, Alessia. *The Ends of Mourning: Psychoanalysis, Literature, Film.* Stanford, CA: Stanford University Press, 2003.

Roach, Joseph R. *Cities of the Dead: Circum-Atlantic Performance.* New York: Columbia University Press, 1996.

Romportl, Jan, Eva Zackova, and Jozef Kelemen. *Beyond Artificial Intelligence: The Disappearing Human-Machine Divide.* New York: Springer, 2014.

Rosenfield, Leonora Cohen. *From Beast-Machine to Man-Machine; Animal Soul in French Letters from Descartes to La Mettrie.* New York: Octagon Books, 1968.

Rothblatt, Martine Aliana. *From Transgender to Transhuman*. Martine Aliana Rothblatt, 2011.

Rothblatt, Martine Aliana. *Virtually Human: The Promise—and the Peril—of Digital Immortality*. New York: St. Martin's Press, 2014.

Ruby, Jay. *Secure the Shadow: Death and Photography in America*. Cambridge, MA: MIT Press, 1995.

"Russian Billionaire Dmitry Itskov Plans on Becoming Immortal by 2045." *Motherboard*. http://motherboard.vice.com/blog/russian-billionaire-dmitry-itskov-plans-on-becoming-immortal-by-2045. Accessed January 7, 2016.

Sandberg, Anders. "Making Minds Morally." GF2045. October 23, 2013. http://gf2045.com/read/276/. Accessed June 6, 2016.

Sandberg, Anders. "My Thoughts and Comments on the Omega Point Theory of Frank J. Tipler." June 28, 2015. http://www.aleph.se/Trans/Global/Omega/tipler_page.html. Accessed January 17, 2016.

"Saying 'Goodbye' to Your Friends on Facebook & Twitter." DeadSocial. http://www.deadsoci.al/. Accessed January 7, 2016.

Scheffler, Samuel, and Niko Kolodny. *Death and the Afterlife*. Oxford: Oxford University Press, 2013.

Schneider, Susan. *Science Fiction and Philosophy: From Time Travel to Superintelligence*. Chichester, UK: Wiley-Blackwell, 2009.

Sconce, Jeffrey. *Haunted Media: Electronic Presence from Telegraphy to Television*. Durham, NC: Duke University Press, 2000.

Sebold, Alice. *The Lovely Bones: A Novel*. Boston: Little, Brown, 2002.

Segal, Alan F. *Life after Death: A History of the Afterlife in the Religions of the West*. New York: Doubleday, 2004.

Segal, David. "This Man Is Not a Cyborg. Yet." *The New York Times*. June 1, 2013. http://www.nytimes.com/2013/06/02/business/dmitry-itskov-and-the-avatar-quest.html?pagewanted=1&_r=0. Accessed February 11, 2016.

Seung, Sebastian. *Connectome: How the Brain's Wiring Makes Us Who We Are*. Boston: Houghton Mifflin Harcourt, 2012.

Sigourney, L. H., Thomas B. Smith, and Howland. *Olive Leaves*. New York: Robert Carter & Brothers, 1852.

"The Singularity Is Near, The Movie—Homepage." http://singularity.com/themovie/. Accessed February 19, 2016.

Sloane, David Charles. *The Last Great Necessity: Cemeteries in American History*. Baltimore: Johns Hopkins University Press, 1991.

Smith, Gary Scott. *Heaven in the American Imagination*. New York: Oxford University Press, 2011.

Sofka, Carla J. "Social Support 'Internetworks,' Caskets for Sale, and More: Thanatology and the Information Superhighway." *Death Studies* 21, no. 6 (1997): 553–74. doi: 10.1080/074811897201778.

Sofka, Carla, Illene Noppe Cupit, and Kathleen R. Gilbert. *Dying, Death, and Grief in an Online Universe: For Counselors and Educators*. New York: Springer, 2012.

Spinoza, Benedictus De, and G. H. R. Parkinson. *Ethics*. Oxford: Oxford University Press, 2000.

Stannard, David E. *Death in America*. Philadelphia: University of Pennsylvania Press, 1975.

Steinhart, Eric Charles. *Your Digital Afterlives: Computational Theories of Life after Death*. New York: Palgrave, Macmillan, 2014.

Stephenson, Neal. *Snow Crash*. New York: Bantam Books, 2000.

Sterling, Bruce. *The Epic Struggle of the Internet of Things*. New York: Strelka Press, 2014.

"Steven Seagal Asks for Russian PM Vladimir Putin's Support in Immortality Research." MOSCOW, May 16, 2011 /PRNewswire/. http://www.prnewswire.com/news-releases/steven-seagal-asks-for-russian-pm-vladimir-putins-support-in-immortality-research-121948323.html. Accessed February 11, 2016.

Stokes, Patrick. "Do the Dead Live on in Facebook?" http://www.academia.edu/1691317/Do_The_Dead_Live_On_In_Facebook. Accessed January 7, 2016.

Stokes, Patrick, and Adam Buben. *Kierkegaard and Death*. Bloomington: Indiana University Press, 2011.

Stolyarov, Gennadi, II. *Death Is Wrong*. Ann Arbor, MI: Rational Argumentator Press, 2013.

"Summerland: An Introduction." Wicca Chat. http://www.wicca-chat.com/gardnarianbos.htm. Accessed February 5, 2016.

Superstorm Sandy Memorial Site. http://www.legacy.com/memorial-sites/superstorm-sandy/. Accessed January 7, 2016.

Svensson, Peter. "Does the Pope Know?" *Associated Press*. Accessed February 23, 2016.

Swedenborg, Emanuel, and George F. Dole. *Heaven and Hell*. New York: Swedenborg Foundation, 1984.

Taylor, Eugene. *Shadow Culture: Psychology and Spirituality in America*. Washington, DC: Counterpoint, 1999.

"Terasem Movement Transreligion." http://terasemfaith.org/. Accessed January 7, 2016.

Terasem Quadrennial Convention, comp. *The Truths of Terasem*. 2012 ed. Lincoln, VT: Terasem, 2012.

Thweatt-Bates, Jeanine. *Cyborg Selves: A Theological Anthropology of the Posthuman*. Farnham, Surrey, England: Ashgate, 2012.

"Transhumanist Values." http://nickbostrom.com/ethics/values.html. Accessed January 17, 2016.

Turing, Alan M. "Computing Machinery and Intelligence." *Parsing the Turing Test*, 2009, 23–65. doi: 10.1007/978-1-4020-6710-5_3.

Turkle, Sherry. *Alone Together: Why We Expect More from Technology and Less from Each Other*. New York, NY: Basic Books, 2012.

Turkle, Sherry. *Life on the Screen: Identity in the Age of the Internet*. New York: Simon & Schuster, 1995.

Twain, Mark. *Extract from Captain Stormfield's Visit to Heaven*. New York: Oxford University Press, 1996.

"Tweet from Beyond the Grave with LivesOn." *PC Magazine*. http://www.pcmag.com/article2/0,2817,2415665,00.asp. Accessed January 7, 2016.

"USC Shoah Foundation." USC Shoah Foundation. http://sfi.usc.edu/. Accessed February 14, 2016.

Vinge, Vernor. *True Names*. New York, NY: Bluejay Books, 1984.

Vinge, Vernor, and James Frenkel. *True Names and the Opening of the Cyberspace Frontier*. New York: T. Doherty Associates Book, 2001.

"Virtual Eternity." ABC News. http://abcnews.go.com/icaught/Story?id=3421 980&page=1. Accessed February 14, 2016.

"Virtual Memorials." http://virtual-memorials.com/. Accessed January 7, 2016.

Waggoner, Zach. *My Avatar, My Self: Identity in Video Role-Playing Games*. Jefferson, NC: McFarland, 2009.

Wardrip-Fruin, Noah, and Pat Harrigan. *Second Person: Role-Playing and Story in Games and Playable Media*. Cambridge, MA: MIT Press, 2007.

Webb, Marilyn. *The Good Death: The New American Search to Reshape the End of Life*. New York: Bantam Books, 1997.

Weiss, Gail, and Honi Fern Haber. *Perspectives on Embodiment: The Intersections of Nature and Culture*. New York: Routledge, 1999.

"Welcome to Catholic Memorials." Catholic Memorials. http://www.catholic memorials.com/. Accessed January 7, 2016.

"Welcome to the Eternal Portal®." Free Memorials. http://www.theeternalpor tal.com/. Accessed January 7, 2016.

"Welcome to Virtual Memorial Garden. . . ." VMG—Home Page. http://www .virtualmemorialgarden.net/. Accessed January 7, 2016.

Wertheim, Margaret. *The Pearly Gates of Cyberspace: A History of Space from Dante to the Internet*. New York: W.W. Norton, 1999.

"What Is a Facebook Memorial?" Digital Memorials. November 29, 2009. https://mediamemoryandhistory.wordpress.com/what-is-a-facebook-me morial/. Accessed January 7, 2016.

"What We Do." Institute for Creative Technologies. http://ict.usc.edu/. Accessed February 14, 2016.

"Who Is Afraid of the Singularity?" NPR. http://www.npr.org/sections/13.7 /2011/03/23/134762846/who-is-afraid-of-the-singularity. Accessed February 13, 2016.

Wilcox, Sue, and Bruce Wilcox. "Speaker of the Dead." http://www.personalar chiving.com/wp-content/uploads/2010/02/finalpresentation-Wilcox.pdf. Accessed January 17, 2016.

Wiley, Keith. *A Taxonomy and Metaphysics of Mind-Uploading*. Alautun Press, 2014.

Winyard, David C. "A Technological God? The Emergence of Religious Transhumanism." ASA/CSCA/CiS Meeting. July 27, 2014. https://www .academia.edu/7791946/A_Technological_God_The_Emergence_of _Religious_Transhumanism. Accessed February 13, 2016.

Wood, Gaby. *Living Dolls: A Magical History of the Quest for Mechanical Life*. London: Faber and Faber, 2002.

Wortham, Jenna. " 'Black Mirror' and the Horrors and Delights of Technology." *The New York Times*. January 31, 2015. http://www.nytimes.com

/2015/02/01/magazine/black-mirror-and-the-horrors-and-delights-of -technology.html. Accessed January 7, 2016.

Wright, John C. "Transhumanism and Subhumanism." *John C Wrights Journal.* http://www.scifiwright.com/2011/12/transhumanism-and-subhumanism/. Accessed January 17, 2016.

Yalom, Marilyn. *The American Resting Place: Four Hundred Years of History Through Our Cemeteries and Burial Grounds.* Boston: Houghton Mifflin, 2008.

Young, William P., Wayne Jacobsen, and Brad Cummings. *The Shack: Where Tragedy Confronts Eternity.* Newbury Park, CA: Windblown Media, 2007.

Your Tribute. http://www.yourtribute.com/. Accessed January 7, 2016.

Zaleski, Carol, and Philip Zaleski. *The Book of Heaven: An Anthology of Writings from Ancient to Modern times.* Oxford: Oxford University Press, 2000.

Zengotita, Thomas De. *Mediated: How the Media Shapes Your World and the Way You Live in It.* New York: Bloomsbury, 2005.

Zsuzsi, Schindler. https://www.facebook.com/zsuzsi.schindler. Accessed January 7, 2016.

Index

About the Author

KEVIN O'NEILL is Professor of Philosophy Emeritus at the University of Redlands where he has taught since helping to found the experimental Johnston Center in 1969. He has studied representations of death for more than 20 years, publishing articles on cemeteries, consolation literature, post-mortem photography, online funerals and memorials, and post-9/11 representations of death in popular culture. Dr. O'Neill received his PhD in philosophy from Yale University in 1967, his MA from Yale in 1965, and his BA from Georgetown University in 1963.